At Last

I Can Witness!

At Last

I Can Witness!

How to Witness to Anyone, Anywhere, Anytime

By
Robert Davis

TATE PUBLISHING
AND ENTERPRISES, LLC

Published by Tate Publishing & Enterprises, LLC
127 E. Trade Center Terrace | Mustang, Oklahoma 73064 USA
1.888.361.9473 | www.tatepublishing.com

Tate Publishing is committed to excellence in the publishing industry. The company reflects the philosophy established by the founders, based on Psalm 68:11,

"The Lord gave the word and great was the company of those who published it."

Book design copyright © 2012 by Tate Publishing, LLC. All rights reserved.
Cover design by Rodrigo Adolfo
Interior design by Ronnel Luspoc

Published in the United States of America

ISBN: 978-1-62147-588-0
1. Religion / Christian Ministry / Preaching
2. Religion / Christian Church / Growth
12.11.27

Dedication

To my wife, Dorrine—thank you
for your love and encouragement

Table of Contents

The Great Commission

Where Do I Fit In?

In the great drama of human salvation, Jesus Christ occupies center stage—in every act, every scene, and every script. His is the only starring role in God's plan for world evangelism. All of us, as members of his supporting cast, are called to focus the spotlight on him. We point the world to his saving grace, his amazing sacrifice of love in giving his life for us, and his freely offered mercy and reconciliation – and let's not forget …everlasting life in a perfect place called Heaven. This should give us great encouragement because, after all, we have good news to give to the world!

In the mind of God, each of us plays a role that cannot be filled by anyone else. While some may be on the "front lines," serving as missionaries in far away places, others, equally important and necessary, occupy strategic positions on the home front. In fact, this is where God has placed most of his people. The odds are that this is where he has placed you.

Wherever we find ourselves, we need to recognize our vital importance in God's plan for reaching the world. No one else on earth occupies your special place in the scheme of things. No one else has the same family relationships as you or the same combination of friends, neighbors, and coworkers. You can search the world over and find no one else who moves in precisely the same circles of humanity as you. No one. Like it or not, *you* are irreplaceable!

Yet unique and irreplaceable though we may be, we do share one trait almost without exception: our silence in the face of God's call to share the gospel with others. In the face of such widespread reluctance to share our faith in Christ, it seems we are compelled to reach but one conclusion. Namely, that many Christians regard witnessing as something that they (we) just don't like to do. Too many of us, perhaps a majority, don't like doing it and don't like hearing about it.

If you doubt the truth of this statement, just look around and ask yourself, "How many Christians are really dedicated to sharing their faith with others on a regular basis?" More to the point, how many believers actually like witnessing, look forward to sharing their faith, and look for creative and resourceful ways of doing so?

What about you? Do you like to witness to people about Jesus? Or do you cringe at the thought, perhaps making excuses in order to make yourself feel better about avoiding it? Would you agree with me if I suggested that this seems to be the state of mind of the majority of believers in the church today—at least in America?

Those of us who fall into this category experience the pain of emotional ambivalence regarding our call to "go into all the world and preach the gospel to every creature." Because, as Christians, we want more than anything to do what God wants us to do. Yet, more often than not, our fears and insecurities hold us back from sharing our faith.

And so we find ourselves in the almost comical position of not wanting to do what we wish we would. Or, to put it more simply: We don't like to witness, but wish we did!

At Last, You Can Witness!

This book is written for Christians who want to witness, but don't. Since you have picked it up and are now reading these words, I'm guessing that you probably fall into one of two categories of readers. If you are in the first group, you are a believer who just likes to look at books about witnessing because you like to witness. If so, great! By all means, I hope you find some enjoyable, maybe even inspirational, ideas here. And while you are not the primary target of this book, I would be quite happy if you found it helpful. But even if you don't, that's okay because, after all, you like to witness, so you'll be just fine!

If you fall into the second category however, you picked up this book because you're hoping to find something here that will help you to finally become the witness you always wanted to be. I want you to know that the answer is yes! And if you give yourself a chance, you will! This book was written especially with you in mind because I know that, as a Christian, your desire is to please the Lord. And since all of us are called to be his witnesses, we can't help but want to fulfill our part in his Great Commission.

Unfortunately, this desire has been thwarted in the lives of many. As we've already seen, many Christians hesitate when it comes to sharing their faith. It's sad but true. Far too many of us are uncomfortable when it comes to the prospect of telling others about Jesus. But because we love our Savior and want to please him, we would gladly share our love for Christ if only we had the confidence to do so.

Many Christians fear witnessing because they feel like they just don't know how to talk to people about the Lord. Yet these same believers would probably love to share their faith if only they knew how to overcome the obstacles that so often prevent them from doing so. If you are one of those people, then this book is dedicated to you. More than anything, I hope to encourage those of you who have been frustrated with your own reluctance to reach out to the people you want to help.

We Really Do Want to Tell Them

When Christ came into our lives and saved us from our sins, we received a new nature from God. Jesus himself now lives in our hearts. And because he lives in us, we have a God-given desire to do what God wants us to do. When we think of how Christ died for our sins we are filled with gratitude and love for him.

Naturally we want to please him. If we sense that we are falling short in doing so, we are unhappy and restless.

Yet when it comes to witnessing, for many of us, there is a wide gap between our desire to please the Lord and our response to his call to "go into all the world and preach the gospel to every creature." In fact, this gap is so wide in the lives of so many of God's children that the last word many in the church want to hear is the word *witness* or *witnessing*.

No doubt if you were to take a poll of believers in an "average" church asking them to name their favorite words in the Bible, one can easily imagine star performances from such celebrities as *love, mercy,* and *forgiveness. Grace* might give even love a run for its money. These and similar words would surely get "top billing" with most of us. This is understandable. After all, it was God's great love for us that motivated him to offer his mercy and forgiving grace through the sacrifice of his son for our sins.

It would be much harder to imagine, however, that the words *witness* or *witnessing* could compete very well with such soothing words as *love, mercy, grace,* or *forgiveness.* There is a sad irony in this, for it is primarily through our *witness* and our *witnessing* that God has ordained for lost people to come to know of his *love* and *mercy* and *forgiving grace.*

Because of the fears we so often associate with telling people about Christ, many of us become uncomfortable when the subject of witnessing comes up. Others feel uneasy because of negative stereotypes that are sometimes evoked when we think about "witnessing"—especially if it is to strangers!

On the one hand, we long to share our faith with the unsaved. We want to reach out to those who are lost, sometimes desperately. But ignorance and fear become walls of separation, silencing our testimony to those who need a reason to hope. We want people we care about to go to heaven. We would spare even our enemies from hell if we could.

On the other hand however, we dread being looked upon as weird or flaky or fanatical. We have no wish to look like fools, even though we should be willing to appear so, if necessary. After all, God did choose "the foolishness of preaching to save those who believe." We know this, of course. Yet naturally and understandably, we want to know how we can reach out to people with the good news of the gospel—but in a way that is comfortable, not forced or strained or…strange.

The Church Has Not Been Trained

Unfortunately, there is a serious lack of training in the body of Christ in the area of personal evangelism. Because of this lack of training, many saints balk when faced with opportunities to share their faith because of uncertainty concerning how to go about doing so. Looking around the church today, one is compelled to wonder, How many Christians go for long periods of time— weeks, perhaps months, maybe even *years*—without telling even a single soul about their faith in Jesus Christ?

They know they should. They are not happy about their silence. But in many ways it has become almost a "normal" part of our (American) Christian culture in the sense that many of us have come to accept it, to dismiss it from our minds as best we can, and to concentrate on those areas of our walk with God where we do not feel so helpless, uncertain, even clueless.

We Teach Everything Else, Why Not How to Share Our Faith?

Looking at the people in the world, we can see that they appreciate the importance of training. They have on-the-job training, simulation training, training videos, apprenticeships, workshops, seminars, and an endless array of creative and innovative programs and courses for equipping people for their designated tasks.

Of course, the church has its programs as well. We have faith seminars and prosperity seminars, seminars on tithing, marriage workshops, and Sunday school programs, retreats, how-to courses in financial independence, and guest speakers to cover all the important topics of "successful" Christian living.

But where are the evangelistic seminars, workshops, training courses, or videos? Some might object to the idea of training courses and workshops for soul-winning and evangelism. After all, their reasoning goes, aren't we just supposed to be "led by the Spirit?" Well, sure. But why assume that the two are mutually exclusive? Does training hinder one from following the Spirit? If so, perhaps we ought to dispatch with our Bible colleges and universities then. And maybe do away with our books and seminars on prayer while we're at it. We certainly don't want to hinder the leading of the Spirit in our prayers...

Teaching and instruction models only become obstacles if they are allowed to become rigid formulas or inflexible methods. No one here is advocating this. The truth of the matter is that, in the area of personal evangelism, many are not being led by the Spirit because they are not doing anything! Most people hesitate to try something new if they are not provided with at least a minimum level of instruction and training—especially if it involves participating in an activity for which they have apprehensions.

If training and practice are obstacles, then why should praise and worship teams use these tools when preparing to lead their congregations in worship? Why, for that matter, should the pastor bother to study, meditate, pray, or take notes when he could just as well be "led by the Spirit"?

How many of us would want to fly with an airline that provided no training for their pilots? Why not just let them "wing it"? Who would want to have his heart operated on by a surgeon who had not practiced on cadavers? How many musicians ever mastered the piano or violin without lessons? Since when did training and practice become incompatible with performance?

There is nothing wrong with training if we are doing it to improve our skills for the glory of God. Doing so does not imply that we are trusting in our skills or in the "arm of the flesh." Of course, we are not to allow our training to stifle our spontaneity. The truth is, training produces confidence, which in turn tends strongly to produce freedom and creativity. Its opposite, lack of training, tends to produce self-consciousness and inhibitions, reactions that tend to stifle and hinder people from focusing on the task at hand—or in the case of sharing our faith with others, to even avoid doing so altogether because of fear and uncertainty.

On the other hand, teaching, instruction, training, exercise, and practice in spiritual activities tends strongly to facilitate *Christ-consciousness* by freeing those so benefited to focus on other people and their needs rather than on one's own fears and inhibitions.

I submit, therefore, for your consideration, the following proposition: practice makes perfect! Practice with an eye to God and a reliance upon his Spirit, as we do our part in preparation. Doing so with a desire to glorify him and meet the needs of others—this is a practice that will honor God and bring those who apply themselves to it to a place of preparedness, enabling them to be instant, in season, and out!

The fact is there are things we can and should do to better equip and prepare ourselves for our individual callings in the ministry of reconciliation. The Bible tells us that we are to "[have] our feet shod with the preparation of the gospel of peace" (Ephesians 6:15).

This book is for those who want to be better prepared to share the good news of Jesus with others, whether those others be family, friends, neighbors, coworkers, or, dare I say it, even strangers! The guidelines and suggestions provided are offered to help you become more confident, more comfortable, and more effective when "witnessing" to people, whether by word or by deed, but hopefully by both!

My hope is that this book may be a tool in the Lord's hand to help you overcome your fears and become a bold and faithful witness for Christ. I pray that as a result you'll fear no more when you hear the words *witness* or *witnessing* and that the idea of sharing the good news becomes *good news* to you! God help each of us to fulfill our part in his Great Commission.

Go Ye...but Where?

In Mark 16:15 Jesus commanded his followers to "go into all the world and preach the gospel to every creature." In Acts 1:8, immediately before his ascension, he declared, "And ye shall be witnesses unto me, both in Jerusalem, and in all Judea, and in Samaria, and unto the uttermost parts of the world."

This commission, given just before his ascension to the Father, presents each of us with both a challenge and a responsibility to fulfill our part in the mission of global evangelism. But this immediately poses a question for you and me: Just what *is* my part?

Since none of us can literally go into all the world, nor can any of us present the gospel to every creature, then what part of the world am I to go into? And which creatures has God appointed for me to preach the gospel to? While some are surely called to go into foreign lands, it seems that Jesus is telling most of us to go into all of *our* world and preach the gospel to those people who are around *us*. This is our unique, individual mission field—*our personal Jerusalem, Judea, and Samaria.* If each person in the body of Christ were to actually do this, to focus on reaching those in his own private world, no doubt the world would be evangelized in short order.

Many Christians are reluctant to accept this challenge. Yet sharing Christ with others is one of the greatest privileges we have as believers. We have seen that through lack of training, many are hesitant, fearful, even hostile to the idea of sharing their faith. Believers must be given the instruction and training they need in order to overcome these negative feelings so as to be able to share their faith with confidence and joy.

The first section, "Reaching Your Private World," addresses the task that every believer is called to, namely, to be a missionary to those in his private world, his (or her) Jerusalem, Judea, and Samaria. This sphere embraces our family, our relatives, our friends, our neighbors, and our coworkers. These are the people in our "inner" and "center" circles of influence, our own personal "Jerusalem and Judea." Those in our outer circle, our "Samaria," are people with whom we come into contact on a fairly regular basis, but frequently overlook when it comes to our personal witnessing. This outer circle also includes our enemies.

For those who wish to go further, "to the uttermost parts of [their] world," Part Two, "Beyond Your Circle," is addressed. This section offers helpful instructions and suggestions for expanding your influence for God's kingdom beyond your immediate circle of contacts. Part Three, "Just For the Fun of It," is an effort to offer some novel perspectives on how we might approach our calling as ambassadors with innovative and creative enthusiasm. Part Four, "To Go or Not to Go," is a challenge to the church to break away from the "slough of despond" we have for too long been mired in when it comes to the Great Commission and to once and for all get with the program of preaching the gospel to every creature...before Jesus comes back!

Finally, Part Five, "Appendices...Not Just an Afterthought," is included to tie up some "loose ends" and to provide a resource for improving your preparation so as to be more instant, in season and out of season. Though the topics covered in the Appendices have been relegated to the back of the book, this was not done because the information they contain is unimportant. They were put there in order to facilitate an easier reading of the vision offered in the main body of the book—that of reaching your own private world for Jesus. I strongly urge you to look them over, as I believe they provide information and insights that will prove invaluable to you in your personal witnessing efforts.

This book limits its scope of instruction, for the most part, to practical suggestions and communication skills as aids to help you overcome the "I don't know what to say or do" barrier—to the end that you might establish meaningful relationships with people for the purpose of winning them to Christ. It is not a book on the more "spiritual" aspects of winning souls. Consider this a "101" class (sprinkled with 201 "isms") to help you break through the silence barrier so that you can be ready to witness for God when opportunity comes along. After all, this is what you want and what God wants for you.

Before proceeding, allow me to offer one caution. Because witnessing is a personal expression of our faith in Christ, Christians sometimes have a less than receptive attitude when it comes to teachings on the subject. This is understandable. As unique individuals, God has ordained that each of us offer a "one of a kind" reflection of his glory. Therefore, it is no small wonder if believers have a wide diversity of styles, manners, and approaches to sharing their faith with those around them. Our personal backgrounds and points of view make this both inevitable and desirable.

This said, we still can and should learn from each other. Some things are of practical value regardless of our personal orientation. It is my hope that you will find at least a measure of practical usefulness for your personal witnessing in these pages. Those things that have no appeal to you may be passed over or ignored. We all do well to respect and appreciate our differences as well as our similarities. God is pleased to have it so. Amen.

Part One

Reaching Your Private World

Let's start by looking at the role God's Great Commission should play in the life of every believer. We've already seen that he wants us to reach out to those in our private world, our Jerusalem, Judea, and Samaria, the world we live in every day, day in and day out, with the good news of the gospel. Every Christian is called to be a living, breathing, walking, talking testimony of the power of Christ to transform the lives of his followers.

God wants those around us to *see* Christ in our lives—that is, in our conduct and in our character, in our resemblance to him, in our lifestyle, and in our actions and reactions to the world and the people around us. He also wants unbelievers to hear Christ speaking to them through us, his chosen ambassadors.

> That is, that God was in Christ reconciling the world to Himself, not imputing their trespasses to them; and has committed to us the word of reconciliation. Now then, we are ambassadors for Christ, as though God were pleading through us: we implore you on Christ's behalf, be reconciled to God.
>
> 2 Corinthians 5:19-20 (NKJV)

God has called and enabled us to glorify him by living holy lives as witnesses of Christ's transforming power. But we must also bring the message of the good news to those who have not heard. When God sent Peter to Cornelius, this Gentile would-be believer implored the apostle to tell him "all the things commanded you by God" (Acts 10:33, NKJV).

Speaking of this same incident in Acts 11:14, Peter, explaining God's command for him to take the gospel to the Gentiles, referred to the angel's message to Cornelius as indicating that he (Peter) would "tell you words by which you and all your household will be saved" (NKJV).

We see then, that we too are commanded by God to tell others words whereby they may be saved. The good news of the gospel is something we must report, or it will be of no use to those who have not heard. Our actions must bear witness to our words. But actions without the life-giving words God has given us are not enough. It is "the truth (which) shall make you free" (John 8:32).

Millions of people know about Christ, but they have never really had the gospel explained to them on a personal level. God exhorts us to "be ready always to give an answer to every man that asks you a reason of the hope that is in you with meekness and fear" (1 Peter 3:15).

We ought not to take this to mean, however, that we should never offer the gospel message unless someone asks us to. Remember, Jesus also said, "Go...[and] preach the gospel to every creature" (Mark 16:15).

God wants us to focus on the "creatures" in our private world. This is the field where we have the greatest opportunity to reach others with Christ's message and love. We will start, then, with the people closest to us, our "inner circle," and then move out in expanding circles of influence beyond Jerusalem, to Judea and Samaria, and perhaps, if you dare, to the uttermost parts of your world.

In Jerusalem

Your Inner Circle

Your personal Jerusalem is the inner circle of your private world—your family, your relatives, and your friends. This group is, in some ways, your most challenging arena when it comes to sharing your faith in Christ. Jesus said it this way: "A prophet is not without honor, except in his own country and in his own house" (Matthew 13:57, NKJV).

We often find this true in our own experience. Those closest to us sometimes seem to be least receptive to our influence. They "know" us. "Is not this the carpenter's son?" (Matthew 13:55).

Even Jesus had to contend with some of his own friends, who thought him to be "beside himself"—that is, not in his right mind. "And when his friends heard of it, they went to lay hold on him: for they said, 'He is beside himself'" (Mark 3:21).

None are so dear to us as our loved ones and friends. We want to do all in our power to reach them and persuade them to come to Christ. Who doesn't long for the salvation of her family? Who can be indifferent to the fate of a friend?

But God has not left us helpless. As we prayerfully trust our heavenly Father and follow the leading of his Spirit, we have good reason to hope for the best when sharing Christ with our families—our wives, our husbands, our children and our mothers, fathers, brothers, and sisters. And yes, our relatives and friends also.

We start then with our inner circle...how can we be the best witness we can be to them so that when our loved ones see us they begin to see Jesus, and come to the conviction that we truly are "new creatures"? Our goal is to so demonstrate the blessing and joy of living for Christ that they too will desire to come to the Savior! Let's see then, how we can be such a witness, "faithful and true," allowing God to use our influence to draw our family into his own.

Chapter One

Your Family: Sharing Jesus with Those Who "Know" You

It is only natural to want to see our loved ones come to Christ. Our spouses, children, parents and siblings are our nearest and dearest relations on earth. Yet, as we have seen, the very closeness of our relation to them sometimes makes sharing our faith more, rather than less, difficult. On the one hand, close kinship can make it hard for family members to receive something "new" from us. On the other, our blood bond can provide an opportunity for deeply impressing loved ones as they see "up close and personal" the changes that are taking place in our lives.

It is important for our family to see such changes and it is equally vital that they understand what has taken place. This means that both our manner of living and our personal testimony need to play a role in our witness. In some instances just coming right out and telling them may be the best way to go. In other situations, it may be necessary to have a well thought out approach inspired and empowered with heartfelt and persistent prayer.

Your Decision to Follow Christ May Cause a Crisis Among Your Unsaved Family Members

While there are sometimes happy occasions when a person's decision to live for Christ is welcomed with curiosity, or even good will, by unsaved family members, this is not always the case. More likely, upon hearing of your decision, your family will be thrown into a state of turmoil and crisis. They, like you, have heard about Jesus all of their lives—certainly in America.

Every human being senses instinctively that his attitude toward Christ is of momentous consequence—even if this is denied on a conscious level. Often families that have no true born-again Christian in the fold have adopted mutually comforting notions about Christ and Christianity, notions that tend to accommodate their shared complacency.

When suddenly, "out of nowhere," one of their own, Cindy, gets "saved," the unbelieving members of her family experience a twofold trauma. First, the trauma of their own shattered complacency. Whereas before these loved ones may have fed and reinforced ideas concerning the place of "religion" in their lives, now Cindy has gone and upset the applecart. This will sometimes cause anger and nearly always confusion and an unidentifiable, but very real, sense of apprehension. These feelings in themselves may lead to resentment. (Why did she have to go and "mess things up"?) Before, it may have been okay to talk about Jesus (once in a great while) and to entertain safe and unthreatening notions concerning him, even as "God's Son" in a kind of meaningless, far off from day-to-day life sort of way—so long as such notions posed no threat to the personal lifestyles of the family members.

When one of the family begins to indicate something else, however, as for example, the idea that Jesus has now become the Lord of her life (Cindy), each of the unsaved members is confronted with one unmistakable and unavoidable conclusion: "Jesus now means more to Cindy than he does to me! More than I ever thought he would mean to me, or to Cindy either for that matter." Which leads like a flaming arrow to the profoundly disturbing question: "Who is right? Me or Cindy? And if Cindy is right, what are the implications for my own life?" All of these thought processes will play out in the minds of Cindy's family, even if she has said very little beyond the fact that she has now made Jesus the Lord of her life.

In addition, this crisis is often compounded by another one. Her unsaved loved ones are awakening to a dawning realization that somehow, in a way they cannot quite put their finger on, Cindy has been lost to them. She is no longer "one of them." In a very real sense, she has departed from the land of the living, or at least the living dead, and wandered off to follow this other worldly Jesus who, until now, had probably been no more than some long-ago, far-away "religious" figure with little, if any, relevance to modern life.

To unbelievers, this is incomprehensible and extremely upsetting. There is the feeling that she is about to throw her life away. "After all," they reason, "how can one really know if there is an afterlife?" This feeling of death is really a projection onto Cindy of their own sense of lostness, for the gospel is to those who are perishing a *savor of death* since it denies the world and all that the world holds dear and puts in its place a promise of *the world to come*, a world which to unbelievers is as alien and unfathomable as life on some forbidden planet.

All of this is very unsettling for the unbelieving loved ones of new Christians. Their emotional reactions are prone to be greater because their love for us is greater. Their sense of loss is very real…and threatening to the tranquility of their own worldview. In a profound way, the "intrusion" of Christ into their family circle has hit home, and even more, *hit them where it hurts*. For our skeptical loved ones, our decision to follow Christ must truly be heart piercing.

All of this should cause us to fall to our knees seeking God's mercy and wisdom for how best to relate to our unsaved (and now unsettled) family members. We ought to have compassion for their dilemma and exercise patience, gentleness, and understanding in all of our dealings with them.

The "Lostness" of Our Loved Ones Can Be Terrifying to Us

When we are first enlightened as newcomers to the faith, it dawns on us that those members of our family who do not know Christ are lost and in a place of great peril. This is profoundly disturbing and, frankly terrifying. We desperately want them to be saved. But we must not allow ourselves to be seized with panic or overcome with despair. Knowing that we are not alone but that God is with us will give us the courage we need to face the challenge of winning those we love without alienating them.

Take comfort in the faithfulness of God's love, the limitlessness of his power, and in the fact that, as a born-again believer, you are now a beachhead on the front lines of your family's homeland, ready to wage spiritual war with the enemy on their behalf. We are the breach in the enemy lines! We are to "stand in the gap" and "make up the hedge." The "weapons of our warfare are mighty through God," and "greater is he that is in us than he that is in the world." God is able and willing, and he has made us able. Determine now that with God you will win, always and ever remembering that "the Lord is…not willing that any should perish, but that all should come to repentance" (2 Peter 3:9). This includes our loved ones.

A Strategy for Winning Your Loved Ones

While no set strategy can apply equally in any situation, you can always trust God to lead you. As a matter of fact, faith— the confidence and determination to believe that God is willing to save your loved ones and that he is eager to work with you and through you to do so—is the essential foundation you need as you approach the prospect of winning your family to Christ. Remember, Jesus died for their sins too! You may be confident of God's love for your family and take courage that now he has someone to work through in reaching them—you!

Determine at the outset that 2 Peter 3:9 is your goal. Like God, you also are not willing that any of your loved ones should perish but that all of them, each and every one, will come to repentance.

What, then, are some practical things you can do to start well in your witness to your family? We will now look at a four-part plan to help you as you share Christ with the people in your family. Each step of this plan is based on Scripture.

Some words of encouragement are also offered for those whose testimony to their family has stalled because of difficulties in communication or because of conflicts or other hindrances. As you trust God and follow the leading of his Spirit, you may be confident that he will work in the lives of those nearest and dearest to you. We begin now with Step One:

Pray to God on Behalf of Your Loved Ones

> I exhort therefore, that, first of all, supplications, prayers, intercessions, and giving of thanks, be made for all (including our families)...
>
> For this is good and acceptable in the sight of God our Savior; Who will have all...(including our loved ones) to be saved, and to come unto the knowledge of the truth.
>
> 1 Timothy 2:1,3-4

Always in everything we do in our service to the Lord, we start with prayer, continue in prayer, and end with prayer. As a blueprint for sharing your faith, this book is not primarily concerned with teaching about prayer or praying for the lost. However, it is understood that nothing can be accomplished to reach the unsaved without God. Yet he has ordained that we co-labor together with him to reach the world. Prayer is simply reaching out to God to do what only he can do while you work with him to do your part to lead lost sinners to Jesus.

So start, then, by asking God to help you. Ask him to lead you and guide you. Ask him for wisdom, and pray for him to open the hearts of your family members to understand and receive your words. Bring him into remembrance of his promises to hear you when you offer prayers in Christ's name.

Pray also that God will help you to be the best example you can be of the power of Christ to change people. Ask him to show your family the difference that he is making in your life.

Which leads us to Step Number Two:

Show Your Loved Ones

Next, be determined to demonstrate and show by your conduct the changes that are taking place inside you. "You are our epistle written in our hearts, known and read by all men" (2 Corinthians 3:2, NKJV).

No one knows you better than your family. If something happens in your life causing you to change, you can rest assured your family will notice. Let them see that the love of God has found a home in your heart. Meditate upon each of your loved ones, beholding them through the eyes of God's love, and ask him how you may demonstrate his love to each one. Look for and seek out ways to show kindness to them. There are many ways you can do this. Here are a few to consider:

1. *Love by serving*: Do things for those you love. This could be anything from cleaning chores to helping with errands, or anything that shows concern and appreciation.

2. *Offer genuine praise*: Look for opportunities to offer compliments and words of praise—from the heart and not just because you want your loved one to "get saved." (Though, of course, you do!)

Robert Davis

3. *Tolerate*: That is, overlook faults, flaws, slights, rudeness, and the discourtesies that are the common stock of day-to-day family life. When conflicts arise, be "swift to hear, slow to speak, and slow to wrath"—and always be quick to apologize. Show a difference in your attitudes and reactions, a difference that demonstrates that you really have changed!

Sometimes your actions may be the only avenue through which you can witness to the life-changing power of God. Some will not hearken to the Word, but they may hearken to the message of your godly life.

> Wives, likewise, be submissive to your own husbands, that even if some do not obey the word, they, without a word, may be won by the conduct of their wives, when they observe your chaste conduct accompanied by fear.
>
> 1 Peter 3:1-2 (NKJV)

Notice it does not say here that the wife did not try to tell her husband. Peter says to these women that if their husbands would not obey the Word, which they must have heard through the wives, then perhaps without the Word they might listen to the message of their wives' holy change in character and conduct.

Because our actions are the foundation upon which our words stand or fall, we have placed "showing" before "telling" here. Showing is the proof of the telling. Yet we must tell as well, for the word of reconciliation has been committed to us for this very purpose: to tell it to others. Step Three then, is to…

Tell Your Loved Ones

Look for an opportunity to tell your loved ones about the change that Christ has made in your life: "Let the redeemed of the Lord say so, whom He has redeemed from the hand of the enemy" Psalm 107:2 (NKJV).

If this seems difficult, try asking your family member directly for an opportunity to do this. Do not be afraid to ask! If you encounter resistance, don't push. Explain that you wish only for a chance to tell what has happened in your life so that they might understand the changes that have taken place inside of you.

More often than not, your loved ones will allow you to do this. If so, try to be natural, yourself—that is, the "new you," without putting on airs. Avoid preaching. Steer clear of religious jargon. Focus on your testimony. That is what will have the greatest impact, and that is what they will be the most interested in!

Sometimes a family member will not want to hear your testimony and may become resistant, defensive, or even hostile and resentful. This may continue on for weeks, months, perhaps even years. In such situations, you will need to be patient and let God work. Your godly lifestyle will continue to witness for you while your attitude of love and acceptance will let your difficult loved one know that you are there for her (or him—see note below).

[Note: In order to be gender fair, we will dispatch with the passé (we feel) custom of always using the male pronoun when referring inclusively to both sexes, or the awkward and wearisome "him/her." Instead we will use both *him* and *her* more or less alternately and interchangeably from here on. This is not motivated from any desire to be politically "correct" (as adherents of this philosophy believe themselves to be), but rather to simply treat all with equal respect.]

For loved ones who are slow to respond, or even resistant, you may need to think in terms of "the long haul." We turn then, to Step Four:

"Campaign" for the Souls of Your Loved Ones

Finally, you should be prepared, in some instances, to take a long-term approach. "Cast your bread upon the waters; for you will find it after many days" (Ecclesiastes 11:1, NKJV).

In cases when a family member resists your attempts to share your faith, having a long-term "campaign" strategy will help you to stay focused and yet patient. Such a strategy will help you to keep your light shining as a beacon, pointing, always pointing, your loved one to Christ. The Random House College Dictionary defines the word *campaign* as follows:

Campaign: military operations for a specific objective; any systematic course of aggressive activities for a special purpose.

There are many ways you can do this without pushing or preaching. Here are some examples:

- Be consistent and faithful to your values and convictions. Through the years, such a pattern of godliness will increase and multiply the impact of your example and witness.

- When appropriate, share testimonies of what God is doing in your life. Do so as a simple expression of your life experience unfolding. You have the right to do this without being accused of soliciting your religious views because people who are close share with each other concerning the things that are going on in their lives.

- Similarly, be alert for opportunities to inject spiritual truths whenever occasions arise where your relation might see a practical application to his situation. Be true to who you are in Christ in your relationships with your family members. That is, do not allow fear of rejection or conflict to cause you to compromise or hold back from expressing your opinions when the situation calls for you to do so. Such exchanges will happen naturally as a result of being yourself and expressing your worldview as situations arise where it is natural and appropriate to do so. Keep in mind that exposure to truth is a necessary means for enlightenment. It is the knowledge of the truth that sets us free (John 8:32).

- Develop a custom or tradition of giving "spiritual" gifts such as inspirational books, cds, tapes, movies, etc., on birthdays and holidays. While you might not want to make these into occasions where you give only spiritual gifts, such a custom is a useful reminder to those you love concerning what is most important in your life.

- Be willing on occasion to write letters, record personal messages, or utilize any other means in order to keep Christ before your loved ones' eyes. Such avenues of communication may be even more vital with family members who no longer live with you. The advantage of such means of communication is that the emotional threat is reduced when your thoughts and words are communicated indirectly. No immediate response is required, and the one receiving your letter or tape can read or listen without having to deal with you in person.

- This is not to suggest launching a spiritual blitzkrieg on reluctant family members. Simply allowing the Spirit to lead will keep you safely on the path of reasonable prudence and moderation.

- The time may come when you may need to be prepared to plead with your lost loved one, even with tears and anguish. While you do not want to be forceful or offensively forward, you must never confuse this with being bold or unhesitating when it comes to sharing Jesus. Fear of offending is a good thing if it is related to actually being offensive. Fear of offending for the truth's sake is a sin, and one should never hold back from speaking the truth in gentleness, meekness, and love when not doing so would constitute neglect of an eternal soul. Understand that spiritual life and death are for keeps. When death comes calling, opportunity dies with it!

- Be willing to back off completely. God may lead you to do this. You might even tell your loved one that you are going to "drop the subject" unless and until she comes to you requesting to discuss it. Explain that you will still be there for her but that you are leaving the initiative with her regarding spiritual matters. This may especially be necessary when dealing with a loved one who has shown hostility or resentment toward your witness.

Resolve to be brave. Face down the enemy. If your small child was walking in the yard and you turned to see a pit bull bearing down on her, fear would not stop you from charging between your child and the snarling beast. Far from it. You would be filled with a fierce, unstoppable determination to save your child and a holy rage of defiant resolve to fight off the killer with your last ounce of strength, if need be.

Determine now that you will not allow Satan to have his way without a fight. Your weapons are mighty through God. Resist the devil, and he will flee. If he comes back, do it again. And again, however long it takes.

Remember that when you fight in Jesus's name, you win. Always! So cast down every thought of defeat, knowing that the gates of hell will not prevail against you. Carry your loved one in the arms of your prayers. Pray in Jesus's name, and know that God hears you. Never give up. Envision your loved ones saved, going to church, serving God, and sharing their faith in Christ with you and others! Amen.

Chapter Two

Your Relatives: "Please Remember My Dear Aunt Susie"

As those who are most in contact with you on a regular basis, your immediate family provides both the greatest opportunities, and sometimes the greatest challenges, for sharing your faith.

Your relatives, those related to you by blood, but less directly than your immediate family—i.e., grandparents, aunts, uncles, cousins, nieces, and nephews, and by extension, in-laws—are people with whom you share a significant and, for the most part, indissoluble relation for life. Though not usually as close as immediate family (spouse, children, brothers, sisters, mothers, fathers), these relations are peculiarly connected to you.

This connection provides a more or less life-long door of opportunity that you can and should use to exert the power of your God-given influence for the benefit of their souls. As special members of your inner circle (your Jerusalem), you should make it your goal to witness to each of your relatives.

All four of the steps listed for winning your family members (pray, show, tell, and campaign) are just as valid and necessary when dealing with your relatives. There are, however, some differences we would do well to keep in mind.

First, since your relatives are not as closely familiar with the day-to-day events of your life, you should not assume that they have knowledge of your decision to follow Christ. Though someone in your family may have told them of your new-found faith, it may be that no one has. If that is the case, then you will need to do this as soon as possible.

Use Your Testimony as Your Starting Point for Sharing Christ

By far the best way for you to go about this is to share your personal testimony—what caused you to give your life to Christ and what has changed in your life as a result.

This is not the same as sharing "spiritual truths." Of course, that has its place. But your testimony should come before this. People who were a part of your life before you were saved (family, relatives, friends, and others) should usually first be told your personal testimony—what happened in your life to draw you to Christ and how he has changed you.

The reason for this is that these people, having known you before you were saved, have certain impressions and opinions about you and who you are. Your personal testimony is your God-given first means of compelling those who know you to consider Christ. It is also a line of demarcation, a line in the sand, if you will, in which you declare openly that something has dramatically and everlastingly changed in your life, in you, and that this change is the result of entering into a new and eternal relationship with someone, namely, Jesus!

Every new Christian should be trained from the moment of conversion to see his personal testimony as the absolute starting point of his witness. New believers should be encouraged, and helped if necessary, to share their testimony with those who knew them before their decision to follow Jesus.

God's Not-So-Secret Weapon for Helping New Christians Share Their Testimonies

God has given the church a powerful institution, or ordinance, to help new believers get off to a good start in sharing their new relationship with Christ. I am referring to water baptism. I believe that God had a two-fold purpose in establishing this ordinance.

First, of course, that the new Christian would experience his own death, burial, and resurrection to new life in Christ through the powerful symbolic nature of water baptism. The church has understood this.

However, for the most part, the church has failed to recognize that God also intended the occasion of this ceremony to be the taking off point for the new believer to *hit the ground running* in the area of sharing his faith. The very act of inviting all of his family and friends to his baptism would accomplish this goal – that is, if it had been properly emphasized for this purpose – which it seems fair to say it has not.

For the most part, the church has also failed to see that the neglect of the proper use of this spiritual ritual is a major factor contributing to the problem of so many Christians in the church who are hesitant to share their faith. Not having been trained at the very outset through the use of this ordinance mandated by the Lord, many believers' first experiences with witnessing are mostly left to chance, happenstance, or dumb luck, with little or no training. Notwithstanding this reality we must make the best use of our opportunities, such as they are.

Our personal testimony, then, is our rite of passage and the open door we are to walk through when dealing with the prospect of first sharing our faith with our relatives. Once we have done this, we have from that time on identified ourselves in the minds of our relations, no longer as individuals in our own right, but as followers of Jesus Christ. From now on we will be watched and listened to as persons representing him. For the rest of our lives we must guard our words, our conduct, and our lifestyles so that whenever one of our relations (or anyone else) thinks of us, they will be led to think about Christ—and that in a positive manner.

What Is Different about Our Witness to Our Relatives?

What comes next then when, having shared our personal testimony, we have a lifetime ahead of us, however long it may be—theirs and ours—to be a witness for Christ to those we love?

While the steps enumerated for witnessing to our families apply here as well, one important difference should be recognized. Just as our relatives will be slower than our family to learn of our decision to follow Christ, due to their less immediate proximity, likewise in the natural course of our lives they will receive less exposure to our experience of living for God. Though this may have disadvantages in terms of numbers of opportunities to influence them, there is one advantage this limitation brings that we may use to the benefit of our relatives.

Knowing that we will not see our relatives as often as our immediate families should motivate us to become more focused on using the opportunities we do have to "let our light shine." This is not to suggest that we preach or sermonize whenever we talk to our kinfolk. That would probably reduce our contacts even further. We should however, recognize the more fleeting nature of these opportunities and be alert to any openings that might present themselves to be a positive spiritual influence.

Family members who see us every day are treated to the spectacle of our day-to-day idiosyncrasies, flaws, imperfections, and sometimes, unfortunately, our inconsistencies. Of course, Christians do have shortcomings, but this does not make us hypocrites. Yet in a way it is good for our relatives to be spared such firsthand evidences of our "earthen vessel-ness." Our limited contacts make it easier for us to put our "best foot forward."

This is not hypocrisy by any means. It is simply awareness that familiarity is best received by family members who are more inclined, because of deeper ties of affection (hopefully), to overlook our flaws. Though they see us clearly in all of our "less spiritual" times, they are inclined to view us in the best light. And provided we are at least sincere in our efforts to follow Christ, they will be no less influenced toward God by our human frailties.

As for our relatives, the knowledge of our Christian convictions will cause them to come to accept and even to expect our new nature to reveal itself in our relationship with them. Over time they will be drawn to see the advantages of living for God as they "behold our good conversation in Christ" and our living testimony that "the path of the just is as the shining light, shining brighter and brighter unto the perfect day" (Proverbs 4:18). We will now consider some additional steps, beyond the ones already cited for witnessing to your immediate family, which you may take to help maximize your potential impact on these relations.

Some Additional Strategies for Witnessing to Your Relatives

- Evaluate the state of your relationship with your relative before you became a Christian. Ask yourself, "How can I take definite steps to improve the quality of this relationship?"

- Determine to find out more about your relative's interests, desires, hopes, and dreams. Look for ways to encourage his aspirations.

- Make every effort to remember her birthday, graduation, anniversary, etc., with thoughtful gifts, cards, and so on.

- Call more often, write more often, and visit more often. Showing such an interest will cause your relation to think, *So and so has become so much more interested in me and my life since she became a Christian.* This is the most powerful testimony you have to demonstrate God's love to your relative.

- Ask God to give you supernatural guidance and revelation concerning how best to pray for and witness to your relative.

- When your relative is dealing with a crisis, be there—in person, if at all possible, but by phone if not.

- Do something unexpected from time to time to show that you care and are thinking of your relative.

- Always be on the alert for any signals of spiritual receptivity, hunger, or even just curiosity.

- Do not shrink from making direct spiritual inquiries or even challenges from time to time. You do not always have to wait for a sign or a signal.

- Pray for God's continued favor and for his Spirit's working in your relative's life.

The most important message you can send to your relatives is to show a sincere and abiding interest in their lives. This interest should stand out as a landmark, directing them to the realization that since coming to Christ, you care more about their lives than you did before.

When this awareness hits home, God will be glorified as your relatives acknowledge that he is showing his love to them on a very personal level—through you! Though they may not show it or say anything to you about it, be assured they will be feeling the impact of your witness. And this will make them wonder, *Does God really exist? Does he really care about me?* And then they will think once more about you, and they will know the answer.

Chapter Three

Your Friends: "Bob, I Need to Talk with You"

When a person comes to Christ, his relationship to the world is radically changed. While family ties and blood relationships are for life, it is not necessarily so when it comes to our friendships. In the world, and even in the church, friends and friendships may come and go.

For the new believer, this change in his relationship to the world necessitates a change in how he views his friendships. Unlike family ties, friendship relationships are optional. Because the Christian must view his optional relationships in terms of their potential benefit or harm to his relationship with Christ, this evaluation can and should cause him to sustain only those friendships that are approved in Scripture.

Jesus, of course, was "a friend of sinners," and so we should be also. But the Christian knows that the only legitimate basis for friendships with sinners is for the purpose of being a witness for Christ. As for friendships in which we participate in activities and pursue interests that have any moral character to them, these are to be limited to those people who share our values and, in essence, our faith. Not that we should not share activities with non-Christians. (See Pastime Evangelism: Bowling for Jesus!) But these activities and interests will only be such as would be allowed in the context of godly living. "Be not unequally yoked with unbelievers. For what fellowship does righteousness have with unrighteousness, and what communion does light have with darkness?" (2 Corinthians 6:14).

The key word here is *unequally*. We are to be in the world as salt but not of the world in our lifestyles, convictions, or in our priorities. This has implications as we consider how best to be a witness to our unsaved friends. These friendships basically fall into two broad categories: first, the friendships we had with non-Christians before we came to Christ; and second, those friendships we make with unbelievers subsequent to our conversion.

Friendships We Had With Sinners Before We Came to Christ

Obviously, our advantage with people whom we knew before conversion is that we already have a relationship with them. Since these people knew us before we came to Christ, they have a unique vantage point in that they knew how we were before. As Christians, we do not become instantly perfect at the moment of our salvation, but we are, nonetheless, changed profoundly. This is bound to make a deep impression on those who knew us as sinners, when we were "one of them." Therefore...

Tell Your Friends What Has Happened to You

The new Christian should seek out the earliest opportunity to tell these friends what has happened in his life. There is no advantage in delaying. As explained earlier, the emphasis should be on one's personal testimony. For those who are receptive, an opportunity may present itself to explain the plan of salvation. If so, the spiritual novice need not be overly concerned with theology or scriptural expertise. The simple story of the gospel—of our Creator's loving hand in making us, of man's subsequent fall from grace, and God's plan of redemption through Christ's death on the cross—is enough to point the unbeliever in the right direction. Even an inexperienced child of God can relate the basic facts of his own conversion and how and why he came to place his trust in Jesus Christ for his salvation.

When sinners discover that one of their own has chosen to follow Christ the affect is profound and lasting. They will talk about it among themselves and compare impressions. More importantly, they will be watching their erstwhile companion in sin to see if the change is real and lasting.

The new believer will want to guard his conduct and take great care to walk worthy of the name by which he has been called. His friends, though skeptical or perhaps even cynical, will be looking for signs of change in their old companion. Such signs, when evident, will be a telling witness to the transforming power of Christ. Most people intuitively sense their own inability to change. Witnessing genuine change in the values, morals, and character of one who was known before conversion is a manifest testimony of the resurrection of Jesus Christ.

Separation from Unbelievers Is Inevitable

There will come a time sooner or later—and usually sooner, when a new believer will have to separate, in a certain sense, from his old friends. With such a radical change in world view as takes place in the life of one who has been enlightened, it is no longer appropriate to pursue the dead works and vain pursuits of those whose philosophy is "let us eat and drink, for tomorrow we die."

Not that the Christian should cut all ties with those he had "hung out with" before coming to Christ. Yet it is the natural tendency of people to prefer running with those whose lifestyles are similar to their own. With the drastic difference in outlook and priorities that exists between the children of God and the children of the world, this tendency is even more exaggerated. It is not unusual for the Christian to find that old friends no longer want to be around him. How could they if they have no interest in the Savior who is everything to him?

God's will is for his children to find fellowship with other members of his family and to find their place in the body of Christ. This may be stating the obvious, but it is important that new Christians understand the difference between spending time with unsaved former companions for the purpose of being a witness of Christ's love and fellow-shipping with unbelievers in their darkness and worldly pursuits. The new believer now has a very different foundation for his relationship with his old friends. Rather than fellow-shipping with them in darkness, the Christian is now a lifeline, a lighthouse pointing his unbelieving friends toward Jesus and the salvation he longs to give them.

When your former companion in sin sees that you no longer care to do certain things that you might have done together before, but that you still care about him—and in fact care more about him since becoming a Christian—he will be confronted with powerful evidence of the truth of the gospel. Godly love pierces the heart more than human love ever can. When a friend who knew you before your conversion experiences this, there will be no escaping the fact that God is real.

When this happens your friend will know that Jesus is alive and well and living in you!

Friendships We Make With Sinners After They Come to Christ

As "a friend of sinners," Jesus was supremely interested in the welfare of people. Everything he did on earth had behind it the intention of glorifying God and drawing lost souls to himself. This was also the motive for his friendships with sinners. By drawing alongside of them in compassionate interest, he sought to win their hearts and loyalties. Herein we find our own motivation and calling to befriend unbelievers.

As Christians We Have a New Motivation For Befriending Sinners

The difference between friendships we had with sinners before we were saved and those we make with sinners after we are saved is that, before, we were drawn to sinners because we were one of them, while after we come to Christ, we are drawn to sinners because we are one of his! Before, we were drawn to sinners because they were like us. Now we are drawn to them because we are like him! Previously, we desired friendships with unbelievers so that we could dwell with them in darkness. Now we desire friendships with sinners so that we can draw them out of darkness!

When we looked at ways to witness to friends we had before coming to Christ, we emphasized the importance of sharing our personal testimony with them. This is essential because, as we have seen, this is our declaration of independence from our old identity. It was necessary to make this declaration to those friends, as well as to our family and relatives, because this old identity we had before we became new creatures in Christ is the person that these people identified with.

While we should never stop sharing our testimony, when dealing with those who did not know us before Christ, it is not always necessarily the first priority. It is important, of course, because these people will still benefit from hearing how Christ has changed us. Still, it remains that people need to be confronted with Christ himself in order to be saved. It is one thing to hear about what Jesus has done in someone else's life and another thing altogether to actually come face-to-face with Jesus himself and to recognize his claims on our lives.

As Christians then, we should look at every relationship we have with sinners as an opportunity to win them for Jesus. Nothing is more important than this. To dwell with old friends (or new ones) and say nothing of the "hope that is in us" would be a tragic neglect of our God-given responsibility to compel them to come in. "…[H]e who does not gather with me scatters abroad." (Matthew 12:30, NKJV).

We want to be on the alert, not only for opportunities to gather in the unsaved, but even to seek out ways to create such opportunities. We are told to have "our feet shod with the preparation of the gospel of peace" (Ephesians 6:15) and to..."Preach the word! Be ready in season and out of season" (2 Timothy 4:2, NKJV).

In time, each new friendship we make with lost sinners will go through phases in which the person's receptivity to our witness will increase, decrease, or close off completely. We must realistically appraise each relationship according to the person's response and the leading of the Spirit. While we do not want to be the one to terminate friendships with unbelievers, it is only natural that we will gravitate more fully toward those who seem to show promise of coming into God's family.

To conclude, here is a list of practical suggestions for being the best witness you can be to your unsaved friends.

Twelve Ways To Influence Your Unsaved Friends For Jesus

1. Pray for an open door, for wisdom, and for God to lead you and help you.

2. Think about your friend, her needs, her hopes, her fears; look up scriptures to address these concerns

3. Do things for your friend; find ways to help him, bless him, and make his life easier.

4. Do things your friend likes to do; share his hobbies, interests, and activities.

5. Look for an opportunity to share the gospel. If possible, take a trip together, somewhere you know your friend has wanted to go—camping, the beach, a weekend getaway. Use this time to share your testimony and to give your friend an opportunity to invite Christ into her life, if you have not done so already.

6. Watch a Christian movie or video together, or a passion play.

7. Tell your friend of your hopes for his future and your desire to see him in heaven and to see God's blessing on his life.

8. Surprise your friend with a gift, a card, dinner, a birthday party, etc.

9. Introduce your lost friend to your saved ones.

10. Meet your friend's friends and family; be friendly to them and alert to their receptivity (they will most likely already know that you are a believer).

11. Always be on the lookout for opportunities to share encouraging words of truth that relate to your friend's needs.

12. Maintain an awareness of the unfolding history of your friend's life. As she faces different challenges, difficulties, setbacks, disappointments, even tragedies, make sure that you are the one who is always there for her.

You Don't Need Magic Formulas

Perhaps as you read these and other suggestions you may be thinking that they are merely statements of the obvious. That is okay. Maybe they are obvious—if one gives any thought to them. However, the temptation to not think of or do what obviously needs to be done is real. The enemy never tires of steering God's people away from doing what is our plain and obvious duty. Therefore, we ought never to tire of reminding ourselves, or of being reminded, to do what we know needs to be done.

In Judea

Your Center Circle

We now move out beyond your inner circle of family, relatives, and friends to those people who, though not as intimately connected to you as these, are nonetheless persons with whom you have frequent or potentially frequent contact. This circle includes those who live near you (your neighbors) and those who work near you (your coworkers).

Because you see these people on a more or less regular basis, we will consider them to be part of that special group of people in your private world—in this case, your Judea or "center circle" of influence—that God expects you to see as part of your mission field. As such, you ought to seek out, and even create, opportunities for sharing your faith with these people.

Our Heavenly Father calls us to transcend the closed circle of family and friends and to reach beyond these borders to expand the territory of our influence for his kingdom. Our calling as ambassadors for Christ is worthy of serious consideration. We do well to weigh and consider ways and means by which we may spread the salt of our influence to those who are living out their earthly lives in close proximity to our own. We turn, then, to consider these two subplots in our mission field: our neighbors and our coworkers

Chapter One

Your Neighbors: "And Like a Good Neighbor…"

The people next door to us, across the street, behind us, two houses down—it used to be that everyone knew everyone. We knew that the Smiths live here, the Joneses over there, the Browns down the street, and so on. In our increasingly mobile society, it is no longer as common for people to know their neighbors.

The tendency is toward more and more anonymity and isolation. This trend works against the promotion of community and undermines the old ways of relating to those dwelling near to us as "the people in my neighborhood." Nowadays we are more likely to see our neighbors as strangers who happen to live next door, whose names we may or may not know, but whose lives are a closed book, as ours are to them. We have even come to prefer it that way. We are content to dwell in our "ceiled houses" (Haggai 4:4), preferring the safety and freedom from obligation or concern that our anonymity gives us.

This, however, is not the way that God wants us to live our lives. As salt, we are to penetrate the world around us with the preserving savor of Christ. This suggests that we are to oppose whatever barriers worldly influences might exert to keep us from other people. To paraphrase the old State Farm Insurance commercial, "Like a good neighbor," we are to "be there" for those who dwell near us, reaching across barriers that would separate us with the love of God and a sincere desire for their friendship.

This should not be difficult to do. The first step we must take is to decide to make the effort.

Make up your mind that you will not be indifferent. You will not stand by and watch your neighbor go to hell without trying to rescue him. Just because you might not succeed does not mean you should not try. How can you know if you do nothing?

As Christians, we have to love better than the world. What is the world's standard? They love those who love them. We need to go further and love those who have no interest in us or thought for our welfare. After all, we're safe. Heaven waits for us. But if our neighbor doesn't know Jesus, there is another place waiting for him.

We must shake off our indifference and stop stalling. We have nothing to be afraid of, so what are we waiting for? Bake the cake. Send the card. Wave and smile. Do something. Start somewhere. Once you take the first step, then all the others will fall in line.

The following suggestions should help you as you seek God's direction for reaching the people in your immediate neighborhood.

Strategies for Influencing Your Neighbors for Christ

- Evaluate the status of your relationship. Are you total strangers, barely acquaintances, friendly but separate? Based on your assessment, seek ways to improve the quality of your relationships with your neighbors. How to do this? "He that would have friends must show himself friendly" (Proverbs 18:24).

- Begin to take specific steps to become friends, or closer friends, with those who live near you. Start by greeting them whenever you see them pull up in the driveway or walking out to the mailbox. Look for avenues and openings to start conversations, i.e., the weather, their lawn or garden, their kids, etc. Anything related to normal, everyday life will do. Most people genuinely appreciate sincere gestures of friendliness and will respond with courtesies and often with curious interest.

- Be alert for occasions where these greetings might turn into opportunities for short conversations. Don't worry about what to say—"How are you?"; "How are the kids?"; "Beautiful day, isn't it?" etc. Sooner or later, such friendly greetings will turn into conversations about the weather, the kids' school activities, the garden, the job, etc.

- At the appropriate time, seek to get together—for coffee, dessert, or even dinner—to discuss areas of mutual interest. Or drop off a cake, some cookies, or maybe a magazine with an article about something you know that person to be interested in.

- Begin to share more about your life, your interests, and your background. From here, you will find it very natural to inject references to your church, your faith, and your testimony. Be careful not to force it or overdo it. By the same token, be true to who you are! When people are getting acquainted, it is natural and to be expected that they will reveal themselves, their interests, their values, and their priorities to each other. Building friendships this way will sometimes result in the person you are reaching out to to actually take the initiative at some point to ask you a reason for the hope that is in you. When opportunities like this come along, be ready to give an answer!

- On other occasions, when the time is right and the Spirit is leading, you will be the one who might take the initiative to bring up the subject of your faith. Usually the way has already been paved through previous conversations in which you revealed your identity as a Christian. One important fact often overlooked by believers is that once you have identified yourself as a follower of Christ, people with whom you have developed a relationship will be anticipating, even expecting, you to talk to them about your religious beliefs. There is a reason for this: unsaved people, at least here in America, intuitively know that Christians are supposed to care about their souls!

- Be prepared to adjust your relationship after such encounters. Whenever you share your faith in Christ with someone, in this case with a neighbor whom you have befriended, the person's inward response to Christ will, from that point on, color and affect their outward response to you. Some will be drawn to you, others will draw back, and still others will be cautiously observant. These are clues indicating their frame of mind toward the Lord. In each case, you must be prepared to adapt your responses in whatever ways are best suited to keep the channel of your influence as open as possible. With those who are responsive, this will not be a challenge. With others who may be less so, you will want to take care not to force feed or overdose them with "spiritual things" whenever you see them. In such cases, it is best to let your conduct be your follow-up commentary on the words you have spoken. Having identified yourself as one of Christ's through your friendship and your words, you can rest in confidence that your conduct and character will be an ongoing follow up "epistle," known and read carefully by those who know who (and whose) you are.

- Be alert for signs of hunger or interest. People change. Things change, as do circumstances. Crises come and go. Your life and example as a follower of Christ should be the rock of reliability, a magnet continually drawing others toward you. As they attempt (with increasing futility) to deal with life's uncertainties, disappointments, and calamities, some, though seemingly disinterested in ear-

Robert Davis

lier seasons, may, as they behold your good conversation in Christ, have second thoughts. When this happens, you may be sure that "a door of utterance will be opened unto you."

- Bear in mind that the flood tide is on the rise in the life of every person who doesn't know his Savior. The floods arise even in our own lives. The difference is that we handle them with the confidence and joy of having under our feet the sure rock of our faith and hope in Christ. Those who do not have this assurance are building their lives, with all of their hopes and dreams, on the sinking sand of fear and uncertainty, however outwardly confident they may appear or pretend to be. As they contrast their private uncertainties with your steadfast confidence and joy, they may be compelled to reconsider their own convictions.

- Adopt the attitude of a servant. This has been mentioned before. Our "neighborly" connection provides unique and varied opportunities to do things for those who live near to us. Be there to help whenever your assistance might be needed. Our lifestyle of humble service is a sure proof of the self-denying, "other person" minded character of the Christ within us.

- Finally, always be ready with fresh "recruits" of truth and further "reinforcements" of faith as opportunities to pass these along come your way. Many are won slowly, patiently, with little rays of light here and there, pointing the way to the lighthouse of our hope.

Chapter Two

Your Coworkers: Character Is "Job One"

Because of the amount of time spent at work in any given week, it is likely that most of us have more contact on a daily basis with coworkers than anyone else in our lives, with the possible (hopeful) exception of our families. This being the case, our job may well be the mission field (or subplot) of greatest opportunity for us to showcase the life of Christ within us.

One thing is certain. Our coworkers will be able to see all too clearly the character of our example and how it stacks up against the content of our witness. The people who work with us, especially those who work alongside us, get to see "up close and personal" our true natures. Our work lives, as our home lives, are the crucible of our daily outworking of obedience to Christ's call to live godly lives in a world corrupted by sin.

It is clear, then, that the way we do our work and the way we conduct ourselves in relation to our coworkers is "job one" of our witness in the workplace. When the people who work with us know of our faith, we can be certain that we will be watched! Our observers will be making comparisons between themselves and us and between the quality of our conduct and theirs and, yes, between the quality of our work ethic and theirs.

To be a vocal witness for Christ in the workplace while demonstrating a work ethic that is less than exemplary, or even slightly suspect, is to send an unspoken message that undermines or even nullifies our verbal testimony. The way we do our work and the way we conduct ourselves in the workplace gives visible evidence demonstrating whether or not we are practicing the faith we proclaim.

Witness...with Caution

Concerning our verbal witness, special cautions adhere. These must be respected lest the very act of speaking of our faith becomes a testimony against it. It stands to reason that, as paid employees, our time does not belong to us but to our employer. It is fair to say that we are paid to do our work and not to spend our employer's time "witnessing" to our coworkers.

Of course there will be frequent opportunities where it may be permissible to share Christ without defrauding our benefactor. Since our time is paid for by another, we must take care to use only those opportunities for witnessing that do not divert us from performing the duties we are expected to accomplish while on the clock.

Sometimes we can carry on conversations, even spiritual ones if the occasion calls for it, while performing job-related tasks. People do talk on the job, after all. And Lord knows, not all of the conversations are work related. But caution must be exercised to avoid any instance of witnessing that might distract ourselves or those we are talking to from our work. The Christian must take care to avoid even the appearance of such indiscretion.

Put simply, there is a right and wrong time and a right and wrong place to verbally share our faith with coworkers in the workplace. We are to be "wise as serpents and harmless as doves" (Matthew 10:16).

See Your Workplace as Your Mission Field

Wherever you might want to be tomorrow, you are where God wants you today. The people around you were important enough for him to put you right there alongside of them. Too often we fail to realize that our employment in a "secular" job has positioned us on the front lines in the battle for souls. Not the pastor. Not the guest speaker. Not even the evangelist—at least, not where you are!

We need to remind ourselves that God sets our boundaries and the times of our habitations. This spiritual war we are fighting is worldwide, and God needs soldiers on every battlefield. Don't look at your place of employment as merely a job to make money to pay the bills. See it from the Lord's perspective...a place he has set you to be a light in the darkness, his beacon to guide lost souls into the safe harbor of his love. You are God's lighthouse!

Some Tips to Help You Be a Faithful Witness at Work

The following points should help us to stay focused on being faithful witnesses for Christ in our place of employment. We want to make the most of our opportunities as God's ambassadors in the workplace—both in the performance of our duties and in the sharing of our faith.

- Demonstrate by your character and the performance of your responsibilities that you are walking in a manner that is above reproach and worthy of one who is identifying himself as belonging to Christ. Do the work you are supposed to do, not minimally, or slothfully.

  Servants, be obedient to them that are your masters according to the flesh, with fear and trembling, in singleness of your heart, as unto Christ; not with eye service, as men pleasers; but as the servants of Christ, doing the will of God from the heart; with good will doing service, as to the Lord, and not to men.

  Ephesians 6:5-7

- Build your relationships with your coworkers. Let them see a difference in you—not just in your work but in the way you relate to them by your interest in them as people, by listening, showing concern, and caring. Make your coworkers feel that you are glad they are around.

- Let your first verbal witness be a simple signal remark or gesture that identifies you as one of Christ's followers. Bowing your head before lunch, reading your Bible (during break!), making casual mention of your church, etc., will alert your coworkers to your identity as a Christian.

- Carefully observe their reactions. Ask God to give you discernment and to show you who to zero in on.

- Ask the Lord for wisdom and for doors of opportunity. Pray that he would show you what to say and do. Wait for him to give you the green light.

- When the opportunity to say something arrives, have an idea in mind, if possible, of how you'll go about starting the conversation. It may be simply mentioning something you read in your Bible this morning or something you heard in church. Be sure it is an occasion when you and the one you are speaking to are either "off the clock" or doing tasks that will not be hindered by your conversation. Observe the person's receptivity and carry the conversation forward in the direction that seems most suited to his needs. Go slow and don't overdo it.

- For those who are receptive, continue this pattern over time, remembering to pray for the Holy Spirit's drawing and conviction.

- As your relationship progresses, seek the earliest appropriate opportunity to see the person outside of the work environment, after hours, if possible. Build on your friendship and keep drawing the person in with spiritual "food."

- Determine a time and a place where you can get together for the purpose of inviting the person to receive Christ. As an alternative, or in addition, you might invite the person to church or to a Bible study, if you have not already done so. Introduce your coworker friend to other friends from your church.

- Offer the person helpful literature to bring enlightenment, conviction, and encouragement. You may also discretely leave such literature around for others, in the cafeteria, in the lobby, etc., but only if you are sure that doing this will not be frowned upon by your employer. (You would probably be wise to ask permission first. Many companies have strict policies against distributing literature of any kind, and these policies must be respected.)

- Finally, make every effort to be the best employee, the friendliest coworker, and the godliest example you can be. Keep sowing and watering and believing God to bless your efforts. Be patient and not pushy. Give God time to work, and be sensitive here, as in all your witnessing endeavors, to do things on his timetable and not yours. (Hint: When the leading comes to your heart, then the timing is smart!)

In Samaria

Your Outer Circle

In the first two sections we looked at how to reach those in our inner and center circles of influence, the people with whom we share close ties either by relation or by proximity. As the people closest to us, reaching them with the gospel could properly be said to be *a minimum required level of response* on our part to Christ's command to preach the gospel to every creature. After all, each of us spends the greatest part of our lives in our personal Jerusalem and Judea. It stands to reason that we ought to do what is in our power to share Christ with the people we come most in contact with.

But there is another circle, our outer circle, or Samaria, if you please, populated with people who, though not bound to us by relation or location, are nonetheless situated within our reach. These people may not share intimate acquaintance with us, yet the opportunity is there for us to change that. I am referring to those individuals whose lives intersect with our own on an infrequent but often regular basis. I call these our *"frequent flyer"* contacts because all of us, for the most part, are "frequent flyers."

Whether it be flying to the supermarket to get food for dinner, or coming in for a landing at the gas station to fuel up our cars, or depositing our paycheck in the bank on the way to the drive-thru for a burger as we head for our child's ball game, we are a nation of people on the move. The beauty parlor, the barbershop, the bakery, the PTA meeting (if they still call it that)—round and round we go, meeting faces, going places, and more often than not overlooking these encounters with our fellow pilgrims on life's journey, even though we know that many of them do not know Christ—and that perhaps most of them do not know that we know him!

As we wander here and there throughout our Samarian borders, could it be that Jesus, who is traveling with us, might be interested in the eternal destinies of these people? Who would suggest that he was not? If so, then maybe we need to remind ourselves that Christ, in a very real sense, is trapped in our bodies. He wants to speak, but his words are trapped in our mouths! He wants to reach out, but his hands are tied to our own! For Christ's sake and for the sake of these people's future, we ought to be looking to turn these strangers into acquaintances and to turn these, wherever possible, into friends. Of Jesus (our example), it was said that he was a "friend" of sinners. We might ask of ourselves, could the same be said of us?

Our Enemies Have Souls Too

On the "outer rim" of our outer circle lie those people who, through conflict or controversy, we place in that category of individuals whom we consider our enemies. Our natural tendency is to revile, or at least to avoid, our enemies. Jesus, however, commanded a different response: "But I say to you who hear: Love your enemies, do good to those who hate you" (Luke 6:27, NKJV).

This scripture forces us to confront the fact that *even our enemies are to be considered as part of our mission field.* God's ways are not our own, but he does will for us to make them our own. Then the world will see in us a reflection of one greater than ourselves and, perhaps, be drawn to the source.

We will now look at these two outlying plots on our personal mission field. Perhaps there may be some opportunities to reach lost souls for God—souls that, heretofore, we may have overlooked.

Chapter One

Your "Frequent Flyer" Contacts: (Not So) Invisible Opportunities

The Christian who desires to be a faithful witness will always be on the lookout for opportunities to expand his circle of influence. The world is filled with lost people. We are surrounded with them. Sinners are everywhere. Upon reflection, it occurs to us that if we are doing what we can to reach our inner and center circles, sooner or later we run out of new people to reach for God. After all, we only have so many people in our family, our circle of friends is usually not very big, and we only have so many neighbors and coworkers.

So what do we do next? Keep up our godly example to those who know us, to be sure. But are we to limit our efforts to people we have relationships with only? It does not seem that this is the gospel mandate. The Scripture indicates that we, as God's ambassadors, are not called upon to proselytize "us four and no more." To be content with reaching out only to those we care about would be to show a love not in any way superior to that demonstrated by the ungodly. "But if you love those who love you, what credit is that to you? For even sinners love those who love them" (Luke 6:32, NKJV).

Since salvation is forever, and damnation too, the eternal soul of every person is priceless. We cannot shut our eyes and turn away. Jesus commanded us to "lift up your eyes and look at the fields; for they are already white for harvest" (John 4:35, NKJV).

When we take this admonition seriously, we will begin to widen the scope of our vision for reaching lost people. This widening of vision is not merely to be the burden and calling of the evangelist. We should all be willing to "enlarge the place of [our] tent…" (Isaiah 54:2) …and our compassion for wayfaring pilgrims on the road to perdition.

With this in mind, we turn, then, to the first of our Samarian circles of influence to seek out ways and means that, with God's help, may be used to draw more people to him. For the purpose of designation, we will call this the circle of our "frequent flyer" contacts.

As stated previously, these are the people we run into sporadically and intermittently on the highways and byways of our life—the waitress in the restaurant, our bank teller, the clerk at the supermarket, the librarian, barber, hair stylist, and so on. It should be obvious that each of these people present us with an opportunity to make new acquaintances, start new friendships, develop relationships, and enter the lives of people who may, as likely as not, have no other connection of any kind with a true Bible-believing Christian who can show them the way.

The biggest reason we fail to reach out to these people is that we are so caught up with our own lives we don't focus on them as human beings with hopes and dreams and problems and struggles of their own—and possibly unsaved souls in danger of being lost forever. If they are living without Christ, then we know they struggle with fear and uncertainty. Think about that the next time you see them bagging your groceries, or making your deposit, or bringing your lunch.

Of all the billions of people living on this planet, with all of the billions who have gone before, these small few—ten, twenty, thirty?—are the only ones in your arena in this day and this time and this hour. The people overseas may be beyond your reach. Those who lived in centuries past will never hear you, but these might. These are alive today, though maybe not tomorrow. Death may take them tonight. Tomorrow might be their last day on earth. Or yours. Today is available, while they live, to hear you.

Robert Davis

Today is available, while you live, to tell them. You can. Through God you are able. Tell yourself, "I will!"

How to Reach Your Frequent Flyer Contacts for Jesus

A thoughtful consideration of these persons as important people worth caring about will readily lead us to ponder ways we may invite ourselves into their lives. Then we will be in a position where we can help them to have a meaningful encounter with Jesus as they see and feel the love of God being shown to them through us.

The possibilities for reaching your frequent flyer contacts are endless in variety and number. With the proper frame of mind you can envision the task of reaching these people as exciting and rewarding, not at all a wearisome or dreadful burden. See yourself as collaborating with God as you "spy out the land" looking for those who are willing to hear his call. Pray. Look into your heart and decide what fits your style. Determine to give God your eyes, your ears, your voice, your friendly smile, and allow his compassion to reach out to these people through you!

To help you "boldly go where [you may never have] gone before," here are some possibilities to consider:

- *Start by looking at your frequent flyer mission as an assignment to make new friends.* Many believers have gone for years, even decades (God help us!), without establishing even one friendship with someone outside their community of Christian friends. Begin to cultivate friendships with the people you see "on the run." Start making efforts to improve the quality of these encounters. Be mindful of the fact that most people are very pleased and intrigued when confronted by someone who shows a genuine, friendly interest. Some simple steps to turn strangers into acquaintances and acquaintances into friends:

- *Smile.* Project a sincere feeling of pleasure in the fact that you are in the person's presence. This is so rarely done toward strangers that it will immediately arrest their attention. Though some will be suspicious, their curiosity will still get the best of them.

- *Develop the habit of easy, relaxed "chitchat."* Show thoughtful appreciation and courteous gratitude toward those who serve you—the waitress, bank teller, store clerk, etc. But don't stop here…

- *Look for openings to turn normally automatic, disinterested encounters into pleasant exchanges.* Be alert for opportunities to compliment, praise, admire, etc. Be sincere.

- As social etiquette permits, *find out, and remember, the person's name*…not necessarily on the first encounter. Avoid appearing too familiar, yet don't let over much caution cause you to miss opportunities to be friendly.

- *Develop a pattern of life in which you increase the likelihood of seeing that person on a regular basis.* Ask God for, and expect favor. Project an "I like you" vibe. If necessary, have in mind a simple conversation helper to increase the quality of your encounter. This may be as simple as a comment on the weather, your day, the surroundings, etc. Increase the person's sense of familiarity with you each time she sees you.

- *Start treating the person as a friend you've already made.* Continue to pray before and after each encounter. Begin sharing more about yourself, your interests, etc. Little comments here and there may be used to tip the person to the fact that you are a "person of faith." Be careful not to overdue it. On the other hand, you need not feel you should hide who you are. This is important because as you gauge the person's receptivity to your friendship, the knowledge that you have casually and unthreateningly revealed your Christian identity helps you to evaluate his receptivity to God.

• *Take the leap of faith, or rather, friendship, by extending an invitation to get together for whatever reason seems good*—coffee, shopping (ladies), lunch, or perhaps for some activity of mutual interest. If the person accepts your invitation, *voila*! Your new friendship is official! From here you cultivate that relationship as you seek whatever way God leads you to begin to draw that person to him. While you want to continue being careful not to come on too strong, don't forget to also be careful not to let fear cause you to hold back and do nothing. After all, a true Christian friend is one who is interested in the spiritual well-being of his friends!

• As opportunities open and trust develops, *begin to share more openly with your friend, using scriptures that relate to his needs.* Communicate your own relationship with God, how you came to faith in Christ, etc. Be prepared, in the right way and time, to invite him to receive Christ. Meditate (and pray) beforehand on how you might go about doing this.

• Make an effort to *expand your new friend's circle of Christian acquaintances* by introducing him to other people in your church. Have several people over for dinner, or coffee and donuts, or meet somewhere—a restaurant, a park, or wherever. Alert your Christian friends about your unsaved guest—not so as to have them gang up on him but to be sure they help to make him feel comfortable, accepted, at home, and above all...special!

- *Invite your friend to an openly spiritual gathering...*a small group Bible study, church, or some special church event. The person's receptivity will become apparent as you begin to "up" the level of spirituality by extending such invitations.

Depending on his response, you can keep moving things forward, slow down, wait, or even stop, if necessary. Rely on God's Spirit and lots of prayer to lead you. As you do these things, the Lord will be there with you, giving you insight, discernment, promptings, cautions, and "go" signals (or "stop" signals) to help you became a skillful fisher of men (and women). Some will be drawn in easily, others slowly, some will draw back, and others will pull out of their friendship with you completely. When this happens, do not take it personally. As Christ's representative, people will be reacting to you as such, and so it is important to keep this in mind. "He that receives you receives me..." (Matthew 10:40).

If a person turns away from you because he is not interested in Christ, you have done your part. It is between God and that person. Do not be the one to terminate the relationship, but if the person makes it clear by word or conduct that he is no longer interested in his relationship with you, respect his wishes and bow out gracefully. Remember, any stranger you change into a friend becomes, through you, a person within reach of the friend of sinners!

Chapter Two

Your Enemies: Fighting Fire with (Coals of) Fire

It may seem odd to look upon our enemies as part of our mission field. Our natural reaction is to loathe our enemies and to make every effort to avoid them. The Christian, however, has no such luxury. On the contrary, Jesus tells us, "Love your enemies, do good to those who hate you; bless them who curse you, and pray for those who despitefully use you" (Luke 6:27-28).

This is clearly at odds with the philosophy of the world. Those who embrace such teaching stand out from the crowd with the clear markings of the cross of Christ. Sinners recognize that to show genuine love to one's enemies is to transcend the deepest instincts of human nature.

What better way to show the surpassing glory of God's unconditional love than to demonstrate it toward those who regard us with disdain and even disgust? What greater proof of godly humility, forgiveness, and good will? Such actions not only proclaim the truth of the gospel, but also offer the most compelling and irrefutable proof of its life-changing power.

Reaching out to one's enemy is neither easy nor pleasant to contemplate. We bristle at the notion. Yet Christ commands it, and obedience is not just a noble option, it is a required submission. So the question is, will we do it?

There is a famous saying attributed to a Mme de Stael: *"To know all is to forgive all."* As Christians, we should absolutely be the best forgivers. What harm could come to us by extending good will to our enemies?

Right or wrong, if you were in the shoes of your enemy, you would no doubt have more sympathy for his point of view. If you have not walked in his shoes, how could you possibly know what the world looks like from his vantage point? Would you be willing to apologize even if you feel you were not at fault if doing so could change an enemy into a friend, or at least cause that enemy to lay down his weapons? Wouldn't it be worth the discomfort, or even the humiliation? After all, God knows the whole story, and isn't that enough?

And besides this, there is the far more important consideration that *an eternal soul may be hanging in the balance.* When all other considerations fail to move us, this one thought alone should not fail to do so. So where do we go from here?

Some Possibilities for Reaching Out to Our Enemies

Now that we are willing, what can we do to demonstrate God's love to our enemies? Since every situation is different, we will need to seek the leading of his Spirit. Here are some possibilities to consider.

- *Call or visit the person* you have in mind. Do so for the purpose of *offering an apology* for anything you may have said or done to offend him. Even if you were in the right, place the burden for restoration on your shoulders. This is not to suggest admitting to anything you were not guilty of. The point is, someone has to take the first step if there is to be reconciliation. We can hardly expect an unsaved person to be the one to make the first move.

- *Offer to make amends.* Ask the person, your enemy, if there is anything you can do to "make up" for the injury. Of course there will be ethical limits to this, and you do have the right to refuse to be exploited or manipulated. But you should be ready to respond to any reasonable and fair request if doing so can demonstrate your sincerity and bring glory to God. Most likely, the person will respond by insisting that everything is "all right" and that it's all "in the past."

- *Explain why you are doing this.* Share, as best you can, the cause of your change of heart…namely, your decision to follow Christ. Make the person understand that you are doing this because you want to please the Lord and that you also want to do it yourself because you would like to "make peace." This will cause the person to give both you and Jesus the credit for the gesture. While you don't want to leave the impression that you are doing this only to please the Lord, you do want to include him in your reasons so that God may receive the glory. (If the person already knows that you are a Christian, you may omit mentioning Christ, as the person will automatically attribute honor to God for your actions.)

- *Be prepared to give some information,* a gospel tract maybe or, better yet, a tape or a book that might point the way to Christ. You might even record something on your own, perhaps your testimony and a few scriptures explaining the gospel. A handwritten letter could be an alternative means of accomplishing the same end. Such a personal touch would make a lasting impression and would have the advantage of allowing the recipient to hear it or read it at a time convenient for him.

- *Be prepared to offer your genuine hand of friendship.* Be willing to invite the person out to coffee or lunch. If your offer is accepted, consider your erstwhile enemy to be your new-found friend, and proceed accordingly. If your offer is declined, be willing to leave your number with an open invitation should the person change her mind.

- *Leave on a cheerful, friendly note*! You have won a great battle against the forces of darkness. Even more, you may have won the heart of an enemy by your powerful demonstration of love, humility, and grace!

Coloring In Your Circle

Before concluding Part One we need to address the vitally important topic of making disciples. This subject is so important that it is fair to say that unwillingness on our part to help new believers in their journey toward discipleship might just disqualify us from taking part in the Great Commission. We should be more than just willing, but actually overjoyed, to help any such believer who desires our friendship and encouragement. Perhaps some have desired to be more useful in this way, but lacked knowledge. We will address the question of how to help new Christians become disciples below.

Also, I want to propose an endeavor that, if taken up by large numbers of believers would, I am certain, do more to help Christians overcome their fear of sharing their faith than just about anything else on the visible horizon. I will disclose the location of this buried treasure in Chapter Two of this section.

Chapter One

Jesus Told Us to Make Disciples... But How?

The goal of all evangelistic endeavors should be to make disciples. Jesus gave us this charge in Matthew 28:19: "Go therefore and make disciples of all the nations..." (RSV)

He wants disciples—that is, people who will follow him. A disciple is one who has disciplined himself to follow Jesus. There is a sense in which we all must make ourselves disciples, relying on Christ to empower us to do so. Yet as our Lord's command in Matthew makes clear, it is also true that new Christians are dependent upon more mature believers to help them become disciples—else why the command?

Discipleship is a life-long process, one that does not end until our earthly sojourn is over. Since new Christians know very little about following Christ, they are in great need of being shown how. They need a flesh-and-blood example. Paul said, "Be followers of me, even as I also am of Christ" (1 Corinthians 11:1).

Decisions or Disciples?

Every Christian should understand that making disciples is a universal call. None of us are exempt. Far too often, however, God's people have pursued "decisions" rather than disciples. By decisions, we mean leading sinners in "a prayer" to receive Christ. Unfortunately, there seems to be a popular notion abroad today that having done this, the "most important" part of the job is done. Such thinking may be a convenient prop for Christians to comfort themselves with when tempted to neglect, or even leave, these new converts to fend for themselves.

But God does not want his people to abandon his babies! In ancient Rome, unwilling women tossed their newborns on the trash heap outside the city. We do not read of any of these little ones scratching or clawing their way out of the refuse to make a life for themselves. Of course the analogy is not entirely accurate, for new Christians are not so helpless, and of course, they must be willing participants in their own walk with God. But they *are* vulnerable.

Are We Talking about "Follow-Up" Ministry Here?

The word *follow-up* is a term that the church has innovated to refer to staying in touch with people who have recently come to Christ. In popular usage, it has come to signify the idea of making disciples out of new converts. In the minds of most Christians, the thought is that we have two separate ministries involved here: evangelism, in which the unsaved person is led to come to Christ, and follow-up, in which the new believer is led to follow Christ.

This separation mentality has caused serious problems in the manner in which the church has dealt with these new "babes." There are many factors that have contributed to this mind-set, and space here does not permit a fuller treatment of these issues. At best, we can provide only a brief outline of the problems. The issues involved, however, go to the heart of what came to be known as the "lordship controversy." For our purposes, we will confine ourselves to those points that seem most essential in advocating a merging, or "reunion" if you will, of the two ministries, i.e., evangelism and follow-up, into one—namely, *making disciples.* This, after all, appears to be the perspective of Scripture.

An Unfortunate Separation

Perhaps it might not be such a bad idea to scrap the word *follow-up* from the Christian vernacular altogether. As this term has come both to symbolize and to perpetuate the notion that "keeping up with" or "staying in touch with" new believers is a ministry unto itself, separate from and different than evangelism (now almost universally understood to mean "leading people in a prayer" to receive Christ), it is an idea we would do well to abandon.

The reason for this is that, by entertaining a notion of evangelism as the ministry in which we "get the person saved" and follow-up as the ministry in which we coax the person to "follow through" on his "decision," such as it may have been, we leave the door open for the enemy to exploit this divided mentality to cause great harm. And this is exactly what he has done!

Here's how it has worked. First, it has led to the idea that getting the person to "make a decision" is the "most important" thing. While there is no doubt that the initial decision to come to Christ is the most important thing that ever takes place in the life of a person, this momentous event was never represented in Scripture as an isolated occurrence, an island pit-stop on the road of one's life. Coming to Christ, in the scriptural sense, is represented as a decision to *follow Jesus.*

The difference between a decision to "come to" Christ versus a decision or commitment to follow Christ is significant. While for many the two are merged into one—that is, their decision to receive Christ was in fact a decision to follow him; for others (it is to be feared, many others) it is not necessarily so. Who can deny that millions, perhaps many millions, have made decisions to receive Christ without ever making commitments to actually go on to follow the Lord? We do not wish to speculate concerning the theological implications involved here. That is for the theologians to wrestle with.

We are concerned, however, with the influence this empha-sis on obtaining "decisions" has had on the way Christians "do" evangelism. The result has been a movement to stress obtaining decisions as ends in themselves rather than as means to the scrip-turally mandated end of *making disciples*. In other words...

Decision-Making Has Replaced Disciple Making!

This phenomenon has resulted in two drastic misconceptions in Christian evangelism, one affecting the way our message is received, and the other affecting the way we go about doing the work of the Great Commission. Regarding our message, believ-ers, sincere though they may be, more often than not convey the impression to sinners that what God wants is for them to "say a prayer" (i.e. the "sinner's prayer"), and that having done this, they have now satisfied the gospel terms for receiving Christ. Granted, the more conscientious believer will, when witnessing to an unsaved person, usually make a passing remark about the importance of "meaning" the prayer. The listener naturally inter-prets this to mean he must be "sincere," that is, that he should really want Christ to come into his life when praying. But sen-timental feelings do not provide a solid foundation on which to build true commitment.

The implications of what it really means to follow the Lord are, more often than not, merely glossed over. Certainly there are those who at the time of praying are intent on really turning their lives over to God in repentance, faith, and submission to his will. Unfortunately for many others, the decision (expressed in the recitation of the sinner's prayer) was made without any clear knowledge of the implications of actually following through with the intentions professed in the prayer itself (typically expressed by phrases such as "I repent of my sins," "I give you my heart," "I make you the Lord of my life," etc.).

It is, for many, as though the saying of these words or the expressing of these intentions were, de facto, the very act of carrying them out. This, together with the typical endorsement and heartfelt approval and rejoicing on the part of the believer who has "led" them in the prayer, serves to validate the notion in the mind of many seekers that the prayer, rather than the *heart intent* expressed through the prayer, was the deed (of repentance and faith), and that all is now well. Well maybe, but then again, maybe not—at least not for those who confuse the saying of the prayer for the carrying out of the intentions expressed therein. And many do confuse the two. But to avoid skirting on the edges of a theological landmine, we'll move on to the second point.

Obtaining Prayers Has Replaced Obtaining People!

How has this evangelistic methodology affected the mind-set of the typical Christian? While we do not presume to read the minds of anyone, the fruit of our thinking will show itself in our conduct. Observing the conduct of many in the church, with respect to their evangelistic endeavors (on those rare occasions when such endeavors are forthcoming), the schism we have been discussing has resulted in a fractured approach to the task of drawing people into Christ's kingdom.

Falling into the same error just described, of substituting words for carrying out the intentions expressed in them, many in the church have adopted an attitude that says, in effect, all that I need to do, all that is important, is for me to lead the prospective sinner in "the prayer," and, "Voila, my job is done! I've 'got them saved', and what could be more important than that?"

Of course not all think this way. And even among those who do, such thinking is usually below the surface of their consciousness, but its affect is telling. Having done what's "most important," the believer reasons, "Whatever else I might do 'on top of that' (by this they mean "follow-up") is, well, though no doubt good and highly commendable, not actually essential because, after all, 'they're saved'—and that's the most important thing!"

And so, conditions are ripe for neglecting to follow-up on the new convert. This is not something that is overtly intentional on the part of the believer, at least in most cases. Yet when viewing follow-up from this perspective—namely, separate, important, noble, even highly commendable but still not, well, you know, "essential"—the door is thrust open to put off or "forget" to do it, or to do it in such a haphazard and, for want of a more tactful way of putting it, lackadaisical manner, as to do more harm to the new would-be follower than good.

This temptation toward laxness in following up new converts accounts for the bizarre phenomenon (so prevalent until the last fifteen or twenty years) of Sunday "morning after" celebration services in which the saints shared testimonies and praises to God for all of the people "won to the Lord" through the latest weekend evangelistic foray, while, in a truly pathetic irony, none of those won were present in the service to take part in celebrating their own conversion!

The Church Has Ditched Community Visitation

We no longer see this activity in most churches for the simple fact that, facing up to the fruitless nature of such endeavors, the church as a whole has pretty much tossed community visitation out the door. Rather than examining her methods to see what might be amiss, the church has opted instead to just throw the quest to birth babies out with the bath water. We are not suggesting that visitation is necessarily the best way to evangelize, but it is one way. Why have we chosen to believe that it is futile rather than to own up to our neglectful and unscriptural way of going about it? "The lazy man does not roast what he took in hunting" (Proverbs 12:27, NKJV). (For more on this see "Community Visitation…Does God Really Go Door-to-Door?" in Part Two)

The truth is that it is easier to simply lead someone in a prayer (get 'em "saved") than it is to devote oneself to an aspiring follower of Christ in friendship and commitment. The prayer can be said in a minute. The friendship takes sacrificial giving of oneself for the benefit of the newcomer to the faith. In other words, treating other people the way we ourselves would want to be treated.

God's Plan for Follow-Up Is Friendship

One of life's great treasures is the friendships we share with others. In the end, all any of us really have is our relationships with those we love—God, our families, and the friends we make along the way. Only these will bring comfort to us as we pass through the vale of eternity.

Jesus came to the earth to make friends with us. He was called "a friend of publicans and sinners" (Matthew 11:19). It is important to understand that Jesus never allowed his natural disposition—that is, his perfect character and purity—to influence him in any way that would create a barrier between himself and those he came to save. It is the common custom among men to react in a far different fashion. We do not, as a rule, gravitate toward those from different social backgrounds or to those with drastically different moral characters and lifestyles.

Sadly, this tendency all too often prevails in the church itself. God calls us to be like Jesus, but more often we in the church behave as though the customs and attitudes of the world are the standards for our social conduct. We choose our friendships based on who we feel is most "like us," who we think will share our values, or customs, our lifestyles, etc.

Of course, there is much that is right and proper in this. God does call us, after all, to "have no fellowship with" darkness: "Do not be unequally yoked together with unbelievers. For what fellowship has righteousness with lawlessness? And what communion has light with darkness" (2 Corinthians 6:14, NKJV).

But while we are commanded to shun unrighteous fellowship, this does not mean we are to shun those whom God is drawing into the fellowship of his family simply because they are different from us. While the world picks and chooses on the basis of fleshly affinities, we are called to esteem each other as worthy of respect and compassion because the same Savior who gave his life for us also gave his life for every other member of his body. We should be willing to give ourselves in friendship to whomever God puts in front of us, without discriminating on the basis of worldly considerations like income levels, educational background, or social skills.

We Can Only Help a Few, But That Is All God Asks of Us

Many aspire to help "the multitudes." Yet in reality, all any of us can do is help one person at a time—usually the one right in front of us. Jesus recognized his single "person-ness" while living among men on the earth. We see, however, that far from limiting his effectiveness, he allowed his bodily finiteness to cause him to focus his energies on a limited number of people, knowing that these, in turn, would greatly multiply his influence through the changes his example of love and compassion wrought in them. Though he ministered to the crowds, he gave his life to those closest to him.

Those special few who become a part of our lives, bringing love, encouragement, compassion, and hope mean more to us than the great evangelist passing through town who preached an inspiring message to the crowd and then moved on. Of course they have their part in God's plan, but it is those who give of themselves to us personally who share our deepest gratitude and affection. We should aspire to be to others what these have been to us.

To Be Born Again Is to Enter Into a Second Childhood

When we came to Christ, regardless of our age, our background, our education, or our experiences, each of us found ourselves embarking upon a journey into new and unknown territory. As beginners, we possessed neither knowledge nor experience in the life of the Spirit. We were literally entering into a new world just like a baby.

Not quite the same, however, for we were not babies but, in many instances at least, full-grown adults with a wealth of learning and experience behind us. Finding ourselves to be ignorant "beginners," though excited in our discovery of God as our heavenly Father, we felt a certain sense of vulnerability and dependence upon others to show us the lay of the land.

We need to remember what it was like for us when we were new in the faith and treat newcomers with the same dignity and respect we wanted to be treated with when we were in their shoes. Our manner of relating to those just starting out with God may have a significant impact in determining the quality of their spiritual childhood, and the impact of those early years is likely to be far-reaching.

As we know, children are prone to make many foolish and hurtful mistakes. On the one hand, we are ideally positioned to help the newcomer avoid many of the pitfalls and snares that the adversary will doubtless lay before him. One the other, we must be mindful that we are dealing with adults who, as such, must be treated with the dignity and respect their equal status deserves.

The spiritual life is not easy under the best of circumstances. The challenge we face in helping others become disciples (or disciplined followers of Christ) is to provide the encouragement and knowledge necessary for spiritual maturity while keeping the relationship on the proper level of mutual equality and respect.

What New Christians Need

More than anything else the new disciple needs to be established and confirmed in his new-found faith in Christ. We must look to God as the most important agent in effecting this confirmation. Through the indwelling of his Spirit, he is faithfully working to bring his new child into a deeper and more settled reliance upon himself.

Working hand in hand with his Spirit, the Lord uses his Word to enlighten, convict, and transform the new Christian—a process that plays out over a lifetime. In addition, the Father has ordained the church, the body of Christ, to nourish and strengthen those who have entered into spiritual life.

The Christian has a value system that is no longer based in worldly philosophies or customs. As a child of God, his priorities have changed, and this change is reflected in his relationships. His relationship to the world has now changed. His relationship to God as his heavenly Father must become supreme. His relationship to God's family—that is, to his new brothers and sisters in Christ—must begin to take priority as the place where he seeks his friendships and fellowship.

This change in relationship priorities is vital to a good start in the Christian life. There are other factors that are considered foundational to a healthy beginning.

> Therefore, leaving the principles of the doctrine of Christ, let us go on unto perfection; not laying again the foundation of repentance from dead works, and of faith toward God, of the doctrine of baptisms, and of laying on of hands, and of resurrection of the dead, and of eternal judgment.
>
> Hebrews 6:1-2

Robert Davis

In addition to the change in relationship priorities and a clear understanding of foundational doctrines, every new believer needs to be made aware of those factors that are necessary in order for him to grow spiritually: systematic Bible study, mind renewal, prayer, fellowship with other believers, and the importance of such things as serving others, giving, and sharing our faith.

Yet while such knowledge is vital, we must keep in mind that the most important thing *we* have to offer the new believer is ourselves. Every mature believer intuitively recognizes that making disciples pretty much boils down to being a friend to the new Christian. It is only in the context of genuine friendship that we may encourage and help him to get off to a good start in his walk with God. A blueprint is not essential, but the friendship and encouragement are.

Even so, a blueprint may be useful in helping clarify our vision, provided we remain open and flexible to the Lord's direction. The suggestions offered here are in the form of general guidelines. They are such as good common sense, compassion, and loyalty to God's Word and peoples' souls require. What follows are eight things every Christian should aspire to as a co-laborer with Christ in "making" disciples.

Eight Steps For Helping New Christians Become Disciples

1. Be a disciple. The first step in helping someone else become a disciple is to *be one ourselves*. We can have little hope of helping anyone else become a disciplined follower of Christ if we are not disciplining ourselves to follow him in our own life. We all know the basic formula for growing in God. Spend time in his Word. Read it. Study it. Pray. Seek the Lord's help and guidance. Trust him. Obey his will. Again and again, day in and day out, always seek

to grow in diligence, in discipline, in faithfulness, and in obedience.

Of course, this will also involve integrating ourselves into Christ's body, usually through the local church, or at least through joining with some Christian group or organization. How can we help others in the body if we are not a part of that body? None of us wants to set an example of "lone wolf" Christianity to a babe in Christ.

As disciples, we should be servers, givers, encouragers, helpers, doing our part to build up and support Christ's church and making an effort to bring others into his body. This is a lifestyle and example the Lord can use to show new disciples how he would have them live.

2. Pray. Next, *our efforts must be built upon prayer.* Prayer puts God first. Prayer puts faith to our efforts and faith in our efforts. We are to intercede on behalf of anyone we would seek to help in his walk with God. We are to pray scripturally, reminding the Lord of the promises he has made to his own, and to add to these prayers and petitions based upon our personal knowledge of the one we are praying for.

Above all, we are to be Spirit-led in our prayers, for "we know not what to pray as we ought." Prayer is so important that we should make a life-long project of studying it in the Word; from Jesus, our supreme example; and by praying ourselves. Regarding those we are helping in their new life in Christ, we should bring them before the Lord at least daily, however brief, and make an effort to spend quality time in prayer for them as the Lord impresses us to do so. We ought to be willing to do this for the first several months at least, in the life of a new Christian.

Our faithful intercession on behalf of the newcomer to Christ can spare her many heartaches. It is especially important to be alert to any promptings of the Spirit should he bid us unexpectedly, in or out of season, to pray for that person. No doubt were this practice more wide-spread in the church, far more of those won to Christ would truly go on to follow the Lord.

3. Be a friend. We must *become the new Christian's friend.* This is so easy. Yet it does take time and commitment. As Christians, however, our time belongs to the Lord. Older believers are to befriend younger ones, period. Though our elder status does equip us to show the way in the spiritual life, this does not imply that we should impose a student/teacher or "discipler/disciplee" relationship on the newcomer. Such an approach would be unnatural and detrimental to the friendship. After all, we all serve the same Master.

   Neither should new believers be looked upon as "ministry projects." Such an attitude reduces the status of the person to a burden, someone we "work" on. We are not called to work on anyone but ourselves in the Lord. People know when they are being treated as friends, and they know also when it is otherwise.

   Those getting started in the faith walk are our brothers and sisters in the Lord, *coequals* in God's family. We are merely predecessors in the things of God. Others have gone before us. Others will follow after. They will likely emulate us in their dealings with those who follow them. Genuine friendship should be the foundation of all our efforts to help those who are new in the faith. From this foundation, all else will flow freely and spontaneously as we walk in love.

Nor should we assume that such relationships are one-way streets. Remember, these new believers have Christ living inside of them, just as we. His manifestation in and through their lives as they learn to walk in the Spirit is just as valid and provoking to godliness as that of any other brother or sister in Christ.

It is true that new believers possess neither the wisdom nor the discernment of those who are more mature in the faith. However, the same spiritual life that flows through the older saint is also being channeled through those who are new in the faith—that is, the life of Christ, who indwells all who belong to him. As Jesus himself said, "Out of the mouths of babes..."

4. Teach the Word. The fourth step we should pursue if we want to help new Christians become disciples is to *guide them into those truths from the Word of God that will enable them to apply spiritual principles in their daily lives.* This does not require assuming the role of a teacher.

Instead, having experience relating biblical truths to situations in our own lives, we share this knowledge in ways that may help new followers to do the same. This is best done in the natural course of daily living. If we are alert, we will find opportunities to relate God's Word in practical ways to various situations in the lives of those whom we are seeking to influence. "Teaching them to observe all things whatsoever I have commanded you" (Matthew 28:20).

We should encourage new believers to develop the habit of seeking answers for themselves by searching the Scriptures and waiting patiently for the Lord's guidance. "For precept must be upon precept, precept upon precept; line upon line, line upon line; here a little, there a little"

Robert Davis

(Isaiah 28:10). This is the technique Jesus used as he lived out godly principles before his followers. He recognized, for example, the legitimacy of physical needs. Yet he drew his disciples' attention to God's faithfulness in supplying the needs of his children and that, knowing this, our primary focus should be on seeking first his kingdom and his righteousness (Matthew 6:33).

The Lord discerned attitudes of mind and heart and brought the revelation of the Word to expose, reprove, and correct those attitudes and values that ran counter to the Father's will. This is not to suggest that we seek out occasions to reprove others. When necessary, however, we ought in a spirit of meekness and gentleness bring the light of the Word to bear on situations when doing so will help a new believer keep his focus on God.

Our chief aim is to keep encouraging young Christians in their new lives and to help them on the path to spiritual maturity. As we keep the relationship Christ-centered while allowing plenty of room for enjoyable camaraderie, we will be faithful collaborators with God in pursuit of the best interests of our new family members.

5. Connect the new Christian to the local church. *Help the new believer become integrated into the body of Christ.* This is a two-way street, of course, and without a commitment to the same on the part of the one we are helping, the effort will be in vain. We help others as they help themselves.

There is, however, much we can do to kindle and nurture a desire for Christian fellowship in those who are new to the faith. By exposing them to others in the local church body, others who will embrace them as new brothers and sisters, we may help them find enjoyment in the friendship offered by God's people. This is extremely vital and may even be a matter of spiritual survival.

The new Christian is called to replace his worldly relationships with new ones in God's family, of which he is now a part. A new believer who has only one connection to the people of God is vulnerable to Satan, who would attempt to sever that connection by disrupting or destabilizing it, thereby cutting off completely that person's ties to the body of Christ.

Yet God does not want any of his children to look to a person or even the church for security, stability, companionship, or love. He reserves this role for himself alone. While we are not in any way to seek to diminish the quality or importance of our friendship to a new Christian, and should never do anything that might deliberately or inadvertently communicate a desire to lesson the friendship, we still recognize that, even as John the Baptist told those who were following Jesus, "He must increase but I must decrease" (John 30:30).

6. Be an example of a servant. While it is important to help new believers become integrated into the church, this alone is not enough. Our relationships with others in the body of Christ are not based upon friendship alone. Each of us are also called to lay down our lives in service to the church, the body of Christ, even as he laid down his life for us: "By this we know love, because he laid down his life for us. And we also ought to lay down our lives for the brethren" (1 John 3:16).

Our manner of living is the paramount means for influencing those who have just come to Christ. What we do will bear greater weight than what we say. The sixth thing we can do for newcomers to the faith is to *demonstrate by example this life of servanthood to God's people.* As unique individuals, our gifts and abilities vary. God, in his sovereign wisdom, has placed each of us in the body as it has pleased him. This is true whether we consider the church as a whole or view it from the perspective of the local assembly.

No one person can contribute to the needs of the church in exactly the same way as any other. But all are of equal importance for the health of the body. This is made clear by the analogy in 1 Corinthians 12 comparing the individual members of the church to the members of the physical body. The new believer needs to discover where her God-given abilities may best be employed in the building up of the church.

Those who are unsure of where their talents lie might be encouraged to serve in little things. All of us can do this. There is never a shortage of opportunities to help out with tasks requiring no special skills or abilities. By trying out involvement in different ministry opportunities in the church, the newcomer can discover where his skills and abilities fit.

God has created us unto good works. He has placed within our hearts a *zeal* for good works. The Christian aspiring to follow in the steps of his master will find fulfillment as he discovers the Lord's special place of service for him in the body.

7. Help the new Christian witness. In addition to helping them find their place of service in the body, we should also *encourage new Christians to begin sharing their faith in Christ with others.* This is something that most of us are not doing. The reason for this is that, more often than not, we ourselves are not sharing our faith in Christ. Yet God

has called all of us to be ministers both to the church and to the lost. It is important to overcome this reluctance. Patterns established early in our devotional lives tend to follow us into spiritual maturity.

We need to recreate our Christian church culture by helping each other to face up to our responsibility to carry out the Great Commission. Ask your new friend if you might go with him to talk with his family and friends about his newfound faith. While the prospect of doing so might frighten him (and you), he will likely take his cue from you. If facing the challenge of sharing his faith with family and friends seems too much to start with, why not take him with you to visit some elderly people in a nursing home? How intimidating could that be?

Or maybe you could sit down together and write letters to people telling them about the good news. (See "Letter Writing as a Ministry Could Revolutionize Evangelism!" in Part Two.) If your own beginning in the faith walk was lacking in the area of personal evangelism and you had no one to help you, wouldn't you have appreciated having someone older in the Lord, experienced in witnessing, to show you the way? Why not be for your new friend that "someone" who was not there to help you when you were getting started?

Earlier we made mention of the profound impact water baptism might have for helping new disciples get off to a strong start in sharing their faith in. In "Maybe We Should All Get Baptized Again" (Part Four), we present a proposal and a challenge for the church to return to this God-ordained sacrament in a way that might help it to realize water baptism's sovereignly intended usefulness for winning the world to Christ and to win his people back to a love for publishing the gospel so characteristic of the early church.

8. Recommend a systematic course of Bible instruction. Finally, there is one more thing we can do to help new believers start well. Knowing the crucial importance of God's Word as the principle agent of change, renewal, and empowerment in the life of every Christian, we should *earnestly challenge every new disciple to embark upon a systematic study of the Scriptures.*

Step Four dealt with helping the new disciple begin looking to God's Word for guidance in his daily living. Here, however, we have in mind encouraging beginners to aspire to a deeper knowledge of the things of God than can be obtained from mere skimming. Such a course of action is essential in order to lay a firm foundation for the Christian life.

Every believer needs to become rooted and grounded in the Word of God in order to become established in the faith. This challenge may be implemented in any number of ways. Many churches have new believer classes, or Bible courses. The sincere young Christian should be eager to avail himself of this instruction. Some may feel called to go further, perhaps enrolling in a Bible school or college, if their circumstances permit. Or a Bible correspondence course, if they do not.

If none of these options are available or practical, it may be necessary for you to offer your own assistance by providing some curriculum or instruction lessons of your own. Most mature Christians should be able to teach the fundamentals of the Christian life to those who are new in the faith. (Note: As a possible aid in this regard, a list of important topics, together with Scripture references for each, is provided in Appendix A: "Lists That Levitate." These may be inserted as Scripture chains in the new believer's Bible for future reference.)

Studying God's Word together can be a powerful means of awakening in the new Christian a deeper hunger for spiritual knowledge. Praying together can provide the same benefits—our example of humble, dependent prayer provides a pattern for the new disciple to follow when looking to God for his own needs.

Before coming to Christ, each of us spent a lifetime learning the ways of the world—a world we now know is under the dominion of Satan. Shouldn't we try to encourage newcomers in the faith to pursue whatever course of action necessary in order to gain a well-rounded overview of the ways of God and the life he calls us to live? Systematic Bible instruction is the means God has provided for us to gain the spiritual knowledge necessary to lay a good foundation for our earthly pilgrimage. No price can be too great to achieve this advantage.

These eight steps are reasonable, achievable, and worthy of our efforts, that we might follow Jesus's command to make disciples. We do not need to be experts. A willing heart, a prayerful, dependent faith in our heavenly Father, and a compassion for those who are just getting started in their walk with God are all we need to fulfill Christ's call.

Robert Davis

Chapter Two

The Tract Nobody Is Using

Looking around the Christian world, it is painfully obvious that many believers are not experiencing the victory God desires for them to have in their personal witnessing. The idea offered here is not new, nor would it be difficult to implement. Yet if it were to ever gain wide acceptance in the church at large, it might be a golden key to unlock the door freeing multitudes of Christians to share their faith with those around them.

The thought of putting one's personal testimony in writing is, on the face of it, so obviously appealing and so laden with promise for generating enthusiasm for evangelism among those who embrace it that it is a wonder God's people have failed to grasp its significance.

Who could deny that having ready at one's disposal a written narration of his personal testimony would serve as a powerful, ever-present motivation for sharing his faith in Christ? Why have we failed to see this? Imagine, no more tongued-tied, frustrating encounters. No more feeling defeated and saddened over missed opportunities to point someone you came to care about toward God's saving grace. I am convinced that if we, as God's people, would decide to make our own personal testimony tracts that our lives as Christ-sharing Christians would never be the same.

Many times we meet someone in a chance encounter and, after just the briefest of exchanges, feel pangs of longing for that person's soul. We are drawn to people that way because we have God's love inside of us wanting to be let out. And what of others with whom we've shared a deeper acquaintance, yet still words we've longed to say have eluded our lips? How much better to have on hand a means of communicating our faith in Jesus, knowing that as we share our trust in the Lord through a written message, we are pointing the way for others, many of whom we may never see again.

It would not be hard to do. If you are looking for a way to easily, yet effectively, share with others what your relationship with Christ means to you, why not sit down, gather your thoughts, and put in writing the words that best express your heart's reasons for trusting in your Savior. If this is an idea that appeals to you, I pray the suggestions that follow may help you to share your personal testimony...in writing!

How to Make Your Own Testimony Tract

- Start by first contemplating your life before you came to Christ. What was your life like before you knew Jesus? What were your struggles, your disappointments, and your fears? Attempt to distill these thoughts into two or three paragraphs, depending on the amount of space you will have in your tract.

- Next, describe the events surrounding your conversion. How did Jesus first become real to you? Did someone witness to you? Give you a tract? Perhaps you were listening to a gospel message on the radio or TV. Describe what happened inside your heart when you first came face-to-face with Jesus. Be sure to include two or three key scriptures that God used to enlighten and draw you.

- After this, describe some of the changes that have taken place in your heart and life since coming to Christ. How did your outlook change? What is different about you now?

- Conclude with an appeal to your reader. Ask him to give his life to Christ. Press the appeal with a sense of urgency. Perhaps a scripture emphasizing the importance of acting now.

- Be sure to offer some directions for those seeking further information. You might suggest a helpful book or some other source of enlightenment and inspiration. Include your church name, address, and phone number on the back of your tract.

Soon you'll have your written testimony right at your fingertips, ready to use whenever you want to reach out to someone with the story of how Jesus changed your life. Do this now and your life will never be the same!

Part Two:

Beyond Your Circle to the Uttermost Parts of Your World

Daring To Go Beyond Your Borders...

If you have read the preceding pages to this point, you have now completed Part One of this book, "Reaching Your Private World." All of us are responsible to do this, to reach our private world for Christ.

We are all equally important in the Great Commission, and each of us has a unique role to play that no one else can fill because no one else can reach your private world as effectively as you. While some of you may be content to reach those in your Jerusalem, Judea, and Samaria, others may wish to go further.

In Part Two, we now consider how we might go out past our Samarian borders, beyond the outer circle of our private world—the world we live in and work in. The evangelistic approaches which follow target people we would not likely meet in the course of our normal daily living.

Keep in mind the following "prerequisites" if you would derive any benefit from the instructions in this section.

1. First, *you must want to go beyond the circle of your private world.* You must have a desire to reach out beyond your

circle, to go places you would not normally go in the course of your day-to-day living.

2. Second, *you must be willing to reach total strangers with the gospel message.* Some are now openly skeptical or even critical of the idea of doing this. The preference for sharing Christ in the context of meaningful personal relationships, while understandable, is not a legitimate argument against reaching out to strangers.

3. *You must be willing to go beyond the borders of your comfort zone,* out past the land of the familiar, into what, for you, will be uncharted waters of outreach to seek new avenues for winning sinners to Christ. You must be willing to be a minority member of the body of Christ and be possessed of a resolute and courageous attitude in the midst of others who may show little or no interest in going with you.

4. *You should be willing, if necessary, to be the object of criticism* (veiled or otherwise) by some well-meaning brothers and sisters in the church, who may take a dim view of your overtly evangelistic approach to winning the lost. You should maintain an attitude of humility in the face of such adversity, and guard against the temptation to judge or resent those not sharing your sentiments. We should respect our differences and appreciate the uniqueness of God's workmanship in each other.

5. Finally, you should be willing to be used by God, not only to reach out beyond the borders of your daily living, but to be available for him to use *to train others behind you who, beholding your example, are provoked with a desire to follow it.*

Robert Davis

...To the Uttermost Parts of Your World

This section is about reaching out to strangers. Ultimately, it is hoped that such efforts will enable you to meet new friends who are open to a relationship with the Lord. The avenues for reaching out to these strangers are divided up, for descriptive purposes, into seven outreaches or ministries, using titles or designations commonly employed by the church when referring to these particular means of evangelism.

These labels have evolved to describe either the location or the method of the outreach or the particular target of the same. Listed in the order they appear in this section, we have: 1) Street Witnessing; 2) Door-to- Door Visitation; 3) Telephone Evangelism; 4) Letter- Writing Evangelism; and, 5) Children's Evangelism. Some of these means for reaching people are found in at least some churches in America—though rarely does a church have more than two or three, and the participation in these is usually limited, at best. Numbers three and four are rarely found anywhere, even among the very most outreach minded churches. We shall see when we come to these two chapters that this is a situation much to be regretted.

Each of these avenues for reaching people has its' own particular strengths and weaknesses. Each, when done properly, has a significant part to play in the cause of reaching everyone everywhere with the good news of the gospel.

Bear in mind that almost any good thing can be abused, misused, mistreated, and misunderstood. Such lapses by believers (along with the personal fears and insecurities so common in the church regarding "direct" witnessing) have caused many in the body of Christ to have little enthusiasm for the evangelistic outreaches addressed in this section—as amply proven by their lack of participation in them. As will be stated repeatedly in the coming pages, however, the fact that some may have, in ignorance, but; (I believe); with the best of intentions, pursued evangelistic activities- ; including those listed above, improperly and even unscripturally, this does not argue against the outreaches themselves, but only against some of the manners in which we have pursued them.

It is clear to those who do these outreaches that God is in them. That is, they see firsthand that his Word goes forth through these avenues, with power, conviction, and life-changing effect in the hearts of those reached.

Furthermore, it is a fact that many people would not be reached any other way without these avenues for doing so. Many lost souls have greatly diminished prospects for hearing the gospel if you subtract all of the faithful Christians who set aside their own agendas long enough to go in search of these people. Think of all of the shut-ins, recluses, and socially deprived people living in their "ceiled houses" who have little or no likelihood of stumbling into any meaningful relationships with believers in their daily lives. Many people in this world go weeks and even months on end without so much as a phone call or a letter in the mail. No one ever stops by or even gives them a thought.

And then, of course, there are the multitudes who have not even the merest acquaintance among family, friends, neighbors, or even coworkers with any genuine born-again believer. Who would dare say that these might not benefit from a "chance" encounter with a Christian on the street, at their doorstep, or even on the other end of the telephone or in the afternoon mail?

We proceed, then, for those who wish to do so, trusting that some of you who feel a special call and challenge from the Spirit will find in theses pages some helpful bit of instruction or encouragement to go forth...even beyond Samaria, to the uttermost parts of your world!

Robert Davis

Chapter One

Street Witnessing

Talking to Strangers Is Good!

Street witnessing, or going out to public places to talk to strangers about Christ, seems to have fallen out of vogue in some Christian circles in recent years. This is an unfortunate development for the obvious reason that, as a result of the decline in the number of Christians reaching out to strangers this way, fewer people have a chance to hear a personal witness of God's saving grace in Christ.

Believers cite various reasons for choosing not to involve themselves in this form of evangelism. Some are openly critical of street witnessing, while others simply have fears or reservations regarding the effectiveness of such a means for spreading the gospel. These might consider it if they were persuaded of the vital role street witnessing could play in the cause of world evangelism. For this reason, we will examine the more prevalent objections and criticisms currently circulating about street witnessing in order to clear the way for those who might desire to step into the waters of this type of evangelism. But first, to put a proper frame of reference in place, we will look at some scriptures on the matter.

What Does God Say about It?

The following scriptures are familiar to all who are acquainted with the Word, yet it will not hurt to look at them again in the light of this seeming fall from grace that street witnessing has suffered in the body of Christ. Those who would prosecute a case against witnessing to strangers, whether it be "street witnessing" or any of the other outreaches described in this section, must contend with God's Word as the final arbiter.

We will start then with Mark 16:15: "Go into all the world and preach the gospel to every creature." While this scripture contains no direct reference to street witnessing (a modern designation), it is apparent that any honest interpretation of this verse would include witnessing to strangers. In light of the command for universal inclusion (every creature), it is clear that many such creatures will never be found unless someone goes out in search of them, wherever they may be.

Then there is Luke 14:23: "Go out into the highways and hedges, and compel them to come in, that my house may be filled." This is a little more pointed. One might argue that "highways" could refer to people in "high" places and "hedges" to those in hidden, private, or even "low" places. Yet such an interpretation would hardly necessitate or justify excluding the more obvious one—that is, people on the highways and byways, the thoroughfares and open "public" places, as well as those in more hidden or private places…people everywhere.

There is also Acts 8:4 (NKJV): "Therefore those who were scattered went everywhere preaching the word." You can picture this quite easily. These believers were driven away from their homes by unbelievers, many of whom were no doubt strangers, strangers who nonetheless knew that these people were Christians. The reason they knew this was because these believers preached everywhere they went. The most obvious implication here is that as they encountered people in the course of their travels, they witnessed to them. Please note that they had not, as yet, had opportunity to "befriend" them.

Space does not permit us to look at the many other examples found in the gospels, in the book of Acts, and in the epistles. A few questions should serve to illustrate the point, however, that street witnessing—witnessing to strangers—seemed to occupy a prominent place in the life of the early church, which, with the scriptures we have just read and many others we might have read, would seem to entitle us to claim that it is scriptural. We share these questions here:

Are there any examples in the gospels where we find Jesus preaching to strangers (or at least to people who did not know him since, as the son of God, he himself knew all people)?

Are there any examples in which we find the Lord instructing his disciples to do the same?

Do we find any instances in the book of Acts in which we see Peter preaching to strangers? How about Paul? What instructions do we find them giving in this area?

Would any honest, first-time reader of the epistles, not previously exposed to any Christian sentiments one way or the other on the matter, gather the impression from his reading that Christians were *not* to witness their faith in Christ to strangers?

An honest answer to these questions would seem to justify concluding that in the life of the early church, this kind of evangelism was practiced and that the written record is sufficient to conclude that it is scriptural for us to share our faith with strangers.

Criticisms, Legitimate, and Otherwise

No one likes to be criticized. But wisdom and humility dictate that one should always be willing to acknowledge truth, even when leveled by the voice of criticism. Regarding street witnessing, i.e. witnessing to strangers, whether they be found in the highways, the hedges, or anywhere else, there are a number of points frequently raised by those who voice skepticism toward this kind of evangelism. We will look at the most common of these and try to appraise the legitimacy factor of each.

Six Most Frequently Mentioned Objections to Street Witnessing

1. Objection # 1: Street Witnessing is intrusive: It is offensive to approach a stranger for the purpose of discussing religion. (Frequently, prejudicial pejoratives are bandied about when referring to this type of evangelism, calling it "button-holing" people, or "Bible-thumping." This is a common technique in debate, i.e. negative characterization, making one thing, in this case, street witnessing [or, talking to strangers about Christ] out to be another—in this case, button-holing, Bible-thumping, "pushing religion," etc.)

    Response: It may be offensive, but not as a matter of course. It would depend on the nature of the intrusion. We have already seen that God does, in fact, want us to "intrude" into people's lives to announce the good news of his love and grace. This being the case, such an intrusion only becomes improper if it violates the universally accepted customs of courtesy, respect, and benevolence.

    Granted there have been those who have violated these standards, yet this does not make a case against sharing our faith with strangers. Careless disregard for good manners or insensitive or offensive attitudes should of course be avoided. On the other hand, approaching strangers with tact, humility, and politeness for the purpose of telling them about Jesus is not something God considers *intrusive* in any negative sense of the word.

2. Objection #2: Too many Christians, when street witnessing, focus on those they are talking to as "objects" to "preach" to rather than relating to them as real people. Likewise, such believers neglect or even ignore their obli-

gation to extend friendship toward those they are talking to—even when there might be signals from some of these people that they would be open to such an offer of sincere friendship, were it forthcoming.

Response: We must acknowledge that this has occasionally been the case—though not nearly as often as some critics seem to suggest, in my opinion. Yet the objection once again does not apply to the act of talking to strangers but to the manner in which some have gone about it. Ironically, the frank recognition by those offering this criticism that there are some who would be receptive to such friendship, were it offered, is in fact a compelling argument to justify talking to strangers.

3. Objection #3: Christians shouldn't "preach at" people, but instead, we ought to live our lives in such a way that "our manner of living will be our witness." (This seems to be a convoluted combination of the previous two objections—attacking both the idea of witnessing to strangers in the first place and then criticizing the manner in which it is done—for good measure.)

Response: The phrase "preach at" is, itself, prejudicial. It seems that some are disposed to characterize those who "take him to the streets" as engaged in preaching *at* people. In other words, not relating to them, not caring to hear the other person express his views, but overzealously seeking to "push" or "shove" their beliefs on these poor, unsuspecting victims.

This has happened here and there, unfortunately, and such instances do reveal a lack of sensitivity on the part of some. To hear it from some critics, however, this is par for the course and standard operating procedure with virtually all of those dedicated Christians who have ever sought to lead a stranger to Christ. The Lord cannot be pleased with such censorious generalizations. We are, after all, family. While some have preached "at" people, most have not. While some have been pushy, most have been polite. While some may have even "thumped their Bibles," most have demonstrated love and concern for the souls they were trying to reach.

As for our lives being a witness, much could be said here, but for our purpose, we offer this response. Of course our lives should be a witness. Who ever said otherwise? But the idea that our example and our testimony are mutually exclusive is as unscriptural as it is unbalanced. It is also unfair to sinners.

How can they know we are Christians if we do not tell them? Remember, we are talking about strangers here. And who would dare to say that all who see us, even if they were to learn of our faith in Christ, would take the initiative to make the first move in "asking us a reason for the hope that is in us"? Some might. But many never would.

4. Objection #4: I don't "have the right" to speak to a total stranger about Christ until I have shown that person the love of God.

    Response: Jesus has earned the right for us to do so, and he has commanded us to do it. Furthermore, doing so is an act of godly love. Certainly deeds and gestures can lend great power to our words or undercut them if such actions are not in harmony with what we say. But for a stranger, whom we may likely never see again, how much opportunity does one have to show by deeds and gestures that God's love has caused us to embrace a new and compassionate way of living?

Robert Davis

5. Objection # 5: Too often, Christians witnessing to strangers are condescending, condemning, and holier than thou.

   Response: If this really has been your experience, then God help you, and even more, those who were so mistreated. I think that the heavenly records will reveal quite the contrary, however. And that, in fact, the majority, probably the vast majority of God's people, have taken great care to share their faith in humility and with proper respect for the dignity and worth of those they sought to reach. In any case, it has no bearing on the debate over whether talking to strangers about Christ is good, right, or "of God." It *is* good if done right, and it is "of God" when done right.

6. Objection # 6: People are intimidated or even offended by strangers approaching them to talk about Christ. (Another variation of Objection #1.)

   Response: Sometimes, yes. But such reactions are not valid reasons for not doing so. Jesus and Peter and Paul, et al, offended many whom they spoke to. Those who resist and resent the truth are obviously going to be offended by it.

   As for the timid, well, God has ways of calming people. Good manners, kindness, gentleness, compassion, and sincerity are usually very effective tools for putting such people at ease.

These then, are the arguments most frequently advanced as objections against talking to strangers. However, we have seen that they do not hold water when we differentiate between right and wrong ways of witnessing to people. Still, this type of evangelism is not for everyone. We have dealt with the more prominent objections to prepare the way for those who might want to try reaching out to strangers for Jesus.

As for those who do not feel so drawn, that is okay. We each have our own callings. We are all called to reach our private world. But if street witnessing or any of the other avenues for reaching sinners, especially strangers, as outlined in this section does not appeal to you, please respect the fact that this may not be the case for others in the body of Christ. After all, we're all different and we each have a part to play in God's great plan to win the world.

Those who are interested should not try to force participation from those who are not. Nor should they try to make others feel guilty who do not share their burden. Such tactics are not approved by the Lord.

On the other hand, neither is it appropriate for those who do not have a burden for street witnessing or the other avenues covered here to engage in recriminations, ulteriorly motivated criticisms, or unjust arguments against such outreaches from a desire to undermine or discredit the evangelistic efforts, or worse, the integrity or character, of those who do.

Some Advantages and Disadvantages of Street Witnessing as a Means of Reaching the Lost

First, some advantages:

1. A willingness to talk to strangers enables a believer to be used by God in a far wider range of situations and circumstances than would otherwise be the case.

2. Sinners living anywhere near such a Christian will stand a greater possibility of being witnessed to in the event of a chance encounter.

3. Since we know that the Word of God does not go out void, it is certain that Christians who speak to strangers on his behalf do not do so in vain. They will be used by God to draw people to himself. Souls will be enlightened, convicted, and saved. Who can argue against that?

4. A sinner, singled out from among others by a believer, will be compelled to wonder why he was "chosen." The Holy Spirit frequently impresses upon the sensitive soul that the encounter was not an accident. And who can say what circumstances that person may have been dealing with at the time?

5. An unbeliever approached by a stranger sharing Christ will be sure to narrate the details of this encounter to others, certainly his family, and probably his friends as well. In telling others what the stranger said, he will, in effect, be passing along the words of the gospel!

6. Those so used of God in this kind of evangelism are blessed in many ways, as his Spirit is always eager to bestow blessings on those who allow themselves to be used to reach others. "He who waters shall himself also be watered" (Proverbs 11:25).

Some Disadvantages Found in Street Witnessing

What about disadvantages? There are some, though these merely advocate the need for other approaches without in any way undermining the legitimacy of street witnessing as an avenue for reaching people. Some disadvantages or limitations encountered in street witnessing:

1. Due to the haphazard nature of the encounter and the likelihood that the person being witnessed to is "going

somewhere," opportunities for future contact are limited. Though some people in public places are open to talking to strangers, and may even be receptive to the possibility of allowing such an encounter to be the start of a new friendship, others are less so.

2. This kind of evangelism is not systematic and, therefore, not the approach to use if systematic coverage of an area is the goal.

3. In an increasingly cynical world, some are inclined to suspect the motives of strangers who approach them.

4. People in public places, because they are usually "in transit," may be pressed for time, in a hurry, and so, less than eager to take time out from their busy day to talk to a stranger.

We have dealt in some detail with the arguments and criticisms currently circulating in some corners of the church regarding the issue of talking to strangers about our faith in Christ. While acknowledging the validity of some of these observations, we have nonetheless maintained that sharing Christ with strangers is good, it is fruitful, and most importantly, it is scriptural.

Acknowledging strengths and weaknesses with respect to street witnessing—the most prominent avenue for witnessing to strangers, we see that it fills an important role in God's plan for global evangelism, a role which cannot be filled by any other means. Yet, neither street witnessing nor any other form of outreach can lay claim to such a lofty position as to render other avenues unnecessary.

It seems fair and justified, in closing this defense of witnessing to strangers, to offer a few criticisms in response to those who are fond of disparaging such endeavors. The truth is that most Christians simply do not want to witness to strangers, whether it be on the streets, door to door, or any other way. There is a tendency to see ourselves as too sophisticated and cultured to "stoop" to such blatant means of "proselytizing."

Perhaps we are deliberately choosing false concepts of pride and dignity to hide our fears and prejudices. Who would dare to suggest that if Jesus were in the flesh today he would oppose taking his message to strangers?

Just because not everyone will respond to the gospel through a house call or a stranger approaching him on the streets does not mean that none will. Millions already have, not withstanding the criticisms of the uninitiated.

It would be interesting to see how many believers would hold fast to their prejudices against street witnessing and door-to-door evangelism if they were told that these were the only means left on earth for reaching their loved ones and closest friends. Truth be told, that may indeed be the case for many who might not listen to a family member or friend but might be open to the words of a stranger. Remember what Jesus said: "A prophet is not without honor, save in his own country and in his own house" (Matthew 13:57).

We need to remind ourselves that people are unpredictable. Life is unpredictable, constantly bombarding us with its challenges, setbacks, disappointments, tragedies, and surprises. Who knows what may lie in the heart of the stranger beside you? Who has the right to assume he will not respond?

And what about God? Does he exist, or doesn't he? If we are so sure that he does, then why are we holding on to the delusion that he is not powerfully moving to reach the hearts of people whenever and wherever he can work through someone who will be his voice in the world?

In fact, God has sworn that he will not allow his Word to be spoken to no affect, regardless of whether it be spoken through a one-on-one encounter on the street, in public, or with a friend over coffee. Remember Isaiah 55:11: "So shall my Word be that goes forth out of my mouth: it shall not return unto me void, but it shall accomplish that which I please, and it shall prosper in the thing whereto I sent it."

And also:

> For the Word of God is quick, and powerful, and sharper than any two-edged sword, piercing even to the dividing asunder of the soul and spirit, and of the joints and marrow, and is a discerner of the thoughts and intents of the heart.

Hebrews 4:12

Perhaps it would be a good idea to spend less time debating about whether God is blessing this manner of outreach or that and more time just speaking the truth in love.

> He that observes the wind shall not sow, and he that regards the clouds shall not reap.
>
> Cast thy bread upon the waters: for thou shalt find it after many days.
>
> In the morning sow thy seed, and in evening withhold not thy hand: for thou knowest not whether shall prosper this or that, or whether they both shall be alike good.

Ecclesiastes 11:4, 1, 6

So, Having Said All of That, Let's Get Started

It is now time to look at some practical ways we can go about sharing our faith with strangers. First, we will briefly consider some ways in which preparation can help. From there we will consider some suggestions for approaching and relating to those

Robert Davis

we wish to witness to. We will also consider strategies for dealing with rejection, should it occur.

How Preparation Can Be of Benefit to Us

In Ephesians 6:15, the apostle Paul admonishes us to "have our feet shod with the *preparation* [author's emphasis] of the gospel of peace." Our confidence must always rest in God, for only he can give the increase. However, it is universally recognized that in any vital undertaking, preparation is crucial if one aspires to do his best. Spiritual undertakings are no different. Preparation gives us several key advantages:

1. We become *more confident* because we feel ready; we know what to do.

2. We are *freed from self-consciousness*, enabling us to focus on other people and their needs.

3. We become *better able to follow the Spirit's lead* because we are Christ-conscious instead of self-conscious.

4. We *no longer worry about "what to say"* because we know how to break the ice and establish rapport with people.

5. We'll be better able *to direct and control conversations* because we know our objectives and how to reach them.

6. We *no longer fear rejection* because we know how to deal with it.

7. We'll be *better able to teach others in the body of Christ how to become more effective witnesses.*

Preparation does not imply reliance upon canned phrases, stock answers, or standard approaches. Nor does it entail adherence or bondage to any step-by-step outline, method, or presentation. Such approaches and methods may serve as training wheels, but over-reliance on any method, no matter how well conceived, tends to limit God's Spirit from having complete freedom in leading us.

Planning and preparation simply provide the foundation of an effective and organized approach to the task. This outline will, for the most part, address the three obstacles of, 1) starting conversations; 2) establishing rapport; and 3) dealing with rejection. The result of knowing how to overcome these three obstacles will be that: 1) you will overcome your feelings of inadequacy; and 2) you will overcome your fear of man.

How to Witness to People on the Streets

The following suggestions are offered to help you get started right away, if you want to, to reach out to strangers for the purpose of sharing your faith in Christ. The purpose here is to get you started. There is really very little you need to know in order to do that. The Lord does not want us to wait until we feel we have achieved the status of "expert" before we start sharing our faith with people. After all, it is "not with persuasive words of human wisdom, but in demonstration of the Spirit and of power, that your faith should not be in the wisdom of men but in the power of God" (1 Corinthians 2:4-5, NKJV).

How Do I Get Started?

If You Have a Tract

It is much easier to approach strangers to witness if you have some sort of gospel tract or literature to offer, especially if you are inexperienced. We will look at some ways to approach strangers without the help of tracts, for those of you who desire to have a greater flexibility, versatility, and preparedness. But first, with...

1. Having prayed beforehand, *decide where you want to go.* Pick a place where you will feel the most comfortable and where you feel "led."

2. Watch the people. *Look for someone who seems nonthreatening* as your "target."

3. *Determine your greeting and what remark you will share* as you offer the tract.

   Examples: "Hello! I'd like to give you this. It's a message from God to encourage you."

   Or, "Hi! May I give you this message? It's some good news to brighten your day."

   If you prefer, write out your own "approach" statement, something that you feel comfortable with. Keep it simple and to the point.

4. Now, do it. *Greet the person, offer the tract with a brief explanation, and smile.* If you like, you do not have to say anything else. Allow the person to take the tract (Occasionally, someone may decline. That's okay. Just keep smiling!)

5. If the person shows any interest, or hesitates, be prepared to *ask a question.*

   Examples: Explain that the tract tells people "what the Bible says about salvation" and ask:

   "Have you ever thought about becoming a Christian?"

   Or, "Have you ever thought about what Jesus did for you?"

   If these seem too direct for you, you might ask:

   "Do you know that God loves you?"

Or, "Do you have any interest in spiritual things?" (C.S.Lovett)

Or, "Have you ever read any of the gospel stories?"

Or, "Do you believe that the Bible is God's Word?"

As in your approach, find a question that you feel comfortable with. If the person is uninterested, be polite and say whatever seems appropriate as a closing remark.

"Have a good day," or, "God bless you," or just, "Thank you."

You might find that in certain instances no closing remark is necessary. The person might take (or refuse) the tract and keep walking, without acknowledging you. Sometimes, no remark is the best comment. In such instances, remain silent and let the person walk away. We will deal with the question of how to handle rejection in more detail shortly.

Draw Out Those Who Are Receptive

If the person is receptive, or even hesitant, be ready to *draw him out*. You can do this in one of two ways:

First, *by asking more questions*: "Can you tell me what a Christian is?"

[Note: The person will *almost always* respond by telling you *things that a Christian does* rather than *what a Christian is*, namely, someone who has been born again by receiving Christ into his heart as Lord and Savior.–paraphrase from C.S.Lovett: 'Witnessing Made Easy']

"Do you believe in an afterlife?"

"Do you believe Jesus will return someday?"

"Did you know that Jesus is coming back soon?"

"Do you believe that heaven and hell are real?"

"Do you go to church anywhere?"

Be prepared to allow the person to talk about himself, even if he somehow changes the subject away from spiritual things. While you do not want to get sidetracked, neither do you want to be insensitive to an opportunity to kindle a possible new friendship. Be alert and show genuine interest. Be aware also that sometimes, one who changes the subject may be doing so, not from a lack of interest, but from conviction that has made him uncomfortable. Changing the subject may be the person's way of groping for a connection with you on less "threatening" grounds.

Second: Another approach with those who show interest, or even just hesitation, is to *share just enough truth to bring the person face-to-face with his need of Christ.* This may be done by...

Moving into a brief explanation of why Christ died for us.

Sharing a brief outline of your personal testimony as the motivation for wanting to tell others about your faith in Christ.

Or (for the brave) explaining your conviction that Christ is coming back soon and that your desire is to see others come to his salvation while there is still time.

If you get this far, the conversation should be beginning to flow naturally, and you'll find you will not be worrying about what to say or do.

Connect with People

Bear in mind that, while you are trying to lead people to Christ, you are also looking for opportunities to establish rapport with people. The tools for doing this are:

1. A genuine concern and interest in the person and what she has to say

2. The use of ice-breaker questions to help the person open up and to help you evaluate her spiritual condition

3. A willingness to relate to the person on the level of her interest, even if it means engaging in non-spiritual small talk

It is useful to build a catalogue of questions both to help establish rapport and to enable you to gauge a person's spiritual condition and receptivity. Here are some more examples to help you do this. Others will come to you as you gain experience.

> Do you have a Bible? Do you read it?

> Can you tell me what the Bible says we must do in order to be saved?

> Do you have any family members or friends who are Christians?

Develop the Skill of Asking Nonspiritual Questions

We all want to cultivate the skill of talking with people spontaneously. A light-hearted, friendly manner and a willingness to engage in nonthreatening "chitchat" can go a long way in opening doors for you to tell people about your faith in Jesus.

Below are some nonspiritual questions you might ask. Take care to avoid the impression that you are "probing." While you do want to find out as much as is needed in order to know how best to respond to a person's spiritual need, asking questions like the following are merely to help you connect through the use of small-talk. Think of them as bridges to help you connect with people.

Use only as many of these kinds of questions as you need to help you do this. Never overdo it to the point that you appear nosey or invasive. Cultivate the skill of socializing with people on things of general interest. And be careful to ask only questions that you can demonstrate sincere interest in discussing. Here are a few examples:

> Do you know if this store has _____ ? (Fill in the blank)
>
> May I ask, do you know any good books about (painting, photography, car repairs, etc.)? (At a bookstore, or library)
>
> Excuse me, can you tell me if the (ribs, salads, soups, etc.) here are good? (At restaurants)
>
> Have you lived in this area a long time?
>
> Do you have any interest in (gardening, art, history, etc.)?
>
> Do you have any children?
>
> What do you like most about school? Or, Do you know what you want to do after you graduate? (To students)

You could also use any situations *when you need directions* or *to know what time it is* as occasions that might open opportunities for "smalltalk" with people.

Be Ready to Share the Gospel

Be prepared to share the gospel when the opportunity is there. You do not need to become a Bible expert before you can share the gospel. Remember, you know how you got saved. If you remember nothing else, tell that! Then give the person an opportunity to decide for himself. Do not be afraid to give the person an opportunity to receive Christ. Ask plainly,

> Would you like to receive Christ into your heart? Or,

Would you like to ask Jesus to come into your life? Or even,

Would you like to get saved?

If you ask the person to receive Christ and he hesitates, do not interrupt the silence. Let the person be the one to respond first. You may, however, offer to help him pray if you sense that the hesitation is due to uncertainty about what to do.

How to Deal with Rejection

What if the person rejects you or your message? This is a question frequently in the back of the minds of believers when they are thinking about sharing their faith with someone. It is really not something to fear. Knowing how to handle rejection will go a long way toward allaying your fear of it. Here are some things to keep in mind:

- Remember that ..."We are of God. He who knows God hears us; he that is not of God does not hear us" (1 John 4:6, NKJV).

- "Two are better than one...For if they fall, one will lift up his companion" (Ecclesiastes 4:9-10, NKJV). That is why Jesus sent the disciples out by twos, so that they could encourage each other and help each other in difficult situations.

- Remember that we are "accepted in the beloved" (Ephesians 1:6). When people reject us or our attempt to share our faith in Christ, they are in reality rejecting him. If he can bear the pain of such rejection, can't we do the same on his behalf, knowing that he has accepted us in his love?

So What Do I Do When It Happens?

One of the easiest and least threatening responses to rejection is to simply *make a gracious exit*: "God bless you," or, "I'm sorry if I've offended you. Have a good day." If the person is very rude, you might just exit *without saying anything*, making sure your mannerisms convey no hint of unkindness or anger. Take care to never appear offended. We are not representing ourselves but Christ Jesus, our Lord. Always walk in love.

If you would like to go a little bit further, you may do so by *expressing your regrets*. Tell the person that you are sorry he feels this way and that you hope he will change his mind. You might add that he can change his mind and God will still receive him. Should you do so, however, it would be wise to mention (if you are brave) that no one is promised tomorrow.

As mentioned before, you can say nothing, or offer a gracious parting remark. You might also express your regrets over their decision. If you would like to go one step further, you might want to *add a final thought*, something to give the Holy Spirit a foothold to work with whenever the person remembers his encounter with you. Some examples:

> "I hope you'll change your mind while there is still time." Or,

> "The Bible says that we need to 'seek the Lord while he may be found.'" Or,

> "Jesus is coming back soon. There's not much time left." Or even, if you dare,

> "Think about the people you love. They have souls, too."

All of these are bold and even unsettling to the unrepentant sinner. Such warnings should only be used in a spirit of meekness, gentleness, and compassionate concern and never as threats or harshly spoken parting shots.

What If You Don't Have a Tract?

All of the suggestions offered for witnessing to people with tracts apply. The only difference is that, not having a tract to offer as an opening gesture, you must *change your approach.* As mentioned, it is easier to approach a stranger for the purpose of sharing your faith if you have a gospel tract to offer as an ice-breaking gesture.

However, it is highly recommended that you develop the skill and confidence necessary to be able to approach strangers you wish to witness to even when you do not have a tract handy, as there are sure to be instances when you will feel like reaching out to people on occasions where you do not have a gospel tract on your person. Here are a few suggestions to help you cultivate this skill:

1. *Develop the habit of being friendly to strangers.* Smile and say "Hello" to people you see and to people as you walk by. This will build your confidence and occasionally even lead to spontaneous conversations.

2. *Pray for, and seek to create , such spontaneous conversations with strangers.* Here are some tips to help you do this:

A. *Be alert to your surroundings.* The environment you share with others frequently offers possibilities for generating conversations. For instance: the weather; the food (at restaurants); the teams (at ball games); books (at libraries), etc.

B. Think in terms of developing the art of friendliness to strangers *without the pressure of telling yourself that you "have to" witness to them.* Practice doing this even if you know you are not going witness to them. Encourage yourself with the thought that you are building your confidence.

C. *Be observant.* Often, you will notice something about the one you are talking to that draws your attention. Maybe there is something about the person's appearance that you can sincerely compliment. If it is a parent with a child, find something praise-worthy about her young one. What parents do not love to here others sing the praises of their children? Be aware of the fact that there are people who welcome the sincere interest of others, even if those others are strangers. Keep in mind that there are many lonely, unhappy, and even desperate, people in the world.

D. 3) *Ask and believe God for "divine appointments."* Who could sincerely make such a request and doubt the Lord's willingness and eagerness to grant it? God is able to so arrange circumstances in our lives and in the lives of others that such encounters occur at the most surprising and, if we are alert and willing, the most fortuitous occasions.

If we, as Christians, would do nothing else but ask and believe God for divine appointments, we would no doubt fulfill our God-ordained destinies in the cause of world evangelism.

There Is No Reason to Wait Any Longer

You now have enough information to help you, 1) approach a stranger; 2) start a conversation; 3) ask questions and establish rapport; 4) present your testimony (how you came to Christ) and/or the gospel (how they can come to Christ); and 5) deal with rejections when they do occur.

By having a plan, you will have the confidence that comes from knowing what you are doing. You know that your preparation has enabled you to overcome the silence barrier while still allowing plenty of room for the Spirit to lead you. It is also worth noting that the suggestions offered in this chapter will serve you well when encountering strangers in other avenues of outreach, i.e., door-to-door visitation, telephone evangelism, jails, and nursing homes, etc.

You are now ready to launch out beyond the borders of your Samaria into the uttermost parts of your world. With God working in you and through you, you will thrill to see Him working in other peoples' lives, altering eternal destinies—and allowing you the privilege of playing a part!

Chapter Two

Dwelling in Ceiled Houses
Does God Really Go Door to Door?

Door-to-Door Visitation: The Pariah of
Modern Evangelism

Of all the means of evangelism employed by the churches in America, none has fallen so completely out of favor among Christians as door-to-door visitation. Most believers dread the very idea of it. We conjure up images of blank stares, looks of disgust, and angry doors slammed in our tongue-tied faces. Not that most of us have ever experienced any of these things, never having tried it. Those of us who have know that such reactions almost never happen.

More significantly, we question the very legitimacy of such a means for reaching the lost. After all, many who have "tried" door-to-door visitation have for the most part come away with little, if anything, that could be called results, especially in terms of numbers added to the church. Of course, little consideration is given to the possibility that our methods might be flawed. It is much simpler and far more convenient to conclude that "door-to-door witnessing" is ineffectual, possibly not even "of God."

With these attitudes prevailing in the church, it seems that most Christians, if they ever do give a thought to door-to-door visitation, share one overriding sentiment, namely, "I don't like it, and I'm not going to do it!" So forays into the community to "spread the good news" have pretty much gone the way of the old tent revivals. In some ways, this is not a bad thing. When one considers the usual manner in which the saints have gone about these "crusades," it seems fair to say that the cause of Christ has probably not suffered much with their passing. But the evangelical Christian community's experience with this kind of outreach is not the whole story.

Do the Cults Share Our Sentiments on the Matter?

The Mormons and Jehovah's Witnesses do not share our lack of enthusiasm for this means of reaching people. It is one of the more bizarre spiritual phenomenon of the past century that, while the evangelical churches experienced little or even no growth in numbers for their efforts in this type of outreach, we see a radically different story, a story still unfolding, it should be added, among these two particular fringe groups.

The Mormons and the Jehovah's Witnesses are still two of the fastest-growing religious groups in the country, and almost all of their increases in membership have come *as a result of a sustained—indeed, unrelenting—campaign to reach people through community visitation, i.e., door-to-door.* And all of this has been achieved in the face of widespread criticism and condemnation of these groups as cults from virtually every segment of the Christian community.

When one considers the fact that, according to their own statistics, it takes the Mormon missionary workers a staggering 732 visits for every convert won to the cause, the prodigious efforts required to sustain this growth are almost beyond comprehension. It is quite possible that the efforts made by any one Mormon temple or Jehovah's Witness center in any given year to reach people through visitation in a typical community is probably greater than the efforts of all of the Christian churches in that same community combined.

No wonder that in many places in America a knock on the door from a religious group is almost always considered to be a visit from one or the other of these two organizations. Rarely, if ever, is it assumed among the unconverted that the visitors must be "those fundamentalists again," or "those evangelicals, Methodists, Presbyterians, Lutherans," etc. Even the notable efforts of the Baptists to reach out to the lost through community visitation–a dedication echoing the efforts of perhaps the greatest personal evangelism and visitation trainer in church history, the Baptist minister, C.S. Lovett, achieve little by comparison. (I say this with the greatest respect and highest esteem for our Baptist brethren.)

What Do the Mormons and Jehovah's Witnesses Know That We Don't?

If there is one defining characteristic that sets the efforts of these two groups apart from mainstream Christianity, when it comes to how they "do" door-to-door evangelism, it is that they spare no effort and leave no stone unturned in their campaign to draw even the most minimally responsive potential convert into their fold. They are like bloodhounds! It is not at all unusual for a Mormon or Jehovah's Witness to return three, four, five, or even ten times to a single home if need be, if even one person in that house shows the slightest interest or receptivity to their visits. How often do we see such grit and determination among ourselves, the "true" disciples? (No insult intended here.)

Whereas the Mormons and Jehovah's Witnesses pursue community visitation with a single-minded determination to follow up every lead, no matter how insignificant, in their efforts to bring sheep into the fold, the typical evangelical crusade is characterized by a seeming obsession with obtaining as many "sinner's prayer" recitals from the neighborhood as possible. The idea of revisiting those "won to the Lord," i.e., led in "the prayer," is treated as an afterthought, if not a downright inconvenience. If we were to place our typical efforts side by side with those of the cults, we observe the following comparisons, or more properly, contrasts:

The cults go door to door to meet people and establish relationships. We go (or went) door to door to "witness." The cults go door to door to find people receptive to revisitation. We (went) to find people receptive to being led in "a sinner's prayer." Cults place the major thrust of their efforts on multiple revisits to draw people into their folds. We (placed) the major thrust of our efforts on one-time contacts to "share our faith."

Whose Wisdom Is Producing Children?

Jesus said that "wisdom is justified of her children" (Matthew 11:19). In terms of evangelistic strategies, it is not difficult to see whose wisdom has been justified with children in this instance. The failure of evangelicals here is rooted in the desire to take the easy way out, nothing more and nothing less. It is worth noting that the cults do not even attempt to lead people in a prayer. They are more interested in leading people into their circle of faith and fellowship, such as they are.

It is neither fair nor reasonable to expect people to instantly respond with arms open wide to gestures of friendship from strangers. It is incredible to expect such a response when the gesture is not even offered. And it is disingenuous to dismiss people as "unresponsive" simply because they are reluctant to come to church after one, or at the most, two visits. The cults don't expect this. Yet they know that if they keep trying, at least with those who show even the slightest degree of receptivity, sooner or later, they will bring sheep into the fold.

We find a strange irony in all of this. On the one hand, those who have ever participated in visitation evangelism know firsthand the joy of seeing God working with them, confirming his Word with signs following. Yet with the "I've led them in the prayer...mission accomplished!" mind-set, those who might have been drawn into active membership in the church body are, more often than not, left to fend for themselves. And then we find Christians questioning the value of it all! The resulting schizophrenic attitude of the church toward evangelism in general, and door-to-door visitation in particular, must truly be a source wonder and exasperation to the angels.

Could it be that our unrealistic, impatient insistence on instant results is nothing more than a device for skirting the commitment and sacrifice that potential relationships with newcomers require? Maybe we ought to join the Mormons or Jehovah's Witnesses for a few months and learn how to do things the right way. After all, why not learn from the experts?

Their doctrinal deviations aside, we are confronted with a disturbing question: *Who is showing more love and interest in people?* Our evangelical churches, with our haphazard, sporadic, here-today, lead-'em-in-a-"prayer," gone-tomorrow tactics, or these fringe groups who actually seem to value people as people rather than as "souls" to be led in a prayer and then left "in the hands of God"?

This may seem a harsh criticism, but haven't we been guilty in this area? We may criticize their love as "phony" and "gooey," but our own lackadaisical attitude toward evangelism of any kind hardly leaves us room to judge.

The Sinner's Prayer: Love 'Em and Leave 'Em?

As a means of inviting Christ into one's heart, a prayer is the natural and appropriate way to do so. As a commission to the church for training would-be followers of Christ, it is not what we are called to do. We are called to make disciples, not to lead people in a prayer. Not that leading someone in prayer to receive Christ is bad or wrong. When used as a substitute for making disciples, however, it is not only bad and wrong, but sinful and damaging to the souls of those victimized by such superficial "ministry."

There are, of course, occasions when such is not the case. Situations occur where there may be an opportunity to lead someone to receive Christ when any chance of further contact is not possible. People we meet when traveling, for example, or chance encounters in which further communication is jeopardized by distance or unforeseen circumstances. These conditions rarely apply, however, in situations involving community outreach in our own town. Clearly re-contact is possible, provided both parties are willing.

All too often, however, the church has taken the instrumentality of the sinner's prayer and used it as a means of forsaking all further responsibility toward the persons we have coaxed into "praying it." Having gotten the person saved, as we suppose, we are freed from further obligation because, after all, the person is now "going to heaven." Anything else is mere icing on the cake. We've taken care of what's really important. It is time to remove this attitude from our thinking.

In reality, praying with a sinner to receive Christ is merely the commencement of our responsibility. Even in situations where future contact is not possible, a sincere effort should be made to establish a written correspondence, or phone contact, or to refer the person to a local church—or, better yet, to refer the person's name to a local pastor or believer willing to take the time to be a friend.

God's definition of evangelism is not leading people into prayer but leading people into Christ.

One can invite Christ into his heart by merely saying a prayer. To invite oneself into Christ's heart, however, is to follow him in the path of discipleship. Discipleship is the path we must follow if we want to enter into Christ's heart, for this is his heart for everyone who comes to him! And this is the path we must lead new believers to follow.

Door-to-Door Visitation: Mormon/ Jehovah's Witness Style

It is time for the evangelical churches to scratch the old way of doing door-to-door visitation. Unfortunately, the church, seeing that what it was doing wasn't working, has simply dispatched with this kind of ministry altogether.

While it may be idealistic, wishful thinking to hope for a full-fledged revival of community visitation among the evangelical churches, there is cause to believe that some have not closed the "door" completely. They need only a reason to believe things might go better with a strategy more in line with biblical principles. At the very least, some intrepid individuals here and there might be persuaded to consider a new approach if given reason to believe it might work—that is, that their efforts might actually bring people into the church. There are several good reasons to hope for this:

1. We have already seen that there are those who have made it work: the cults. They have done so despite the tremendous obstacle of having a widespread reputation *as* cults. It would not take near the effort for mainstream churches to find favor in the community.

2. There are people who are open, even eager, for the friendship of a stranger. All they need is to see that such friendship is sincerely being offered. The plan offered in the following pages will communicate that sincerity.

3. At any given time, there are people going through crisis of various kinds: the death of a loved one, severe illness, financial hardships, family conflicts, and other difficulties. At such times, many are open to the love that God wants to offer them, provided he has someone to offer it through.

4. We all know that there is not much time left. Instead of sitting around in church waiting for a "move of God," we ought to be out among people trying to make things happen.

5. In spite of all the church's misgivings, community visitation is still the only systematic method for reaching her neighbors on a personal level. And what church would not want to at least reach out to the people living in homes right in their own neighborhood??

It Is Time for a New Vision

Most people are open to trying new things, provided they can be persuaded that their efforts will pay off. If we can go further and actually kindle an excitement and a vision to stir our hearts, then neither the cost nor the burden will feel heavy. The joy of seeing fruit come as a result of our labors will more than outweigh any sense of sacrifice we may have felt.

The plan that follows is an effort to create such a vision. The steps in this plan are exceedingly simple and such as require only a modest but consistent effort. Each step is reachable. Those who follow this outline will feel a sense of accomplishment and victory in knowing they are doing their part to reach people for Christ.

Taking a page out of the cults' playbook, the premise behind the plan is simply this: that repeated, nonthreatening, pleasant encounters with people through creative "revisitation" will produce consistently positive results, both in terms of believers' participation and in new people being discipled into faithful church membership.

The key ingredients that make this plan appealing are as follows:

- *It is easy*: This is important because people don't like to do things that are hard.

- *It is simple*: Each step is so simple that the intimidation factor usually associated with this kind of outreach is reduced to almost zero.

- *It is not time constraining*: Each step takes no more than half an hour, as little as twice a month. For the more persevering souls, weekly outings of equally brief duration might be pursued.

- *It is exciting*: Each step builds on the previous ones, resulting in deeper acquaintances, causing more barriers to be broken down, increasing favor and influence.

- *It is rewarding*: Sooner or later, a relationship will be formed that will draw someone into your church. The reward to the one who participates in making this happen will be great indeed.

A Phased Approach to Community Visitation

We call this plan a "phased" approach because each step is sequential, building on previous visits until, inevitably, breakthroughs occur in establishing new relationships with people in your community. In an ideal scenario, each person would begin with those closest to him, his next-door neighbors, and those in the immediate vicinity.

It should be understood at the outset that, though the ultimate aim of any evangelistic effort is to win souls, that is not the particular goal of any one of the steps outlined in this plan. The purpose of each step is to improve the quality of the relationships between those doing the visiting and those being visited.

Starting with total strangers, we turn these into acquaintances, then friendly acquaintances, and wherever possible, turn these into genuine friends.

In practical terms, this is "friendship" evangelism, but from a different starting point in that we begin, not with friends that we already have but, starting "from scratch" with strangers, we turn these by degree into friends through the re-visitation plan that we will describe in detail below.

It is important to emphasize that the goal of each visit in addition to deepening relationships is, wherever possible, to leave the person wanting more. We want to be careful never to overstay our welcome. Likewise, we should avoid the mistake of trying to unnaturally force a relationship with anyone. Friendship is, after all, a two-way street. We do not want to cross the boundaries of natural etiquette or infringe on anyone's comfort zone.

Of course, no approach will win everyone. We do not live on that planet! We must keep in mind that we are searching for people who are open and receptive while giving those who are understandably cautious a chance to warm up to us.

The Plan

In this plan, each participant will choose or be assigned by the pastor a small number of homes to visit on a recurring basis. The standard sequence for re-visitation may be monthly, bimonthly, or some other agreed upon interval. The interval itself will be flexible to suit the receptivity level of the people you are visiting.

The numbers of homes visited may vary but should be small enough in number that the visitations may be completed in thirty minutes to no more than an hour. This will keep the commitment level from becoming too intimidating.

A typical approach might be to have each pair (two is usually best; one is inadvisable, and three tends to be a little overwhelming—we must consider the comfort level of those we are visiting and not just our own) be responsible for visiting seven homes on a monthly basis for three to six months, depending on the responses generated.

Each visit should have a specifically assigned and limited task that may be accomplished in a very small amount of time, usually two to three minutes per house, allowing for peoples' varying responses. Afterward, the team members compare notes and evaluate each visit in terms of receptivity or lack thereof. Brief written reminders should be used to summarize these observations, to use as guidelines for prayer, and to refresh the visitors' memories for the next encounter.

As the visitation progresses, it will become apparent which homes have people who seem to be hopeful prospects for winning to your church. Please note: the goal of this plan is to win people to your church!

Of course you want to win them to Christ. But this should not be allowed to supercede your primary goal. The reason for this is that you want to avoid the error so prevalent in typical evangelical visitation crusades of leading people to Christ—or should we say, leading them in a prayer, only to abandon them afterward with self-comforting notions of having done what was "most important," too often a line of reasoning used to avoid the inconvenience of making any further contacts with those we've led to the Lord. But we've already covered this.

Here, then, is the plan, step by step. As you use these guidelines, allowing yourself to be led by the Spirit as you go, you and your church will increase in favor with the people of your community.

Here We Go!

Step One: On your first visit, your goal is to *introduce people to yourself and your church*. That is all. In this first foray, you will not seek to "win souls," preach the gospel, or even witness to people directly. You are there to simply tell people, 1) who you are; 2) where you are from—that is, your church; 3) and why you are there, which, in this first visit, is to give people you meet some literature telling them about your church.

Some will wonder, *How can you suggest that I not "witness" or "win souls"?* First, in the plan we are offering here, your primary goal is to make connections leading to meaningful relationships. Your visit itself is a witness. Obviously, when you meet someone who is wide open to hear your testimony or witness, or even to receive Christ, follow the lead of the Spirit. Under no circumstances, however, should you lead someone to Christ if you have no intention of making an honest effort to establish a meaningful relationship with that person. This is the thing we most want to avoid! We have thoroughly dealt with this issue in the preceding pages.

If you need an example, try something like this:

> Hello, my name is _____ and this is _____(your partner). [*who* you are] We're from _____ Church on _____ [*where* you are from]. We're visiting your neighborhood today to introduce ourselves to you and to give you some literature to tell you a little about our church [*why* you are there].

At this point you simply offer your literature, thank the person for allowing you to introduce yourself, and say, "Good-bye."

You then *make as though to leave.* The person will likely be quite surprised that you have not sought to press the occasion into a "witnessing" encounter. This will immediately elevate your stature and favor with the person. People appreciate the fact that others, especially strangers, respect their privacy and do not presume to impose themselves upon those whose homes they have visited. By the same token, they tend to appreciate and respect people's spiritual dedication to reach out to others when done in a manner that is sensitive to their rights.

After you have accomplished your purpose and are beginning to make your exit, many, if not most people, will respond

Robert Davis

in one fashion or another. Some may indicate kindly, but firmly, that they "already have a church" they attend. In such cases, you respond with a positive affirmation and thank the person once again as you are leaving. (Those who respond this way are telling you that they are happy where they are and have no intention of leaving. Of course you should make no attempt to change their minds. Jesus didn't call us to beg, borrow, or steal sheep from each other!)

Look for Those Who Are Receptive

When you have clear evidence that a person does not want you to revisit him, then note the address and respect their wishes. Even if you never see the person again, you have done what you could. If the person gives strong indication that he is not interested simply because he is not interested in church or Christ, this also must be respected. In such cases, for those of you who dare to go the last mile, the instructions for leaving *one last thought* as detailed in the chapter on street witnessing may apply here.

Sooner or later, however, someone will indicate by their words or manner that he is open and receptive to you. Usually those who are will either ask you for more information about your church or they will begin to tell you a little bit about their own religious or spiritual background, i.e., "I used to go to such and such church," etc. When this happens, simply engage the person in a natural way and pursue the conversation in the direction indicated by his response. Let the Spirit lead you.

At this stage, it is important to point out that, because the strategy of this plan is based on revisiting each home a predetermined (but flexible) number of times, it is not necessary or advisable to approach this first visit, or subsequent encounters, as you would if you knew you were never going to return.

Naturally you want to allow each person's receptivity to determine your reactions. If someone you meet makes it apparent early on that she is interested in knowing more about your church, about Christ, about salvation—then you will want to meet her need without delay.

On the other hand, with many people a more gradual approach, based on increased favor and trust, will enable you to exert a cumulatively increasing influence with each subsequent visit. At least this will be the case with those you encounter who have an underlying hunger for God.

The key is to properly gauge each person's receptivity. Do not be concerned if you feel unsure of your ability to do this. With prayer and experience, you will gain the wisdom and confidence needed. Regardless of where you are at, rely upon God and do your best. When in doubt, follow the steps of the plan, trusting the Lord to work behind the scenes.

Define Success in Terms of Your Overall Plan

Before proceeding to Step Two, one more point is in order. It is important to define success in terms of your overall plan, one step at a time. In Step One, after introducing yourselves (*who* you are), telling the person the name of your church (*where* you are from), and offering your church literature packet (*why* you are there), you are successful! You have completed Step One!

While leading someone in a prayer to receive Christ is exciting, this should never be your definition of success. For one thing, it is God who gives the increase. For another, leading someone in a prayer is practically worthless if the person is then deserted and left to make it on his own. In fact, such tactics may do more harm than good. A person treated in such a fashion would hardly feel loved by someone dealing with him in such a manner. Worse, he may question God's love for him in sending such a half-hearted, disinterested "laborer" to his home!

So then, follow each step in order, deviating only when the person's interest or lack of interest dictates a change. For all but the clearly disinterested, we proceed to Step Two.

Robert Davis

Come Bearing Gifts

Step Two: Return to the homes approximately one month after your first visit—sooner for those who show clear interest. Your assignment on this second visit will be to *offer the person a gift from your church*. This gift could be anything—a Bible, a musical recording, a message from the pastor (though this is best saved for later), or an inspirational book of some kind. Or perhaps some simple but elegant handcraft made by those in the church who are artistically gifted.

Look for something that communicates a genuine interest in, and appreciation for, the person receiving it. The church might bake some cakes or cookies or some novelty treat. Whatever you decide, be sure to include a church bulletin, or flyer, or a card from the pastor to serve as a reminder of the source of the gift.

Follow the same guidelines described in Step One for evaluating each person's receptivity. After presenting the gift, make your departure with gracious well wishes. Be careful not to communicate any sense of expectancy on your part so as not to make people feel uncomfortably obligated. Rather, let them see your simple joy in giving to them.

There will, of course, be a natural obligation of good will created, which will pave the way for your next visit. Do not be too surprised if one or two people decide to just show up at your church the following Sunday. People are deeply touched by sincere generosity and goodwill. However, by no means should you define the success of Step Two based on whether or not anyone comes to church. Your definition for success for Step Two, as in all of the others, is simply this: you did it!

Have Your Church Make a Special Events Calendar

Step Three: This time come armed with another gift: a calendar (*not* a bulletin but a bona fide calendar listing all of the special events in your church's schedule for the coming year). It is worth the time and expense it will cost to do this. Many people will put this calendar in a place of prominence where they will see it almost daily throughout the entire year. You might choose a Norman Rockwell calendar, or any other with fine illustrations and inspirational thoughts. (Do not be deterred if it is midyear; calendars are always welcome!)

Each time they look at it to see what day it is, they will be subtly reminded of your church and remember the feelings of goodwill you have created with your low-key, nonthreatening, but friendly visits to their home. As a valuable bonus they will also be kept abreast of those intriguing special events you have planned for the upcoming year—events tailored, hopefully, toward the interests and curiosities of nonmembers.

Your church should carefully weigh the potential impact such a tool might have for reaching out to its community. It is well worth putting your best effort into every aspect of its planning, design, and creation.

Extend a Special Invitation

Step Four: By now you are likely increasing in favor with at least some of the families you are visiting. No doubt you are also beginning to zero in on some who are showing continued interest in you—and by extension, your church.

It is now time to offer a special invitation to those you are revisiting, preferably to some upcoming special event on your church calendar. You'll want to make this an occasion to remember. Your church needs to think outside the box here. We ought not be content to settle for business as usual. Perhaps you could stage a dinner theater production or a quality concert. Maybe a parenting seminar or a creation/evolution debate. You might want to choose an event geared toward children, a big screen Disney movie or children's play. Of course, the children will arrive with parents in tow, providing another opportunity for you to get to know each other better.

The event should be geared toward attracting not just Christians, but non-Christians and members of the immediate community. Whatever you decide upon, it must be free of charge—at least to nonmembers. Be sure to extend your special invitation no more than two weeks before the scheduled event.

For those who come, you will want to pull out all the stops to make them feel like the honored guests that they are. Your church must be prepared to have those who are gifted in the social graces to reach out to make these people feel at home. This task cannot fall on the inviter's shoulders alone, for it is imperative that your guests be introduced to others in the congregation as well. This will greatly magnify your church's favor with the visitors.

Take the Relationship to a More Personal Level

Step Five: At this stage, your knowledge of each home and the people living there will have reached a point where you should have a good feel for who may or may not be potentially interested in joining your church body. Perhaps one or more relationships have progressed beyond the need for a planned approach. Yet to pursue every possibility, continue to reach out to the others in your original seven—or ten, or whatever number of homes you may have started with—excluding only those who have made it clear that they are not interested.

For that special one or two, however, you will attempt to take the relationship to a more personal level. On this, your fifth visit to the homes in your target zone, attempt to build on your previous efforts with each person while seeking an opportunity to get together with the one(s) who are especially receptive *in some setting other than their home or your church.*

For those who do not fall into this category, you may want to think in terms of bringing your visitation efforts to a decision point. That is, by gently upping the ante, you can more clearly evaluate these people so as to determine if it is worthwhile to continuing to visit them. You may do this in any number of ways. Here are some examples to consider:

- *Ask the person if he has ever thought about a personal relationship with Christ.* Be prepared here to present the gospel, should the occasion permit. Such an inquiry will reveal where your neighbor stands spiritually, if you have not yet been able to gain this information. As an alternative, you may...

- *Ask the person if he might be interested in participating in a Bible study series, either in his home or at some other convenient location.* Once again, the person's response will help you gauge his spiritual hunger and receptivity. Or you may...

- *Ask the person to consider being your special guest for a Sunday morning service.* Your goal in each of these options is to confront the person with a gentle, but significant, challenge to allow the relationship to progress to a more spiritual level.

Obviously the person's response to whichever invitation you extend will help you to better evaluate the merit of continuing visitations. It stands to reason that those who fail to show any interest in spiritual things must be recognized as not meriting the continued investment of time you could better employ in seeking out those with more promise. If your evaluations are informed and sincere, you will merely be showing yourself a good steward of your time. In such cases, however, always take care to leave the door of friendship open should the person have a change of heart.

Robert Davis

Zero In On Those Who Respond Favorably to You

We return now to those who continue to show promise. Seek to engage that person or persons outside their home or your church, thereby maneuvering the relationship to a place where it may experience a dramatic and positive breakthrough. Many people, open to spiritual things and a relationship with Christ, nonetheless may find the thought of visiting a new church frightening and intimidating.

By extending an invitation to get together on neutral ground, you are presenting the person with an offer to deepen the friendship. As a representative of your church, and therefore of Christ, the person's response to you will be a strong indicator of his openness to Christ himself. The challenge to meet outside of the security cocoon of one's home is also a test of true interest in the friendship itself.

If you have not already done so, ask the person if you might explain God's plan of salvation.

Step Six: This is the final step or visit to your target homes, at least as far as the formal plan is concerned. It is reasonable to assume that if you have been unable to win the friendship and interest of those you have visited by now, it may be time to move on.

With those who have received you, continue to build on your relationship with them as you seek to draw them in. By now you may have invited the person to church, or to a Bible study, or to get together with other friends from the church informally. People who show positive responses to your efforts should begin to show signs of increasing spiritual hunger.

Allow your knowledge of the person's spiritual condition and background to guide you in determining how best to proceed. At some point you will need to address the issue of the person's salvation, if you have not already done so. Based on his previous positive responses, if he is not saved, the person will likely be ready to receive Christ at this time.

For those who have been noncommittal, Step Six will be your last attempt to break through. In Step Five you challenged the person to respond with interest to your offers of spiritual encouragement. Quite possibly you elected with some who were unresponsive to make that your last visit. If, however, you decided on "one more try," then approach the encounter as if it were that person's *last chance* to hear the gospel. Tell the person that you would like to share God's plan of salvation with her. You may do this as follows:

Upon greeting the person, after engaging in any small talk that seems appropriate, *tell her that this is the last of your "church sponsored" visits.* This sets the tone for the more direct approach of this visit, as compared with your previous ones. Meditate beforehand, and pray for guidance as to how to go about this. For example, you might say, "Mr./Mrs._____, as you know, we've been visiting your neighborhood now for the last several months. This is the last of our church-sponsored visitations to your area..." (Here you may select from the following options, choosing as you feel best):

"If you could give us a few minutes of your time, we'd like to show you some scriptures that explain God's plan of salvation for us."

Or, "We would like to take this opportunity to invite you to a special service our pastor will be having for visitors from your neighborhood."

Or, "May I ask if you've given any thought to the importance of having a good home church for your family?"

If none of these suit your taste, by all means use something that you feel comfortable with. The important thing to bear in mind is this: *Unless you get some positive feedback, this will be your last visit to this person's home.* Therefore, having built up some good will from your previous visits and having informed the person that this will be your last "church-sponsored" visit, it is appropriate, *and even expected*, that you will be a little more direct and to the point.

These people know, after all, what your intentions have been all along. You have been trying to interest them in your church and in a relationship with Jesus Christ. This will be the time, if ever, for both parties to open up and be candid with each other. Not as though heretofore you have not been. On the contrary, you have demonstrated great tact and patience, making every effort to win favor for both yourself and your church. You are entitled to get to the point here, if you have not yet done so.

Any of the example questions cited earlier, or similar ones of your own choosing, will clear the way for this dialogue. Your response, as always, will be determined by what the person tells you. For those who indicate that they are not interested, you may leave graciously and in peace. If you are so inclined, you may leave a last thought, as described previously. Be sure also to leave a church calling card, and always leave on a positive note, encouraging the person to call "for any reason" in the future.

As in Step Five, continue to strengthen your friendship with those you have found favor with. Keep up with efforts to help these to forge friendships with others in the church, regardless of whether your new friend has made the leap of visiting your church or not. It is very easy to just sit down and look up a few scriptures together when visiting him at home, especially after you have established a friendship relationship with the person. And remember, if you can get your friend to meet you and some others in an informal setting away from his home for the same purpose, he is that much closer to the point of feeling comfortable visiting the church.

Remember that you are not alone. God is working in the hearts of those you find favor with. So hang in there with them. Do not be the one to terminate a relationship with someone who is responding to the call of God. Be sensitive to the Lord's direction. If he gives you a "caution" signal, slow down and give the person some space. Let her know that you are there and trust God to show you what to do next. And always, pray each step of the way!

Old Wine and New

As a postscript to the plan you've just reviewed, it is worth noting a principle that Jesus made reference to when talking to his disciples about how people come into the kingdom. He said in Luke 5:39, "No man, having drunk the old wine, straightway prefers the new: for he says to himself, the old is better."

I believe that what Jesus was saying here was that the appetite for spiritual things is an acquired taste. All sinners, before coming to Christ, and in a very real way, even during their initial acquaintance with him, have a natural preference or "taste" for carnal or worldly indulgences. This includes sinful appetites but is not limited to these only. Non-sinful preoccupations and pursuits seem to be included as well. While such desires may become sinful if allowed to usurp the place that rightfully belongs to God—and frequently do so—in themselves, these things are not inherently evil.

These activities, hobbies, pastimes, recreations, and interests are "old wine," which we, as mature believers, may use to our advantage as we seek to stir an appetite for the new wine of the Spirit in those we are seeking to win. We are not suggesting here that mature saints have set aside all of their pastimes and entertainments...only that such interests are held in proper perspective.

By drinking of this old wine with those whom we are attempting to draw to God, that is, by sharing in their hobbies and interests in the fellowship of just having fun, we have increased opportunities to offer the new wine that God freely gives to all who will drink it. Simply put, sharing in otherwise harmless activities with the unsaved may give us a foothold of common interests in the pursuit of which we may draw them in with "better things than these."

"He that wins souls is wise" (Proverbs 11:30).

Behold, I Stand at the Door and Knock...

Somewhere in your neighborhood, there is a family going through a painful divorce. No more than two or three blocks from your house, there is likely a widow raising her children alone. Within walking distance, some teenage girl lays on her bed in her room, wondering why her daddy left her, thinking about whether the boy in school who told her she was "pretty" might be able to make her happy.

In the next year, someone on your block will likely lose a loved one—hopefully not you. Some may be told they have cancer or heart disease. Someone not far from where you sit will file bankruptcy. Others will leave, never to tread any path crossing yours again. Who will be killed in the next car wreck or go to war...and come home in a coffin? Would God go door to door if your lost loved one were home alone getting ready to have din...a heart attack? Jesus said, "He that gives a cup of cold water only, in my name, verily I say unto you, he shall in no wise lose his reward" (Proverbs 25:25).

Those who reach out to others on Christ's behalf know that he is with them. No theological arguments or sophisticated spiritual reasonings to the contrary can shake their convictions. Those who offer them are to be pitied—and prayed for.

Many sit alone or in the company of another, each alone in his or her private world of broken dreams, love gone sour, and life grown strangely empty and achingly void of meaning. How can we say no one will listen? Are we God?

If you die five minutes after reading this and all opportunity to reach your lost loved one is taken from you forever, would you hope that God would go "door to door" in her neighborhood? Do you think he could find someone who would hear if he asked?

Like you, I would rejoice with tears of hope to see some intrepid soldier of Christ marching fearlessly, *or in spite of fear,* up my loved one's drive way, your loved one's driveway, to the porch, and reaching up, to knock, knock on their door…the door of your lost loved one, bringing…what? *Everything!* Jesus, all she will ever need, all he will ever need…to eternity!

Yes, you would want that for your loved one, wouldn't you? Then why not give it? Be the answer to someone else's prayer, even as your own ascend to the throne. "Give and it shall be given to you…" (Luke 6:38, NKJV).

Chapter Three

The Telephone...
How Could We Let This One Slip
Through Our Fingers?

When Jesus told us the story of the woman with the lost piece of silver (Luke 15:8-10), he was showing us the kind of attitude he wants us to have when it comes to seeking lost souls. This woman "swept her house" and "searched diligently" until she found her missing coin. It seems she could think of nothing else until she found it.

He also gave us the example of the shepherd who left the ninety-nine sheep who were safe (in the church?) to seek out and find the one who had strayed (Luke 15:4-7). It seems clear that he wants us to leave no stone unturned in our efforts to lead sinners to him.

By the same token, as Christians, we should leave no options unexplored when it comes to finding ways to reach out to people. Our churches are filled with God-loving saints holding back from heeding the call. Every child of God would like to be used to win souls for his kingdom, but many are hesitating.

With the thought of face-to-face encounters striking fear in the hearts of so many believers, it would seem that if some other, less-threatening way were available, the church would leap at the opportunity to take advantage of it.

As a matter of fact, there is such a means right at our fingertips, something most of us have used almost daily for all of our lives. How is it then that the church has failed to realize the potential of this means to reach out to people for the gospel's sake? I'm speaking, of course, of the telephone. The telephone is one of the most overlooked potential instruments for promoting the gospel in the last hundred years.

Perhaps you are one who finds it difficult to share your faith with people in person. Or maybe you are someone who has difficulty getting out for one reason or another. Stay-at-home moms, shut-ins, and people with handicaps do not always have the liberty to just come and go as they please. Or maybe you are simply intrigued at the novel possibilities of using the telephone in ways you may not have thought of before. Who knows? You might discover that reaching people this way could be a dream come true for you.

Though the idea of using our telephones to spread the gospel may seem a bit unusual, it is really not so strange. We use them for a million other things. Why not use them for God? Whatever your situation may be, perhaps "dialing for Jesus" is a way you can "let your fingers do the walking" as you "reach out and touch someone"…for him!

Not Just for Counseling

Let's be clear concerning what we are talking about here. First, we are not talking about a telephone counseling "hotline." While these are fantastic ministries and serve a vital role in helping others, we are thinking more in terms of how the telephone may be used as a means of evangelism—that is, as a tool for reaching out to others rather than just waiting for them to call us. This is the great opportunity the church has ignored for so long, to *use the telephone as an avenue for making new contacts with people.*

Why has this almost never been done? The Word of God tells us that "all things are [ours]." How is it that we have overlooked the tremendous potential for using the telephone, not only as a means for reaching out to the unsaved, but as a vital tool to help those who have held back from sharing their faith through fear of face-to-face encounters? There is no need to wait any longer. The Lord expects us to make use of every means within our reach to publish the gospel. In the words of the Apostle Paul, "That I might by all means save some" (1 Corinthians 9:22).

We have used the television, the radio, newspapers, books, tapes, cds, videos, and music.

Why wait for people to call us? God is calling. Jesus is calling. The Holy Spirit is calling. So what are we waiting for?

So How Can We Use the Telephone to Reach People?

The answer to this question is that there are many possibilities. With just a little imagination and enough desire to try it, we can make the telephone a multi-stranded lifeline reaching out in all directions to our community and beyond. Here are just a few examples to get your wheels turning. We can make phone calls...

> ...*to invite people to church—not just for services but (even more) for special events such as concerts, plays, festivals, or any other happening of interest.*

There are endless possibilities for putting together fun and interesting events to draw in a crowd—plays, dramas, skits, even talent contests. Why not have debates on special topics, or art shows (with community participation), even treasure and "scavengers" hunts; horse riding, instruction classes in archery, fishing, computers, mechanics, chess, etc., etc., etc! (see "Butchers, Bakers, and Candlestick Makers"). How about a special movie night or dinner theater or anything beyond just "business as usual"?

In the frontier days of our nation's youth, the church used to be the cultural center of the community. Why can't we try to be so again? People are tired of the mall! They realize that shopping is a poor way to find meaning for an empty life. We need to draw these wanderers into the community life of God's people so that they can see the hope and joy we have in our lives! This is not becoming worldly to win the world. Such a thought is a blight on the ones who are trying to be innovative and appealing to a skeptical world—a world filled with people who are accustomed to looking at the church through the stained-glass windows of tradition and religion!

...to offer special messages from the pastor to the community.

Such messages could be tailored toward the peculiar needs or concerns of people in your hometown or to special target groups. The idea is to get out the message (literally) that your church cares. Tapes or cds could be offered on an endless variety of topics: marriage; child rearing; overcoming poverty, fear, anger, emptiness, alcohol, drug addiction, etc.; setting goals; healthy living; and on and on. Such messages could be made available as often as your church could afford to send them out. They could even be made available to download off of the Internet – at no cost to the church!

Your pastor need not be the only one to come up with messages. Perhaps you and some other people in your church might like to record your own. You could teach on something spiritual—but then again, you might teach something like "How to Make the Best-Tasting Thanksgiving Turkey" or "How to Fish in Fresh-Water Streams," or any one of a million different things. (Again, see "B's, B's, and CSM's.")

People are not stupid. Anyone receiving such a message from someone in your church will know that you are endeavoring to be a good witness for Christ—whether the message is spiritual or not. Just imagine the impact we could make on our communities if Christians were to seriously pursue such an enterprise. And the fact is, outreach projects such as these would be fun and fulfilling. After all, who doesn't enjoy talking about the things he is interested in?

...to "see how you are doing"—a sort of courtesy call on behalf of your church.

Such simple gestures of kindness are not lost on those receiving them, and their affect will linger long after the call has ended.

The "see how you are doing" inquiry may be followed up with an offer to put the person on your church's prayer list. (This is usually better than offering prayer in a first-time conversation with a total stranger…who may feel awkward or even resentful at being put in a position of having to decline to "be prayed for" over the phone. Of course, some would welcome such prayer, even with a stranger. The important thing is to be sensitive.)

Some people, when asked if they would like to be put on your church prayer list "for anything," may take the occasion as an opportunity to share their problems. Not all will, of course, but some might. These are the ones you are searching for. Who knows what some of these families might be struggling with? Your phone call could cause someone to feel as though God has reached out to her in a very special way, which would be true! And of course, doors of opportunity for future contact may open.

…to see if people would like to have a visitor from the church.

This may seem rather direct. Yet who knows who might be open or even eager to receive a personal visit from a friendly Christian. Every community has lonely people and shut-ins. Many might gladly receive a visitor from the church if made to feel comfortable and cared about by a friendly caller.

There are Christians in every community who are unable to make it to church. They may be elderly or handicapped or whatever. Most of these people are eager for fellowship. Some have no Christian friends to visit them. What does the Lord think about these people? God may want you to find one such as these even more than having you look for "new" prospects. If you doubt this, then try putting yourself in that person's shoes, as well you might be someday. Would you imagine Jesus being indifferent to your need?

…to promote activities of special interest to children or teenagers.

Often, the church limits its promotion of such events to radio or newspaper advertisements, posters, or church marquee notices. Why not go a step further and extend a personal invitation? Parents of children will recognize such an invitation as an act of Christian love toward their children—and by extension, to them as well. God will see to that. Whether the person responds or not, he will regard your church with respect and often even appreciation. Soon your church will stand out from the crowd, gaining a reputation as one that cares about its community and its neighbors.

Should a sudden whim or urge strike the person to "go to church this Sunday," whether it be that very week or next month, or even a year or more from now, it is more than likely that your church will be the first one to come to mind. And even if such a person decides to go elsewhere, because of personal background or denominational affiliation, you will have helped to "nudge" him along the way.

...to take telephone surveys.

Though people may not be eager to submit to long, involved surveys, some are willing to answer questions if told at the outset what to expect, and reassured that it will be brief. Surveys are very useful for canvassing the spiritual inclinations of your community and as instruments for provoking people to examine their own spiritual attitudes. On another level, they may serve as bridges to help build relationships with people through the spontaneous conversations that are sure to ensue with those who are open. (For more on surveys see Appendix C, "Survey Says...")

...to invite people to holiday gatherings.

The Christian origin of our three biggest holidays— Christmas, Easter, and Thanksgiving— are ideal occasions for reaching out to others. Of course, churches have been doing just that for years. However, when it comes to bringing in outsiders, just as in bringing people to Christ, many will never come to such events without a special invitation. Most churches have used the standard means for announcing and promoting holiday events (posters, church marquees, newspaper and radio ads, etc.). The telephone provides a uniquely convenient means for extending a personal invitation.

If your church, for example, wanted to offer a community dinner why not offer it in the context of a theater production, or a choir presentation, or some other entertaining event. Not only would it be fun, this would go a long way toward allaying fears of awkward conversations with strangers. People need to know that they will not feel either isolated or "targeted." This calls for creative approaches, and even more, for the church to brush up on the social skills and amenities necessary to put people, especially new visitors, at ease.

...to promote special causes of concern to the community.

There are many ways this may be done. Food and clothing drives for needy families in the community; neighborhood renewal projects; supporting the needs of the local shelter for the homeless; and many other worthy causes. Your church might also promote issues addressing the spiritual well-being of your town. Anything from shutting down pornographic movie theaters to picketing to clear out the drug dealers from the local park could serve as worthy causes for lifting God's banner of righteousness and compassion. In such cases, phone calls could be a means of soliciting votes, or signatures for circulating petitions (See Appendix C: Survey Says...), or to promote letter-writing campaigns to civic leaders. Such causes, judiciously pursued in a spirit of Christian benevolence, help to raise the "Christ-consciousness" of your community and set your church on a hill as a beacon of moral righteousness.

Regardless of what purpose you choose when calling, those you reach will not soon forget a phone call from a stranger representing Christ. Such an encounter will leave a lasting impression, compelling even the most cynical to wonder if perhaps, just maybe, "God might be trying to tell me something." His spirit will be convicting them, witnessing to their need of the Savior.

These are just some of the possibilities for using the power of the telephone to reach people for Jesus. God is not limited in his thinking, and since we have been given the mind of Christ (I Corinthians 2:16), his church should not limit itself in seeking creative and innovative ways to promote the gospel.

All of the objectives we have looked at are potential means through which you will have opportunities to make connections that may lead to relationships. Having a wide variety of purposes for calling people gives you a greater number of occasions for making contact and, through such contacts, to establish friendships with people you might then lead to Christ and into your church fellowship. After all, that's our ultimate aim, to win friends and influence them for Jesus!

Get the Vision

You have before you an exciting vision for reaching people using the telephone. Why not at least try it? Have a church pizza party, or get a friend to do it with you, or if you prefer, try it alone in the comfort of your own home. How hard could it be, really?

Choose to believe God. Trust him to give you divine appointments. Determine to focus on the person at the other end of the line instead of any fears or worries you may have about what to say. God is faithful. He will lead you. He will give you bread for the hungry and water for the thirsty!

"Behold, I have put my words in thy mouth..." (Jeremiah 1:9, NKJV).

Robert Davis

Chapter Four

Letter Writing as a Ministry Could Revolutionize Evangelism

If the telephone is one of the great unused instruments for evangelism in the history of the church, then letter writing would have to receive top billing as the candidate most likely to surpass even the phone as a weapon that could have changed the world. After all, the telephone has been around for just over one hundred years. The art of writing letters, however, goes back to the very dawn of civilization.

In 1839 the English author, Edward Bulwer-Lytton, famously declared that "the pen is mightier than the sword." Those of us who believe the Bible to be the inspired Word of God know that this is true. We know that Paul's letters have turned the world upside down: "For his letters, they say, are weighty and powerful" (2 Corinthians 10:10).

Of course, we also know that his letters were God-breathed scripture from heaven. But our letters don't have to be God-breathed in order for God to breathe life into them! Were the church ever to embrace letter writing in a big way, the problem of vast numbers of believers sitting restlessly on the sidelines of global evangelism would evaporate overnight. The fears that hold so many back from sharing face-to-face (or even "voice to voice") simply do not apply when it comes to writing letters.

As a means of communicating the gospel, writing letters is *a fear-proof way of getting involved in the Great Commission.* There is no possibility of direct face-to-face rejection. Worries about what to say prove to be obstacles without substance.

The constraints of time and circumstance are not a factor where letters are involved. The writer can write in the place and in the time of his own choosing. The words chosen can be carefully reflected upon. Things said may be "taken back" if necessary, through rewriting. Scriptures can be looked up without hurry and placed most strategically with a forethought and deliberation not available in spontaneous face-to-face exchanges. Not that we ever trust in wisdom of words, mind you. But the studied approach available to one expressing his words in writing is an advantage to be considered, especially when preceded, accompanied, and followed by prayer.

Furthermore, letters may be read again and again, and yet again...on through the years. A letter may be stored away carefully (or carelessly) in some forgotten box or drawer, to be rediscovered at the most opportune and fortuitous occasion. There it lies, waiting patiently, quietly, in no hurry, but poised, ready in an instant to pierce the heart of the unsuspecting discoverer.

Letters are more powerful than tracts. A personal, handwritten message has the power to be received as direct communication from God. The reader is compelled, in spite of himself, to wonder, "Why did this letter, from a total stranger, find its way into my hands? Could God be trying to tell me something?"

Surely we have not seen the power and potential of such a ministry. How can this be? Not that Christians through the centuries have not written thousands, and yes, millions of inspired letters to people for Christ. But let's be honest here. Most of these were written to family, friends, or colleagues, at least. *But what about strangers?* Who can tell the awesome power our letters may hold to reach the hearts of souls we may never meet personally? One day we will see. Hopefully, it will not be with regret.

I believe that this is something worth looking into! Let's do so, then, with our hearts open to receive a vision of the awesome potential our God-inspired letters may hold to bring light into darkness and hope where there was none.

How to Write Letters for God

As we embark on our quest to find ways to use letters to reach people for Christ, it is acknowledged that most of the ideas and suggestions offered here would probably occur to a thoughtful reader pondering the possibilities on his own. In fact, the same might well be said for much of the material offered in other chapters as well. But it is good to "write the vision and make it plain, that he may run that reads it." With that said, we will now consider a few of the many exciting avenues that lay before us. No doubt, you may come up with your own variations. The more the merrier.

We'll start by focusing on strangers, looking at different possibilities for using letters to reach them in unexpected ways. We will not leave out family, friends, and others in our personal "Jerusalem," however. In some cases, letters may provide a back-door opportunity to communicate what might otherwise, for myriad reasons, be difficult to share with those who know us. For as we have seen, people who have known us for a long time are sometimes less receptive to more direct attempts to share our faith, try as we may.

So, beginning with strangers, we will first set our sights on the how-to of targeting those whom we want to reach. We find, in doing so, that there are an endless variety of intriguing and even down-right adventurous possibilities before us. Here are a few to get the wheels turning.

Deciding on Your Target

First, who do you want to reach? Where might you look to find strangers to write to? Here are some possibilities:

The Phone Book: an obvious first choice. With thousands of names to choose from, letting your fingers be guided by prayer, select a page, then a column, and finally, a name: Mr. and Mrs. Curious on Wayward Ave.

The Internet: Facebook. YouTube. E-mail. Chat rooms. Blogs. Twitter. Who knows what's coming next. Never before available until this generation, the Internet has become the most widely used form of communication on the planet. You now have the power to make direct electronic contact with people as far away as the other side of the world in a matter of minutes. It is now possible to Google names and addresses of people on white-page listings from websites in virtually any language. The Internet has the capability to function as a virtual worldwide electronic phonebook to practically any town or city in the world. Try to imagine how you would feel were you to receive a letter telling you how much God loves you from a total stranger in some foreign country, thousands of miles away. It would be something you would likely tell your grandchildren, as well as everyone else you know and care about!

The Drop: This is a letter written with the intention of "dropping" it in some strategic location, with the prayerful expectation that God will cause just the right person to find it. The strange and unexpected nature of the discovery cannot fail to leave a permanent and profound impression on the finder.

The Profiled Target: With this guided missile, you zero in on a specific kind of person you want to reach. You may, for example, imagine you are writing to a teenage boy or girl. As you prayerfully put pen to paper, you trust the Lord to give you just the right words to hit home. Feel the excitement and anticipation as you carry that letter with you, in your purse or in your pocket, waiting for that moment when God taps you on the shoulder and says,

"This is the person I want you to give it to." Wow! The power of such tailored messaging is sure to leave the recipient asking, "Why did that person give this letter to me? God, what are you telling me?"

The Long-Lost Friend or Acquaintance: Here again, through the power of the World Wide Web, you now have the possibility for literally traveling into your past to reach old friends, classmates, neighbors, and acquaintances…people who, not too many years ago, you would have had almost no possibility of ever communicating with again- certainly not without great effort, expense, and perseverance. Not so with the www. In many, if not most, cases, you can now find them…and if you can find them you can reach them!

Family, Friends, and Acquaintances Whom You Find Difficult to Speak with Face-to-Face: We addressed this earlier. Sometimes people who know us are not so open to hear what we have to say about "religion." Or it may be we have tried to talk with them but have felt hindered or fretful about provoking resentment or hostility by being too direct. To avoid conflict, we may have succeeded in only partially sharing the truth of God's grace. Letters have the power to overcome this hindrance.

And one more, just for fun…

Messages in Bottles, or Helium Balloons (!), or Secret Places Waiting to Be Found: Who would not be profoundly moved at the experience of receiving such a message? The thrill of discovery, the incredible unlikelihood of such an event occurring in one's life, would be a hallmark moment, to say the least! Think about this for a moment. As you read this right now, do you think that such a thing as this has happened today to anyone *anywhere in the world*? What about yesterday? Or the day before that? The odds are that many days, weeks, and months during any given year go by without such a thing happening anywhere—in the whole wide world! But you have the power to make something new happen in the earth. More importantly, to make something new happen in someone's life that could make a difference in eternity!

You can see that the possibilities are unlimited. Your letters may reach out across space and *even time* to touch the heart of some soul you may never meet in this lifetime. But in heaven... "Cast your bread upon the waters; for you shall find it after many days" (Ecclesiastes 11:1).

Keep in mind that, exciting as the possibilities might be for reaching faraway people in far-flung places around the world, our first allegiance and responsibility ought still be to our own Jerusalem, Judea, and Samaria. As a means for influencing people to consider Christ and our home church, letters directed to this end—and to the possibility (we'll say it again) of leading us into new friendships for the gospel's sake—should be our first priority when deciding who we wish to target. Okay, so we have our target in view. Now what?

Hitting Out Target: What Do We Say in Our Letters?

As in all of our witnessing efforts, God's desire is for each of us to find the style we are most comfortable with, the one that most reflects our unique personality in him. Since most all of us are experienced in writing letters, the advice offered here is merely to loosen up your thinking and help you get started. The important thing is that you pursue your own heart and your own unique style of self-expression. Here are some pointers to get you started as you give your pen to God and let him make it the "tongue of a ready writer" (Psalm 45:1).

- When writing to a stranger: Decide whether you want to target a certain "type" (lawyer, banker, factory worker, adult, teenager, child, etc.) If so, then pick your target and prayerfully meditate on themes that seem especially relevant to the one you are writing to. Select scriptures peculiarly suited to that person's station, background, cultural orientation, etc.—at least to the degree that you can do this with strangers. (Pray for wisdom.) Cultivate the art of thinking outside the box. *Try not to limit yourself to letters giving standard explanations of salvation.* Look for the personal touch. What might be the special burdens, challenges, aspirations, and concerns of the one you are writing to? If you are not targeting a specific type of person, then pray and ask the Lord to impress upon you the words and thoughts he wants you to share. Explaining salvation is never bad. Yet trusting the Lord for his supernatural leading will put you in the place where he can use you to write words that are *peculiarly suited* to the needs of that person.

- When writing to an old friend: If you are writing to a long-lost friend or acquaintance and think it unlikely that you'll ever see the person, you need to carefully gauge how far you want to go in sharing "spiritual" things. Perhaps your letter will be the beginning of a mutual correspondence, in which case you will have further opportunities to share your faith with the person. If, however, this turns out not to be the case and you feel that you may not have a likely possibility for further contact (for whatever reason), it may be wise to write the words you would want to say if you knew that either you or she were going to die before you ever had a chance to communicate again. What would you say to someone if you knew you would never have another chance to say anything to him again in this life?

- When writing to family members: If you are writing to a family member, evaluate the history of your previous attempts to share your faith with him. Has there been hostility, resentment, or resistance? Do you feel you have been hindered from fully sharing what you desire to say or perhaps have been unable to communicate, for whatever reason? You should use your letter to address those things that you wanted to say but have been unable to communicate. Be as tactful as possible. Yet we do not want to shun from "declaring the whole council of God" for fear of being rejected.

- When writing "on behalf of" your church: Determine the content of your message from the purpose of your letter. If it is to share your testimony or your faith, then do so, making reference to your church as your "calling card." If it is to extend a personal invitation to some special event, then make it appealing and gracious.

Do not allow yourself to be limited! You may use your letters to tell people how they may receive Christ, but you might also write to...

- Help someone see that God wants to meet all of our needs as we seek him first.

- Help someone understand God's longing to have fellowship with us and that this is the reason he made us.

- Show someone that the Bible reveals that God wants to be our heavenly Father, as well as our healer, our protector, our provider, and our shepherd to guide us through life.

- Describe what the Bible says about the last days.

- Share a variety of scriptures on a variety of topics that God may use to enlighten, quicken, comfort, heal, warn, rebuke, or exhort.

Robert Davis

- Share how Christ has saved you and helped you find peace and fulfillment in your life. (See Part One: "The Tract Nobody is Using")

- Encourage people in an endless variety of ways to look to God for meaning and purpose in their lives.

- Offer friendship, continued correspondence, even a personal visit, if possible.

A Closing Thought

What if you had received a letter from an anonymous source, many years before you came to Christ? Suppose that this letter inspired you to believe that God was wanting you to see how much he loved you and cared for you. Imagine that this experience had such a profound impact on you that you sensed the call of God on your life far earlier than you actually did. Who can say what added blessings this might have brought to you, and even more, what lives you might have touched in those added years of walking with God.

You do not know how the Lord might use a letter from you to impact someone, perhaps even changing the entire course of that person's life. But one day you will find out, when God reveals it to you—that is, if you try it. (For some example letters see Appendix D: "Letters in Lights")

Chapter Five

Children: the Most Important Ones!

As a child, I remember riding my bike up and down the streets of my neighborhood, wandering over hill and dale for hours at a time. Sometimes alone, sometimes with my friends, it rarely occurred to us to be on the alert for kidnappers, molesters, or child murderers. It was summertime. School was out, and homework was a thing of the past—at least for those few blissful months of perpetual play when our greatest worry was where we would round up a couple of more guys to play baseball.

Back then we were filled with a sense of adventure and anticipation, dreaming of bright futures filled with unlimited possibilities. We gave little thought to danger, terror, or monsters lurking in the shadows. To be sure, we were told, "Don't talk to strangers," and, "Look both ways before you cross the street," and so on. But we never had to worry about planes being smashed into buildings, skyscrapers falling on top of us, or pedophiles in the churches. And though we grew up under the shadow of "the bomb," even practicing getting under our desks at school a few times (which was more exciting than anything else), it always seemed far away, off in some distant future too remote for a kid to worry about.

Nor did our parents give thought to sinister threats around every corner. They let us roam far and wide, reminding us only to "be home for supper." No doubt they kept many private worries to themselves—after all, they knew about the Lindbergh baby, the concentration camps, and of course, the fact that we were all going to die, a fact we were becoming aware of too, but like most kids put on the shelf as something to deal with later…much later. Like all parents, they tried to keep these things a safe distance from us and seemed, at least, to offer a world full of wonder and promise.

For those of us who are parents of the new millennium, however, that is not so easy to do as it may have been for our parents or their parents before them. The world is a very different place than it was when we were growing up, and not just because we no longer see it through the rose-colored glasses of childhood. It is a darker place, more dangerous, more threatening, and more evil.

A World Gone Mad

We look around and it seems that everywhere we turn there is hatred, suspicion, and violence. Democrats and Republicans no longer just disagree; they revile each other. Many Americans hate their own government. The media and our university professors (mentors of our youth) seem to portray Uncle Sam as the mother of all that is wrong in the world. We have "wars and rumors of wars," just like Jesus said there would be. Murderers running around everywhere, and not just murderers, but repeat murderers, curiously mythologized with the darkly compelling title "serial killer." We even have video games offering to train our children in the skills required to emulate the Mansons, theBundys, and the Dahmars of the world.

As if that were not enough, we have the Internet, replete with video-taped beheadings, calls to "Jihad" (it's a "holy" war), pornography, and not just pornography but "kiddie" porn…to wet the perverted appetites of every parent's worst nightmare—the child molester, or, for the politically "correct" among us, those "afflicted" with pedaphilea (it's a "disease").

In a society where good is called evil (prayer in schools, public posting of the ten commandments, religious people in politics, creation science, et al.) and evil is called good ("peaceful" Islam, liberal judges, evolution (only) in public schools, "parole" for violent killers, etc, to infinity), we wonder, how shall we navigate our children safely through the turbulent waters of a world gone mad?

For those of us who are bringing up our children in the "like precious faith," the prevailing decadence and degeneracy of our once righteous nation causes us to look with alarm at the evils they will have to confront as they come to terms with living life in a fallen world. Only through our faith in Christ may we take courage to arm ourselves, and our little ones, with the protection of God's love.

The knowledge that Jesus will soon be coming to take us out of this world with all of its darkness encourages us to press forward through the trials and challenges. Yet in the light of his soon appearing, we are confronted with another reality. If time is short and this age is coming to a close, then where does this leave those who do not know the Savior? More particularly, where does this leave the children who have not had opportunity to come to Christ?

When I look back at the history of my own life, I am faced with the realization that, if Christ had returned when I was a child, I would not have been found to be among those who were trusting in him. I did not come to the Lord until I was twenty-two years old. If he had returned when I was a teenager, I would have been left behind. No doubt the same is true for many of you...

The "Age of Accountability" Question

Some may find the subtitle above vaguely disturbing. The word *question* may seem to have a suggestion of doubt about the matter of accountability as it pertains to children. In response to that thought, may I answer: "Not exactly, but sort of...maybe."

In fact, there is some controversy, or at least uncertainty, regarding this doctrine. For those unfamiliar with the term *age of accountability*, it is generally understood to mean something like this: the age at which a child arrives at an understanding of the difference between right and wrong, together with a moral sense of obligation to choose the right and reject the wrong.

The uncertainty lies in the fact that, first, there is no direct mention of this doctrine in scripture, though some, or many, would argue that it is implied, or at least that it is in harmony with everything which, biblically speaking, suggests of mercy, grace, and the Father's tender love for his earthly children—a line of thinking we all feel strongly compelled to embrace.

The second difficulty involves the uncertainty regarding the age at which a child arrives at this level of understanding in which he is thereby made accountable. Again there is no direct mention of a specific age given in Scripture, though some might argue that the Jewish bar-mitzvah, celebrating a boy's initiation into manhood at age thirteen, represents a sort of type of accountability. Most, however, myself included, suspect that any age of accountability, as such, arrives a good deal earlier than this.

The general opinion is that the age differs from one child to the next, depending upon his level of maturity and understanding. By this standard, it may be that one child, advanced in moral sensitivity, becomes accountable at, say, five or six years of age while another, slower to comprehend the moral difference between right and wrong, reaches accountability at a later age, maybe eight or nine.

The truth is that none of us really knows, and to make matters more difficult, the whole issue is extremely delicate and charged with emotion. After all, we are not just talking ivory tower theology here but about the fates and futures of the very most precious of our kind: our children! Some readers may be upset that such a topic as this is even being addressed here.

I have no wish to make anyone unnecessarily uncomfortable. And I have no intention of debating unknowable matters of faith or doctrine. However, if we are resolved to fix upon the wisest course of action with respect to children and their future happiness, then we oblige ourselves to set our spiritual compasses in the direction that seems most likely to yield a harvest of safety and security for those who are most vulnerable, our own feelings being secondary to the question of what is best for these "least" among us. In fact, most of us would agree that children are the most important people on earth and their souls should occupy first priority in the Great Commission.

Better Safe Than Sorry

The arguments for an age of accountability are reasonable. The notion of accountability commencing with conscious awareness of right and wrong resonates with the human notion of justice and fairness. Yet we should never blithely assume that our limited understanding of spiritual truths may be used to comfort us in our own complacency.

With reference to the subject at hand, the point we are stressing is this: We should esteem the souls of children greater than any others. Any other attitude is tragically unfair to them. Whatever our theology may be regarding the age of accountability, when it comes to the eternal souls of children, we do well to abide by the time-tested philosophy: *better safe than sorry.*

It seems needful to say this because some believers convey the impression that young children, especially those who are too young to know about right and wrong, and thus under no moral obligation, do not have as great a need for Christ as others. The result of this thinking is a tendency among some to take it for granted that children have less need of the gospel because, after all, they are not yet accountable.

This is not to say that anyone in Christ's church dismisses the importance of children!

It is just that this kind of thinking seems to make room for an attitude that, like the disciples in Jesus's day who shooed away the little ones, seeing them as a distraction, so, on a lesser level, we in the church might unknowingly fail to see the urgency of reaching children right now. This line of subconscious reasoning never affects us when considering our own children, however.

Certainly nothing should be more important for Christian parents than to raise their children in the knowledge of the Savior's love. And we can hardly impact the lives of other children as profoundly as those of our own. This is to be expected and is in the general nature of things.

Yet the need for other children to be introduced to Christ is real. And though we are unable to do as much for these as for our own, this does not mean that we can do nothing. Of course there are many dedicated saints devoting themselves to reaching children not fortunate enough to have Christian parents. Thousands of "Vacation Bible Schools" attest to this.

However, we should recognize that, good as these are, there is room to do much more. This should not be doubted for the simple reason that most of God's people *are doing nothing* to reach these children.

Children Do Not Need a "Vacation Naughtiness School" to Teach Them How to Sin

It is unnerving to realize that sinful tendencies manifest themselves very early in the lives of most children. They seem to have a highly developed talent for throwing tantrums, ignoring parental directives, and general all-around rebellion. It is hard to ignore the fact that such behavior, rather than its opposite (docile submission, instant obedience, and angelic serenity) are the near universal norms of conduct for even the youngest among us.

We have to train them in obedience, good manners, consideration of others, and so on. No need for instruction in naughtiness; each child comes into the world with a natural proficiency in the finer arts of misbehavior without any coaching from outside. Observing such behavior it is not hard for us to understand the words of the psalmist, "They go astray from the womb" (Psalm 58:3).

Indeed, if David had said, "They seek to please their parents at every turn," we would have thought he had taken leave of his senses. Even atheists and agnostics recognize that children need no instruction in disobedience and that godly traits of selflessness and saintliness are not naturally existing features of childhood character.

Not that children are all bad, of course. But their sinful nature asserts itself from the earliest moments. Selfishness and self-pleasing are the guiding lights of their nature, even as was the case in our own childhood.

Even so, we love our children. They are adorable and more precious to us than life itself. But it is folly to suppose there is no need to point them to Jesus before they reach an "age of accountability," especially when their ability to stray begins to assert itself even before they utter their first words.

But though little children need no classroom instruction to demonstrate proficiency in sin, it is also true that children of all ages are far more responsive to the gospel than any other age group when given a chance to meet their Savior.

The heart is never so tender, never more trusting, never more humble than in those first years of life—before the years of sin, rejection, betrayal, and cynicism have taken their toll.

There is no such thing as a hard-hearted child. Even those who may seem such are still desperately hoping to be loved and cared for, their indifferent or hostile exteriors merely a pitiful coping mechanism to protect themselves from more hurt.

If We Really Are Living in the Last Days…

We see the prophetic signs all around us pointing to the end of the age. No one knows how much time we have left. But we do know this. However much time remains for us, there is that much less for the children who do not know Christ. If you are twenty-five years old as you read these words and Jesus comes back in three years, you will be twenty-eight at his appearing—assuming of course, that you live that long. A three-year-old today, too young to read these words, would be six. Age of accountability? Maybe. Who knows? Were you saved when you were six?

Perhaps we hadn't thought about it that way. Maybe we should. We know the time is short. How much shorter if you were just a five- or six-year-old, barely out of the crib, full of wonder and awe and magic anticipation of the great adventure of life stretching out before you…little suspecting what lies just ahead. But you and I know exactly what's coming for those without Christ: "A day of darkness and gloominess, a day of clouds and thick darkness" (Joel 2:2); "For behold, darkness shall cover the earth, and gross darkness the people" (Isaiah 60:2).

How would you like to be a kid who doesn't know Jesus when all of this happens? Christians everywhere are slumbering and sleeping while God is calling us to: "Cry aloud, spare not, lift up thy voice like a trumpet…" (Isaiah 58:1); "Multitudes (including children) in the valley of decision: for the day of the Lord is near in the valley of decision" (Joel 3:14).

There is no more time to lose, especially for the youngest ones. Children are the ones who deserve the most attention, the greatest effort, and the first priority. Sadly, many will not believe this. Many will say, "I am not 'called' to this 'ministry.'" But who said you needed to be "called"? Jesus already called us: "Let the little children come to me (by making a way?), and do not forbid them (by not helping them to?); for of such is the kingdom of heaven" (Mark 10:14, NKJV).

Is There Some Child Somewhere You Can Help?

If you are a Christian with children, then you are likely doing everything in your power to bring them up in the nurture and admonition of the Lord. This chapter is not aimed at helping you with your own children. It is about you helping to reach other kids, not just your own. Could you possibly consider expanding your compassion to include these "other" kids, the ones in your neighborhood, your apartment complex, next door to you who have not been told of Christ's love for them?

Look around you. Is it possible that some child or children in your neighborhood or some other part of your private world might be within the reach of your influence? If thinking about the many overwhelms you, then ask yourself if there might be just one or two or some other small number that you can help.

You can do this, even if you've never had experience working with children. You don't need any. All you need is a willingness to try and a desire to share God's love with some little child who doesn't know any better and may never know any better unless someone (like you?) does something to make a difference.

You Should Have a Plan

It is not as easy to reach "other" children as it used to be. Understandably, parents don't want their kids talking to strangers. Who can blame them? But God can still make a way if he has someone to co-labor with him.

The most popular programs among churches attempting to reach children are the summer "Vacation Bible Schools." These have been around for years and have proven to be a wonderful avenue for introducing kids to Christ who might not otherwise have the good fortune to come to him through other means. While many of the children attending these gatherings are kids whose families are members of the church, there are usually a good number of other children who find their way there—some from bus ministries provided by the church, others from parents who heard about the event through church marquees, advertisements, etc.

These annual events (usually run for one week during summer vacation) have continued to hold favor among un-churched parents in the community who feel safe leaving their children in the hands of the church staff for a few hours a day during the "VBS" week.

Unfortunately, un-churched parents willing to drop off their kids for the week of the VBS (sometimes for no other reason than to be free of them) are not nearly so enthusiastic when it comes to bringing them the remaining 51 weeks of the year – which would require their own attendance. Granted, the churches do make an effort to stir the spiritual interests of the parents by inviting them to their child's Sunday graduation ceremony and expressing hope that they will "come and see us again." And many of these churches do have excellent year round children's ministries. But most of the un-churched (and often unsaved) adults fail to respond unless other measures are taken. Usually these measures are not forthcoming and the child is left to fend for himself, perhaps until the next VBS comes around.

This in no way invalidates the need for, or benefit of, Vacation Bible Schools. It does seem to indicate, however, that perhaps something more is needed to fill in the gap for these children during those long eleven months between annual events. It is this need that is the focus of the remainder of this chapter.

A God for All Seasons

When the "VBS" vision was first conceived in the heart of some believer who had a compassion for children and a desire to see them come to Christ, we might imagine that her (or his) thinking went something like this: I want to introduce young children who do not have the good fortune of growing up in Christian homes to their Savior by giving them enough information in a short time to enable them to understand and believe the gospel.

As a vehicle for accomplishing this task, the Vacation Bible School ministry has succeeded beyond anyone's wildest hopes or dreams. What is needed, however, is some means to help the children whose parents do not bring them back to church after the VBS week. The unfortunate reality of their parents' spiritual apathy presents a formidable obstacle. As we have seen, the sad outcome of mom and dad's indifference is that these kids will usually not see the inside of a church building again until the next Vacation Bible School rolls around.

Like anyone else, children need to grow in the "grace and knowledge of our Lord Jesus Christ."

These kids face the daunting challenge of holding on to their faith in the midst of, in many cases, a Christ-less home. With unbelieving parents who neglect church attendance and have little thought for their own children's spiritual welfare, the situation is ripe for Satan to come in and steal the precious seed of hope that was sown in their hearts.

The church must face this challenge with unflinching compassion and determination. One week out of the year devoted to the cause of reaching un-churched children is not sufficient to do more than lay the barest foundation of faith. Granted, the church can never take the place of godly parents and a warm Christian family life. But it can and must keep its helping hand extended to those children who have reached out their hands to the Savior!

It is only through ongoing contacts sustained through continuing encounters that there is any realistic chance for these children to enter into meaningful, life-changing relationships with godly people. The lasting effect of such relationships offer one of the greatest, if not the single greatest, potential benefit for the long-term spiritual welfare of these children.

Why Not Share the Burden?

The biggest reason that most churches do not follow through with a year-round ministry to these children is that it is usually too difficult to find anyone willing to assume the burden for such a demanding ministry.

Fortunately, this need not be an obstacle to meeting the ongoing spiritual needs of these kids. What is needed is for the congregation to spread the burden around among the members in such a way that no one individual or group is overextended.

This would not be hard to accomplish. All that would be needed is for twelve members to volunteer ten weeks of the year to sustain a year round outreach. These would not need extensive experience or training. A heart for kids and a willingness to help out are all that is needed.

Here's how it could work: The calendar is divided up into four quarters of thirteen weeks. Each thirteen-week period would have ten weeks of "kids' club" meetings, followed by three weeks off.

Each quarter would be assigned to one group of three people. These would commit to holding the meetings for the ten-week period of the quarter to which they are assigned. After that, their commitment is fulfilled! During the three weeks before the commencement of the next quarter, the next team of three is readied. These three then lead the kids' club for the next quarter (ten weeks), and so on.

The program is only planned for one year at a time. The people who volunteer for this ministry for the year in progress would assume no further obligations. As the year-end approaches, new volunteers for the upcoming year would be solicited from the congregation. This promotion would be especially convenient if the new year commences either in the summer week following the VBS or during the holidays as church members begin to think about the coming new year. The wonderful thing about this approach is that each volunteer could receive virtually all the training he or she needs by sitting in on, or helping out with, the church's regularly scheduled children's church for as little as two or three weeks before taking their turn.

Robert Davis

"Kids' Clubs" Are Different from Children's Church—and Bus Ministries

Children's church services and kids' club meetings are not the same thing. The Sunday school bus ministry comes close and is surely the greatest outreach to un-churched children in our nation's history.

However, a Bible "club" for kids differs from a bus ministry in significant ways, and there are important advantages to consider in contemplating an outreach to un-churched children separate from the typical Sunday school bus ministry.

First, a kid's Bible club may be held anywhere, in a home or someone's backyard, a community room, a park, or, if preferred, at the church. A bus ministry, on the other hand, is always centered around the church—the purpose of the bus, after all, is to bring the kids *to* the church.

With kids' clubs, the flexibility of location allows for greater opportunity to reach children in the neighborhoods in which they live. This usually has the further advantage of allowing parents greater convenience insofar as checking in on their kids is concerned. Also, for the parents who are themselves not attending church, it may pose less of a "threat" to look in on their child at a nonspiritual place like a backyard or park, etc.

Second, a kids' club may be held almost anytime—after school, on a Saturday, even early evenings, depending on the needs of those participating. A church-centered ministry, on the other hand, can usually only be held during the set time of the church service—namely, Sunday morning.

Third, having the meeting time and location in a nonconventional (non-church) setting creates a more club-like atmosphere. It is not just *church*, a word that may have negative connotations in the minds of children whose parents are likely unsaved. Many sinners are very prejudiced against churches in general, and children very early pick up on these parental attitudes.

Fourth, the central concept of a kids' club (which may also be called a Bible Club, Adventure Club, God's Explorers, or any other name you can think of) is to have fun while learning about Jesus. It is supremely important for young children growing up in spiritually impoverished circumstances to have happy, joyful experiences with lots of fun, and sometimes, even adventure, with their kids' club so that as they grow up those wonderful memories will be like magnets attracting the child to Christ and his church. By not limiting a child's spiritual experiences to the confines of the church building, these gatherings have a greater potential for offering varieties of experience, and a sense of adventure for those participating.

Beachheads in the Community

Another advantage of kids' clubs is that the more immediate location (the child's neighborhood, the park, a community room, sometimes even the homes of the children themselves) tends to facilitate a more significant impact on that child's parents. Intimate community venues help to create a spiritual lifeline to the parents, connecting them with Christ's church and his people. These outlying locations, together with the children they reach, become spiritual beachheads, giving the Holy Spirit a foothold to work with in drawing other family members to Christ. The flexible location concept also increases the likelihood of reaching more children in other areas.

The children's joy in learning to trust their savior, as well as their spontaneous sharing of the "fun things" they do in the kids' club, will be powerful instruments in the hands of the Holy Spirit to convict the parents and other family members again and again.

There is an advantage for the church leadership as well. Because of the rotating shared burden approach, these kinds of ministries are usually more able to produce a steady stream of volunteers. A bus ministry, on the other hand, usually relies upon one or two stalwart church members to carry the load year after year. When they can no longer serve, it is often difficult to find anyone willing to replace them due to the long-term, open-ended nature of the commitment required—unless, of course, they also were to adopt the shared burden approach!

This is one of the main factors that have contributed to the "fading out" of the once grand tradition of the local Sunday school bus ministry. Perhaps if the shared burden concept were applied here we might see a welcome resurgence of this once proud and noble pillar of community outreach.

Mapping Out Your Blueprint for Action

To achieve the best results in ministry, as in most things in life, it is wise to sit down and map out a strategy for implementing your plans. The best place to start is to define your vision. Since the focus of this chapter is reaching un-churched children for Christ, we might define our vision as follows:

We want to start a club for children in which they can experience the love of God and receive his free gift of salvation by trusting Jesus Christ. We also want to provide a fun-filled atmosphere of warmth and acceptance inspiring these children to cherish the memories of the times we shared.

This is just an example. You may define your vision however you like. The important thing is to "write the vision and make it plain, that he (and she!) may run that reads it Habakkuk 2:2." Having done this, you are ready to get down to the nuts and bolts of your action plan.

Here Are Some Pointers

1. Decide who you want to reach. This is the place to start. Pray and ask God to show you where the need is. Perhaps your neighborhood or apartment complex. Maybe some other area in town. Sometimes the only way to know is to go, trusting the Lord to lead you to the open door (Rev.

3:8). Of course, you can't know if the door will open until you first knock. Knock until an effectual door is opened to you. Trust your instincts and your spiritual intuition. God will make known his will through prayer and by acting in faith.

2. Get one or more people to help you. It is possible to do this kind of ministry by yourself, but it is much easier if you can find at least one, and preferably two or three others, to help you. If you present the "shared burden" concept to your pastor, he should be able, by presenting the vision from the pulpit, to find eleven others to help—even though you need only two additional people to start the first ten-week period. Pray together with your team members for direction and favor, not just with the children you hope to reach, but with their parents as well.

3. Map out your strategy. You will need:

• A plan for reaching your target children and meeting their parents. (See "Guidelines for Recruiting Children" below.)

• A gathering place and provision for transportation, if necessary.

• You will also need to decide what curriculum you will be using. Perhaps you may use the church curriculum, or if need be and you prefer, you may choose to develop your own or to purchase some instruction materials from your local Christian bookstore. Remember, for this plan you will want to map out a ten-week lesson outline so that you know ahead of time what ground you will want to cover.

Robert Davis

- Decide how long you want your club meeting to last. (Generally, an hour and a half to two hours is ideal.) What will be your starting date? What day of the week? What time will it start? What time will it end?

Some Guidelines for Structuring Your Meetings

While structure should never be a straight jacket to limit the leading of the Holy Spirit, scriptural wisdom admonishes us to, "Prepare ye the way of the Lord, and make his paths straight" (Luke 3:4).

We are to seek after the mind of the Spirit, making every effort to prepare ahead of time. This will enable us to wisely and effectively communicate the things that are most needful for the children to understand to enable them to hold fast to their trust in Jesus.

Therefore, it is prudent to have both a curriculum outline, as mentioned earlier, and a structure to enable you to effectively communicate the lessons you have planned. Begin by deciding on the major elements of your meeting and the order of each. The following outline may serve as an example, keeping in mind that flexibility, creativity, and innovation are hallmarks of the Spirit's leading.

Sample Outline For a Kids' Club Meeting

1. Start your meeting with informal fellowship.

2. Lead the children in some songs of praise

3. Teach a Bible lesson or tell a Bible story

4. Teach a Bible memory verse

5. Teach an "object" lesson or an illustration

6. Do a puppet show or have some arts & crafts

7. Prayer time (may also be done after the Bible story)

8. Something new and fun and "out of the ordinary"

9. Serve refreshments and hand out literature

As you can see, a typical kids' club meeting may be structured similar to a regular children's church gathering. There are some important differences to keep in mind, however, in addition to those we've already discussed. These will be considered shortly. But first, a few points about each of the above.

1. Informal Fellowship: You want to have a relaxed, informal atmosphere to transition from arriving at the meeting place and the commencement of the kids' club proper. Care should be exercised to see that each child is warmly greeted and made to feel welcome. Be sure that quiet or shy children do not feel left out. It may be a good idea to have an "ice-breaker" game or activity to loosen things up and get everyone in a good mood. There are plenty of resource materials for such activities in bookstores, on the Internet, and your imagination.

2. Sing Some Praise Songs: It is a good idea to write the words to songs on poster boards or handouts so the kids can follow along. They may not know the words. Remember, you are targeting "un-churched" children here. Also, you should understand that children who do not have a relationship with Christ are incapable of worshipping God. They can sing, however, and as they do the Spirit will be working his "magic" in their hearts!

3. The Bible Lesson or Bible Story: If teaching a lesson, keep it simple and focused on one theme only. If telling

Robert Davis

a Bible story, clearly communicate the significant moral lesson to be learned from it. (Refer to "Guidelines for Teaching the Bible Lesson" and "Guidelines for Sharing Your Testimony" in Appendix E: More Stuff for Kids.)

4. The Bible Memory Verse: The verse should relate to and exemplify the Bible lesson or story. It should not be long or complicated. Modern translations are preferable, and paraphrased renderings are frequently more suited to the child's comprehension level. It is vital that truth be communicated in language capable of being understood by young children. The verse may be memorized by having the kids read it over as a group several times, with the teacher or helper erasing one or two words each time, until the children can recite the verse from memory. (It would also be beneficial to make individual memory verse cards for each child to receive after the exercise is complete. Not only will this assure that the Word will not be stolen, but Mom and Dad and other family members will likely see it as well…and as we know, God's Word never goes out void.)

5. Object Lessons/Illustrations: Object lessons and illustrations are very effective devices for communicating spiritual truths in practical, down-to-earth ways. An object lesson involves using physical objects in ways that demonstrate their interaction with the environment. Comparisons are then drawn to show how these interactions may exemplify or parallel spiritual laws and principles. An illustration is a comparison or example intended for explanation or corroboration.

It is important that, when using object lessons or illustrations, these be correlated in some way with the Bible lesson or story so that the lesson may be amplified. As with icebreakers, there are plenty of good resource materials available in your Christian bookstore, the Internet, or your local library.

6. Arts and Crafts/Puppets: Some people are extremely talented artistically. Others may feel that their creative juices sputtered out somewhere between kindergarten and junior high school. Of course, artistic talent can be very helpful for leading arts and crafts projects. But for the less gifted among us, help is readily available through the same resources mentioned above. The important thing to remember is that children love arts and crafts! Even a modest effort in this direction will significantly increase the "fun factor" for your kids.

   Similarly, you need not be a "puppet master" to keep the little ones spellbound. Children are simply mesmerized by puppets! A little bit of practice (rehearsal) is all it takes to get you ready. If you are willing, God will make you able! [For suggestions on how to make your own puppet skits, or prepare your own teaching plans, share your testimony, and other helpful material, please consult Appendix E.]

   [Note: For expedience and time's sake, it is generally advisable to choose either an art/craft project *or* a puppet show in a given meeting. If you like, you might alternate from week to week.]

7. Prayer Time: This may be done right after the Bible lesson or after the object lesson, illustration, or puppet show. There is no hard and fast rule or formula. Do what seems good at the time. The prayer format itself may also be varied. You may pray together as a group, individually, or in smaller groups with a helper leading each. Let the children learn by watching you pray. Allow for each child to participate, while avoiding coercion.

Breaking up into smaller groups is an ideal way to allow each team member to review the lesson on a more intimate level with the children. This also gives the workers an opportunity to establish closer personal relationships with each one.

8. Something New, Fun, and "Out of the Ordinary": The idea is to keep the kids in a state of happy anticipation from week to week. What to do? We will offer a small number of possibilities to get your mental gears in motion, but the best thing to do when contemplating what to do each week is to "let go and let God!" He never has creative dry spells. Treasure hunts or scavenger hunts (look that one up yourself); "blind" kickball—the blind-fold comes off after you kick the ball so you can see to run the bases (your teammates tell you when to "kick"!); team races "to the tree and back"; "guess who I am" games—kids write down a secret about themselves; others try to "guess who"; sorry, no more hints here…

9. Refreshments: A must! The kids will look forward to tasty snacks and cold drinks!

Some Additional Points to Consider

- It is useful to have a handout to give each child as a review/reminder of the lesson taught. Additionally, such a review would be an affective means of communication to the parents, informing them about the things their child is learning and doing. A few written words addressed directly to the parents in such a handout might pay dividends in maintaining favor and rapport, enhancing your prospects of continued ministry to their child.

- It is the leader's responsibility to orchestrate the helpers in order to see that every task is covered and to help each member to discover his or her special gifts and talents. Ideally, everyone should be given an opportunity to participate in a variety of different activities and responsibilities. This will facilitate growth and versatility in their ministry to the children.

- It is also advisable to have someone prepared to function as the leader in the event that you cannot make it to a meeting. Of course, it is always good to train up leaders as a matter of policy for the simple reason that leaders make things happen!

Guidelines for Recruiting Children

The key to having a kids' club is to have kids! Recruiting children, therefore, is one of the most important tasks you will face in starting a club. The following suggestions are offered to help you do this. The tips here are for visiting house to house. While it may be possible to hand out flyers to children returning from school as they get off of the bus, you must be especially careful to avoid any appearance of suspicion. Please read the list of "cautions" following these suggestions.

- Greet the parents with a friendly smile. If a child answers the door, it is best to ask for the parent and to talk to her first. Explain that you are visiting the neighborhood to tell everyone about something "fun and exciting" for children that will be starting soon in their area.

- Give a brief and enthusiastic description of the kids' club. Mention that there will be Bible stories, puppet shows, skits, arts and crafts, contests and games, refreshments, and lots of fun activities. (To boost your confidence, you

Robert Davis

and your helper might practice giving a one-minute description of the club to each other before going out.) If there are other children in the neighborhood who are already attending or are planning to go, mention their names to the parent—and the child, if she is also listening. This may stimulate further interest and motivation.

- Explain to the parent that the purpose of the kids' club is to teach the children about Jesus and what he has done for us.

- If the child is present and you feel comfortable with the parent's reaction to what you have said, invite her to the kids' club. As you do so, offer the flyer to the parent and briefly mention when and where the club will meet. Be sure to invite the parent to come as well, even if just to see what it is all about. (If necessary, explain to the parent that you will not be "pushing church" or trying to change anyone's church affiliation. You are simply teaching Bible lessons and stories to help children learn to trust God and his Word.)

- If the child and parent give an immediate positive response, be sure to get his name and address. Review the when and where, and answer any questions the parent may have. If transportation is provided, you might ask the parent if she wishes to accompany the child to the pickup point or watch from the door. Suggest that the flyer be taped to the refrigerator door as a helpful reminder.

Important! If The Child Is Home Alone...

Occasionally a child will answer the door and there will be no parent around. The child may be home alone. If this seems to be the case, give the briefest explanation to the child regarding the purpose for your visiting and state that you will return "soon" when the parents are available to talk to. You may leave a flyer, but do not ask the child to open the door (if it is a screen). Simply leave it in the door handle. Of course, if the child has already opened the screen door, or if there is none, you may hand him the flyer with the brief explanation and then leave immediately. Be sure to leave your phone number on the flyer, encouraging parents to call for further information.

Some Words of Caution

Due to the high incidence of kidnapping and other crimes, great care must be taken to avoid any appearance of suspicion when dealing with children.

Choose only the most open and visible avenue. Door-to-door visitation is probably the safest means of promoting your kids' club. Newspaper and radio advertisements are also good, though less personal.

1. Be positive and unapologetic. We have nothing to hide!

2. Never talk to a child if you are standing near your car or any place that might appear hidden or secret.

3. Do not distribute candy, except at the kids' club. Distribute only the flyers when you are engaged in recruiting children.

4. Never talk to a child who is separated from his parents. This includes door-to-door visitation, except for briefly explaining why you are visiting her home. Then, give out the flyer and leave. The only exception is when you are

distributing flyers at school drop-off zones. This is usually okay because there are almost always several children, and you are well out in the open. There is a risk, however, that some parents may frown upon this activity.

5. Never enter a home where a parent is not present even if the child invites you in!

6. If possible, avoid going alone or at night.

7. Always carry flyers with your church name and phone number.

8. Always carry proof of your personal identification.

9. Pray before and after your outing, to bind the powers of darkness from hindering your efforts, and to request God's presence and favor to go before you and with you.

It may be advisable (and in some states mandatory) to require those who wish to participate in this ministry, or any other that deals with children, to submit to a background investigation with the local police or sheriff's department. While this may be offensive to some, the interests of the children must come first.

Though this may not always seem necessary, as in instances where you are so familiar with a person and his or her character and background as to be beyond doubt, it is better to be safe than sorry whenever there is the least uncertainty. Those who are innocent have nothing to fear. Those who are not innocent are *forbidden by law* to have any involvement with activities in which children are present. Always err on the side of caution and always on the side of the children.

Some Important Dos And Don'ts

In Matthew 10:16, Jesus tells us to "be wise as serpents and harmless as doves." This is never truer than when working with children. Here are some common sense suggestions to help you be both.

1. Always meet the parents: Never allow a child to participate in a kids' club without first meeting his parent(s). And of course, never under any circumstances bring a child to a club meeting without the parent's knowledge and permission.

2. Be sure to invite the parents to attend. This will go a long way toward putting them at ease, since you have made it clear that you have nothing to hide. If a parent should accept the invitation, all the better. You may have an open door to start a friendship with that person.

3. Always follow through on your word. Be on time every time. Get the kids home on time. If you promise a special activity or treat for the next week, make good on your promise.

4. If you must cancel a meeting, make every effort to give a reminder notice to each child the week before.

5. When talking about sin, avoid condemnation.

6. Never tell a child she is sick because of sin or because his faith is weak.

7. Never administer corporal punishment! If the child is disruptive and will not cooperate, have a helper separate him from the others to give him special attention. If this works, allow the child to return to the group. Gently but firmly tell persistent disruptors that they will not be allowed to return to the group unless they behave.

8. Never yell at a child. Never embarrass him in front of other children.

9. Avoid teaching any doctrines of a controversial nature, no matter how firmly you believe in them! Stick to teaching the children to trust in Jesus and follow his Word.

10. Keep the parents informed about their child's activities in the kids' club. Lesson outlines, letters to parents, and special gifts or cards to the parents are the thoughtful gestures that may help keep the door open to minister to their children, while also being a blessing to the family.

11. Remember to pray for each child during the week.

12. Try to keep a supply of helpful children's literature on hand, as well as literature with a special appeal to the parents. These printed materials (as well as your handouts) can work long after you are gone. Be careful to select literature that is not overly geared to proselytizing, such as gospel tracts. It is better to look for materials that address themes and issues of concern to parents, with spiritual truths related to practical daily living.

Special Needs of Un-churched Children

In some ways, children who are being raised in homes without Christ (homes in which neither parent is a Christian and where spirituality is nonexistent) need the same things as any other person living in ignorance of God's salvation. They need Jesus, first and foremost. They need to be taught to understand God's love and his provision for their salvation through his son's death on the cross for them. These are the universal needs of all mankind.

However, children growing up under parents who do not know the Lord (and who may never come to know him) have special needs, both emotional and spiritual, that are important to be aware of if we want to most effectively help them. The following list offers a starting point for understanding these needs. It is important to be alert and sensitive to the unique needs of each individual child and to tailor your approach, as much as possible, in whatever ways will achieve the greatest good for the greatest number.

Children With Low Self-Esteem

While any child may suffer from low self-esteem, it is important to understand that those who are growing up in non-Christian homes may have never been told that God loves them. This simple, life-changing truth may make all the difference in determining whether that child will succeed in life or fail. It is a proven fact that no one can live a happy or successful life by any definition of those words if he is burdened with a poor self-image. While many parents, sometimes even Christian ones, can inflict terrible damage on the vulnerable psyches of their own flesh and blood, if the child can be persuaded of God's unconditional love for him *early enough in life*, great damage may be avoided and even undone.

Children With Fear of Rejection

Very often children living in unbelieving homes suffer the fear that one or both of their parents will abandon them. This is a terrible cloud to have hanging over one's childhood. Such a child needs to be constantly reassured that God will never abandon her and that he is big enough and powerful enough to take care of her in any situation.

Single-Parent Children

Whether growing up in a Christian home or not, divorce is one of the greatest scourges assailing our nation's children. Some children, born out of wedlock, have never even experienced the feeling of being able to come home to a normal family. Nearly half of today's kids are growing up in homes in which the father is either absent or nonexistent. Only God can be a Father to these fatherless ones. As for those who have no mother to care for them, an even more pitiful situation, the Lord still promises us that "when my father and mother forsake me, the Lord will take me up" (Psalm 27:10).

Children of Alcoholics

A child growing up with an alcoholic parent (or parents) is living a continual nightmare. The widespread nature of this problem does nothing to lesson the painful and tragic consequences for kids who have to endure such a situation. They need to know that, though their home life is far from happy, they can go to their heavenly Father with their troubles and their burdens, and that he will give them grace to endure. We need to pray for these kids and do all we can to give them the assurance that God cares.

Children of Drug Addicts

These children face the difficulties described above, except that with drug-addicted parents it is usually even worse. It is not enough to simply reassure children in such tragic circumstances that God is with them. We have to pray and resist the powers of darkness that would seek to destroy children living in such a hell.

It is vital for the protection of the child, and for the preservation of your opportunity to minister to him, that you never address a parent's sins or make any comments or remarks regarding the child's parents, even indirectly, which might be reported by the child to the parent, causing him to misinterpret or simply take offense at what was said. This might jeopardize the child's future participation in the kids' club. However, see below.

Abused Children

Prayer and encouragement are not enough here. *You are required by law to report any instances of suspected child abuse of any kind to the proper authorities!*

Attention Deficit Children

This is largely a latter day phenomenon. Our modern society, with its unrelenting bombardment of the senses, the general chaos of the times, and the lack of peace on the home front converge to assault the attentions of today's kids. Only "the peace of God which passes all understanding can keep (the) hearts and minds" of these children. As his Word begins to take hold in their hearts, healing will come. Promises and declarations of God's love and the peace and security he gives will be bridges in the hearts of these kids to give them the assurance of his presence.

Life After the Kids' Club

It is not easy to contemplate the future for those children who move on with their lives, passing out from under our influence. Inevitably however, every child grows up and the kids' club becomes just another memory, one of the few bright spots on an all too often unhappy childhood. We must entrust them to the unfailing love of God and do all in our power while they are under our care to instill in them a hope and faith in a heavenly Father who "will never leave [them] or forsake [them]."

Life in a World a Terror

The world has never been a safe haven for anyone. But the reality of our post-9/11 world is more uncertain and perplexing than ever. Mankind can find no solution to the myriad problems caused by his fallen, sinful nature. And sooner or later, every child sees this. It is up to us to show these "adults in waiting" that God is faithful to protect those who look to him. While this promise of protection is not a blank check on a tomorrow that is promised to no one, by placing our lives in the hands of our Creator, our future is secure. We can rest assured that our hope for a new world, in which "there shall be no more death, nor sorrow, or crying, [or] any more pain" is a hope we can look forward to as a certainty, for the One who has promised is "faithful and true"!

The "Why Me?" Question

Children growing up with the gradually dawning realization that their circumstances are not as fortunate as that of many others are faced with the added burden of confronting life's unfairness. This is a very painful realization and one that should not be ignored or swept under a rug by those who would seek to give encouragement to children struggling with such issues. While there are no perfect answers to life's difficult questions, we must do our best to help those who face these issues to understand that God's love is not based upon the circumstances of one's life, whether favorable or not. These children need to be reassured that God has no favorites, and that he gives special grace to those suffering under hardships through no fault of their own.

Could You Donate One Season of Your Life?

The vision presented here is doable for almost any church. If just two or three members could donate one brief season of their lives, and then two or three more after them and so on, a mere eight to twelve people could carry forward a children's evangelism mission to their community for an entire year. Think about it. Once a week for just ten short weeks. And yet, what a difference it could make in the life of a child growing up in a home without Jesus.

One day our time on earth will be over. If you will do this ministry for just one season of your life, you'll look back on this time as one of the "red-letter" experiences of your life in Christ. You'll be glad you did it, and the memories will bring joy and comfort to your soul. When you stand before the Lord to give account for your life, that special season will jump out as a highlight, a true "hallmark moment"—one you'll give account of to Jesus with joy!

Robert Davis

Part Three

Just For the Fun of It

Can Witnessing Really Be Fun?

Recreation is good for the soul. We all need the refreshment and stimulation that comes with just having fun. Enjoyable activities provide a welcome relief from the stresses and demands of our day-to-day existence. God tells us in his Word that, "A merry heart doeth good like a medicine" (Proverbs 17:22).

There is nothing wrong with having fun. After all, everything has its place. It seems a shame, however, that far too few of us have considered the possibility that having fun is not incompatible with being a witness for God. Why shouldn't we look at our recreational activities as opportunities to let our light shine for Jesus? Even more to the point, what could be wrong with seeking out new and exciting and creative ways to share our faith?

I think that God would be all in favor of this. Paul tells us that "it is God who works in you both to will and to do for His good pleasure" (Philippians 2:13, NKJV) and that "we have the mind of Christ" (1 Corinthians 2:16).

God never runs out of new ideas. Jesus is the vine from which all spiritual creativity flows. If we desire to allow our recreational activities to be opportunities to share Jesus with others, we can be confident that he will give us the inspiration and the opportunity to do so.

The ideas in this chapter are simply being passed along from Jesus through me to you. I have used some of them, but not all. I anticipate using as many as possible and am excited about the prospect. Hopefully you will become excited as well, and catch a wave of new vision and renewed purpose in your personal efforts to reach others and shine your light for Jesus!

Chapter One

Pastime Evangelism—Bowling for Jesus!

We acknowledge that recreation and enjoyable activities are good for us. When we got saved, we didn't suddenly become indifferent to the desire to have fun. Of course, many of the ungodly have made an idol out of entertainment and recreation. The god of sports is, after all, alive and well in America. As God's people, we are warned against placing our affections on things of the world. We have not always listened. "As it is written, the people sat down to eat and drink, and rose up to play" (1 Corinthians 10:7).

Idolatry is one thing. Wholesome fun and recreation to rejuvenate the soul, however, is another. The rhythms of life demand that cycles of work be interspersed with recreation, relaxation, and enjoyable, carefree pastimes. In short, the desire for such is God-given and good, if kept in proper balance with life's great priorities.

When it comes to serving God, however, why must we assume that the call of the Great Commission and the things we do for recreation must always be mutually exclusive? More to the point, why can't we let our lights shine for Jesus while we are out and about having fun?

Sinners also love to enjoy themselves. Of course, many of the ways they pursue such enjoyment are sinful—but not all! Sporting events, games, and recreational activities of all kinds are perfectly innocent and normal avenues for people to get some enjoyment out of life. While some pursuits are solitary by nature, many others are fraternal—meant to be shared with others.

Here in this "field of dreams" lies a great, and largely untapped, potential for reaching sinners with the gospel. For if many of the activities we pursue for enjoyment require the participation of other people, why should we then limit those other people to include only our church friends? Wasn't Jesus also "a friend of... sinners" (Luke 7:34)?

Adopting such an attitude of inclusiveness would do wonders for enriching our encounters with the unsaved. What better way of getting to know each other in a nonthreatening atmosphere than while pursuing a mutually enjoyable activity? Why not include sinners in our fun?

Do you like to bowl? Even a little? Then join a league, and not for recreation alone but as an "under cover" agent for Jesus. See the league members as your mission field; your target is not the ten pins only, but those who might be hungering and thirsty for something they'll never find in a bowling ball, not even in a "perfect game." If you look at your weekly league night that way, God will be sure to arrange divine appointments with some of your fellow bowlers.

Of course, bowling is not for everyone. Good! If it were, then who would be left to join the bridge club, the chess club, or the softball team? Dozens of sports, hobbies, and recreational activities have venues providing opportunities for people to get together and get to know each other while pursuing a pastime both enjoy. Not to mention the endless variety of social and civic organizations offering the same.

Perhaps this idea doesn't appeal to you. But why not? You are a Christian, or else you wouldn't be reading this book. You do care about souls, or you would not be a child of God. Reading this book is proof that you do care. Then what is the problem? Not the "joining" type? Then let Jesus change you. Too busy for one afternoon or evening a week...for the Lord?

You may want to reconsider and then adjust your schedule accordingly. After all, you might find an activity you really come to enjoy. More importantly, you might make a friend who would never have come to know you, and possibly never come to know Jesus were it not for your friendship, example of faith, and loving interest in her as a person.

If you are ready and willing to have some fun bowling (or bicycling, backpacking, "yogaing," knitting, "aerobisizing," or even skydiving) for Jesus, here are a few pointers:

How to Have Fun in the Son While Turning Sinners into Winners

1. Let the first thing your companions notice about you be your friendly interest in them. You do not need to try to be someone you are not. Just be your best "you" and God will be with you.

2. Allow your identity as a Christian to become known passively, that is, as a natural, unforced outgrowth of self-disclosure in the context of getting to know people.

3. Be alert to detect divine clues as to who you are to zero in on—not with proselytizing, but with efforts to deepen your friendship.

4. Seek for opportunities to get together, outside of the recreational venue.

5. When the iron is hot, strike. That is, when the door is open to bring up the subject of "spiritual things," walk through it!

6. Continue on course, building the friendship, sharing truth in ways that relate to the person's needs, and enjoying your non-spiritual activities together.

7. As God leads you, gradually increase your involvement in the person's life by, a) suggesting that you get together "for coffee"; b) inviting the person to a home group or church; and, c) by seeking to lead the person to Christ and into active fellowship with the church body.

8. Pray and believe. Be friendly, low key, gentle, always interested, and always persevering! "Cast thy bread upon the waters…" (Ecclesiastes 11:1).

Chapter Two

Clubbing, Gospel Style

Nightclubs, or simply "clubs" as they are called by the hip young party hoppers of today's generation, have become, more than ever, the place to be for those looking to have a good time, i.e., to drink, dance, mingle, and maybe "hook up" (as they call it) with members of the opposite sex.

Of course, "partying" has always been popular in our hedonistic culture. But now more than ever, many are pursuing clubbing (going all night from club to club) as a way of life. Social drinking, raucous music, and opportunities for "casual" sex are the dark magnets pulling many into a lifestyle that promises more than it can deliver while exacting a price no one in his right mind would want to pay. Alcoholism, drug addiction, venereal disease, and dissipation are the heavy wages all too often paid by those who channel their fleeting energies into the partying lifestyle. The spiritual costs are even greater…cynicism, despair, and hardness of heart—conditions causing their victims to become more and more desensitized to the gentle call of grace.

Few Christians would ever think of these places as mission fields. Yet a curious irony exists in the midst of these clubs with their "happy hours," carousing, and single-minded dedication to pleasure. Many, perhaps even most, of those who frequent these places are unhappy, unfulfilled, and uneasy about the future, especially their future, and in spite of the crowds, the partying atmosphere and the occasional "one night stands," lonely. Alone in the crowd. Alone with their private doubts, fears, and disappointments.

In the 1970s movie *The Big Chill*, former classmates gather to pay their last respects to one of their recently departed comrades. Gradually we are introduced to the inner realities of the characters' lives. Each has experienced, in one way or another, the "big chill" of disappointment that awaits each new generation in the years after they leave school and go out into the world pursuing their dreams. For many, these dreams die young. Others may cling to the illusion more tenaciously. But sooner or later reality comes home to roost. Landing the "perfect job" didn't bring the promised fulfillment, the knight in shining armor turned out to be a self-absorbed philanderer, Cinderella sprouted horns, or life just didn't seem to be turning out the way it was "supposed to."

Even the theme song from the former hit television comedy *Friends* struck a note of recognition concerning this unanticipated disillusionment: "Well, it hasn't been your day, your week, your month, or even your year." Or, in the words of the popular Bee Gee song from the ultimate party era, the disco decade, "We could never see tomorrow. No one said a word about the sorrow."

But it came anyway, uninvited and, for many, unexpected. The bad year. The big chill. The knawing, unsettling realization that life just might not get any better than this, and that "this" is not so hot after all. This is what happens when people come face-to-face with the God-void, though they usually fail to recognize it as such. High school fantasies of a perpetually rosy future, if such fantasies were ever entertained at all (some see the handwriting on the wall very early in life), just aren't working anymore.

When young people begin to come up hard against the harsh reality of life's indifference, it is small wonder that many flee into the netherworld of partying and clubbing and the mindless pursuit of pleasure. The pain is there, run though they may...life as one dreary day after another of unfulfilling work, unfulfilling relationships, and unfulfilling indulgences, until...what? A plot of ground six feet under. And then what? Nothing? Forever?

Robert Davis

No wonder it is "eat, drink, and be 'merry' for tomorrow we die." When hope is aborted, despair is waiting in the shadows. For many, "clubbing" is the soul's desperate flight into "one last party" (which they endeavor to keep going for as long as possible!) before "settling down" into a sort of resigned acceptance of hopeless, meaningless, day-to-day existence, waiting for the end.

Raiding the Enemy's Camp

The club-hopping lifestyle is a dead end. Many who are looking for love in all the wrong places know they are on the fast track to nowhere. Some may be open to the message of the gospel. If we are to win souls "out where the sinners are" (T.L. Osborne), then why not infiltrate these chattels of dark dreams and illusions to bring the true hope and fulfillment that Jesus, and only Jesus, can give?

Granted, this not a ministry for everyone. Those with a background of involvement in heavy drinking, drugs, or casual sex would be wise to stay away. God would not approve of one of his children with a history of entanglement in such vices deliberately making himself vulnerable to their temptations—not even "for the sake of" the lost.

Some might respond that anyone would be vulnerable in such an environment. While we all have our peculiar vulnerabilities, there are some who *are* able to stay focused on the cause of rescuing sinners, even in such places as these. After all, God calls some of his people to reach the prostitutes and drug addicts on the streets. Why should those who are inside the bars and clubs be ignored?

The truth is, temptation is everywhere. Access to alcohol, drugs, immoral sex, and other sinful vices are easily available in America and much of the world. All of us must guard ourselves from the snares of the enemy.

Safety First...and Second

Naturally, special care should be taken to avoid unnecessary exposure to temptation. But for those who are qualified, two simple but effective safeguards are suggested here. First, there should be a willingness to submit to pastoral oversight. This does not mean that the pastor need or even should go with you. It simply recognizes the wisdom and safety of having one in spiritual authority to watch out for the safety and preservation of those who would go into the club scene for the purpose of winning souls.

Second, can you hold yourself accountable to other qualified, like-minded believers as part of a team effort? No one should pursue such a ministry alone. Sooner or later, the devil may find a chink in your armor. If it is there, he will find it. Going as part of a team, in which each member looks out for the other, will provide the safety net of accountability necessary to protect the participants.

Going with others, however, should not be interpreted as an endorsement for launching large-scale invasions. We are talking infiltration here, not inundation. Three or four, and probably no more. Never less than two, but never so many as to draw widespread attention to the group.

Can You Relate to These People?

Even if you meet the above qualifications, you need to ask yourself if such a ministry is right for you. Are you generationally, socially, and culturally equipped so as to be able to relate to people as peers in such places? Can you communicate on their level, as one like them, though not of them?

Do you have a genuine heart for people in these environs? Can you ignore the sideshow and not be distracted by appearances? Do you see past the flirting and posturing to the hurt below the surface? Or are your thoughts more judgmental and inclined to view these as heading for their just deserts? Only those who

Robert Davis

see the lost soul more than the straying sinner should consider themselves suited for reaching out to people such as these.

One Last Test

For those who meet these standards, there is still one important hurdle. We alluded to it briefly earlier. It bears greater attention here as a sort of final "litmus" test for those who might think themselves suited to this kind of outreach. Anyone giving thought to embarking on a ministry to the "clubbing" crowd should be willing to submit the idea for such an undertaking to your pastor first, or to an ordained elder of the church.

The spiritual oversight of your pastor (or qualified elder appointed by your pastor) is a necessary hedge against the enemy and his devices. Put simply: If you are unwilling to confer with your minister about an outreach of this kind, you should honestly question your motives.

A Christian with a sincere and humble attitude before God will have no problem submitting to the will of his pastor, as God's appointed spiritual authority in his life, even if his pastor is opposed to the idea. After all, when God really does open a door, no man, not even your pastor, can close it. If God really is leading you in this direction, he will go before you to prepare the way and to open the door—and that would include having your pastor's approval.

With these safeguards in place, we have the necessary groundwork of qualifications and conditions for a ministry to the "clubbing" crowd. Here then, for all who have "dotted their i's and crossed their t's," are some practical suggestions.

How to Go Clubbing—For Jesus!

1. When venturing with your team into a club, avoid being caught alone with members of the opposite sex. This refers to people in the clubs, not your teammates. Never go off

to some isolated area with someone of the opposite sex. Avoid every appearance of evil. And avoid such situations as obvious setups for temptation.

2. Men should zero in on men as their targets, and women should zero in on women. Not that you can or even should avoid members of the opposite sex. But as a general rule, focus on establishing friendships with members of your own gender while being friendly to everyone.

3. Determine that your goal will be to "win friends and influence people." Don't go in to preach. Of course, you are there to be a witness for Christ. You will be able to quickly, easily, and inoffensively begin to reveal your Christian identity in the next step.

4. Order only nonalcoholic beverages, especially such as may be easily recognized. Orange juice and coffee, for example; but soft drinks are okay.

5. Play darts with people if there is a dartboard. Not just with your teammates. Mingle! Occasionally, there might be a pool table. Ditto.

6. Don't dance with anyone, including your teammates. This will tend to dilute your effectiveness, as dancing, or at least "worldly" dancing, is rightly perceived by sinners as unbecoming of a Christian. If you are asked, politely decline. Just say, "I'm sorry. I don't dance." Be careful, however, to avoid saying anything judgmental or negative about dancing.

7. Make excuses to make friends. Smile. Greet people. Make small talk. Pray for favor and open doors. Don't leave God out! When you meet new friends, be sure to introduce them to other members of your team. Look for the lonely, the hurting, the vulnerable, and the receptive.

Robert Davis

8. When you do engage in conversation with members of the opposite sex, avoid all suggestive looks, glances, tones, or body language. If you are on the receiving end of such gestures, simply pretend not to notice. Steer clear of questionable conversation.

9. Establish a reputation as sociable, caring people who are interested in meeting new friends while preferring not to indulge in the customs of the crowd—drinking, dancing, flirting, "hitting" on members of the opposite sex, and so on.

10. Allow your "Christian identity" to become known in the natural course of conversation as you get to know people. This need not be forced or awkward. It is appropriate and even expected for people to make self-disclosures in the course of getting to know each other. A straightforward confession such as, "I'm here with some of my friends from church because we want to meet new people," would be sure to arouse the interest and curiosity of no small number of patrons as word spread about "those church people." Nonjudgmental, friendly interest from a hip young group of Christians would be sure to spark many cocktail conversations among those accustomed to viewing believers as "preachy" or "holier than thou."

As a final suggestion, it is advisable to limit your club visitation to no more than once a week, and then, for a period of probably no more than an hour and a half to two hours per visit. Leave before midnight, as a general rule. Also, determine to visit a place for no more than two or three months, looking for those you might win over as friends to meet away from the club. Be sure that before doing this you have firmly established your Christian identity while tactfully making it clear that your primary interest is the spiritual welfare of those you have befriended.

When the time frame is over, terminate your visits but not the friendships you have made with those who are open to God. Of course, you may feel differently about the length of time necessary to adequately "cover" a particular club. This is best handled as a matter to confer about with your pastor. It is generally advisable, however, to have some ending date in mind, as you do not wish to become looked upon as a permanent "part" of the clubbing community!

Chapter Three

Painting the Town Red
(for Artists…and the Color by
Number Crowd)

Growing up in New Jersey in the sixties and seventies, I suffered from a malady common to adolescents of every generation. I had an excruciatingly poor self-image. I didn't like myself. I didn't really understand why I felt this way, though I was to learn the answer to that question later. All I knew or cared about back then was that whenever I looked in the mirror, I minimized every positive feature and magnified every flaw, real or imagined. Needless to say, life is not very pleasant when you feel this way about yourself.

In my senior year, I met a new teacher who was brought in to teach vocational education. He did not have a classroom, as such. I don't even recall how I met him or how it came about that I found myself taking photography lessons from this man.

Interestingly, I was his only student at that time. I have since concluded that my guidance counselor had referred him to me to try to salvage me from self-destruction. He had tried to reach me himself when I was a freshman, without success, though not for lack of effort. (Later, God did what man could not.)

There are two things that make this teacher stand out in my memory. For one, he became my friend. Because of my low self-esteem, I had pretty much withdrawn from the world in general and most of the people in it. This man treated me as an equal, and looking back, I can see that he was showing by his attitude that he believed in me as a person.

The other thing that made him not just memorable, but unforgettable, was a gift that he gave me. One day he suggested that we go to the school store so that he could take some pictures of me. The front of the building, which was actually a trailer in the front of the parking lot, was the school store. The next room was a place set up as a sort of miniature printing press operation. There was a window in the middle of this room, letting in sunlight while giving a perfect view of the athletic fields beyond.

Here in front of this window, he set up his camera. He positioned himself about five feet from me for a full front headshot. Taken from this angle, the photos were framed in such a way that the sunlight from the window fell on one side of my face, leaving the other side in shadow.

We then went back to a small area he had converted into a dark room to develop the pictures. Naturally I was curious to see the result, but also a little apprehensive. Whatever qualities I may have possessed at the time, I knew from experience that being photogenic was not one of them. In fact, for many years I would cringe at the prospect of having my picture taken, so mortifying was the invariable outcome.

But this day would be different. As the first picture began to come into focus under the developing liquid, I could hardly believe my eyes. Without the slightest trace of vanity, I can tell you that the face staring back at me was…beautiful. Me! Youthful, handsome, unblemished, symmetrical, and dare I say, fascinating! The effect of the light and shadow and the ethereal quality of black-and-white film combined to create an aura of mystery and intrigue, and it was my face that was both mysterious and intriguing! Even my seventies hairstyle, parted in (of course) the middle, halfway to hippydom (I could never go all the way), was neat, natural looking, and so cool! I can hardly begin to describe the effect this had, not only on my morale, but on my way of seeing myself.

It is now over thirty years since that photo, that portrait, was taken. Unfortunately, I have not seen it in over a quarter of a century. It lies buried somewhere quietly in my dearly departed brother's attic, in the home where we grew up together, waiting hopefully for me to find it someday. But I can still see the image in my mind, and I will never forget that face. And though many years have rolled by since that long ago afternoon, that photograph, taken by someone who cared enough to try to bring out the best in me, remains the single most compelling and uplifting image of me ever captured on film.

Such is the power of the photographer, the painter, the sculpture...the artist. Art, in the hands of God, has the power to transform. I do not recall that photographer friend of mine ever making mention of God. I am certain, in fact, that he did not. As a Christian, however, these many years later, I can clearly see the hand of God in the gift that he gave me.

And what stands out in my mind with sterling clarity now is this: That if that man had said something to me that had revealed himself to be a person of faith, a believer, a Christian, then all through the intervening years I would have been compelled to see God's gentle hand guiding his, causing him to see me through the eyes of divine love. In other words, I would have given God the glory and gratitude and not my friend only. In other words, that portrait would have become an ever abiding witness reminding me of my Creator, drawing me to want to know him.

Which leads to one conclusion, as I see it. If art has such power, why are we not offering it on the altar of God's glory to create a new vision for the world—or at least for the people in it? If the transforming nature of images can so recreate the landscape of the heart, why then do we fail to see how art, the very fulcrum of imagination and imagery, might be used to lift the spirits of those who are cast down, and perhaps, just maybe, cause the disheartened soul to look up to the very One who sees him despite his flaws, as beautiful, unique, and special?

That man did not charge me for the portrait he took of me that day. But as sure as there is a God in heaven, I know that he was repaid many times over by his Maker. If he had spoken even one word to me on behalf of Christ, then every time I thought of that picture I would have thought of Jesus. And the blood that Jesus shed for me on the cross would have left its indelible mark on my portrait. Years later I can give God the glory, from whom comes every perfect gift.

I do not have the artist's ability to draw or paint, and I never really developed as a photographer either. But if I did, or had, I like to think that I might be used by God the way my friend was so long ago. Only I would want people to know that it was God working his magic through me. Because in the end, only he can make the difference in their lives.

Robert Davis

Chapter Four

Singin' in the Rain (for Musicians…and Karaoke Crooners)

Not long ago I had the privilege of reading one of the all-time Christian classics, *In His Steps*, by Charles Sheldon. The magic of the book lies in Sheldon's ability to brilliantly and passionately capture the dream of what life would be like in a world (or at least a town) filled with Christians so completely and uncompromisingly consecrated to Christ that every decision and every direction of their lives is determined only after first asking the question: *What would Jesus do?* (Yes, of "WWJD?" fame.) As the story unfolds, each of Sheldon's characters is faced with the dilemma of what it would cost if they were to base all of their significant life decisions upon the hinge of that all-important question.

The story is made even more powerful, however, because its characters are forced not only to ask themselves, "What would Jesus do?" at each important moral crossroad of their lives, but they were compelled to ask it as though they were, individually, no longer themselves, but actually Jesus in person living his life through their own. In doing so, we the readers are confronted with the same question—not only "What would Jesus do?" but, "What would Jesus do if he were me, living his earthly life disguised as me, right here, inside my body, using my hands and feet, my eyes and ears, my mouth and tongue, and even my very heart and soul?"

In the end, we are left with the sobering realization that this is exactly how we are to live our lives—as though we were Jesus, disguised as "us," reincarnated, if you will, through you and me.

(...not I, but Christ lives in me. Galations 2:20!) Each of us must face the question, "What would Jesus look like to others if he were to come back to the earth disguised as...me?"

Among Sheldon's memorable pantheon of characters, we meet Rachel, a beautiful young woman gifted with a voice to make the angels weep. Blessed with social grace, a member in good standing of society's upper caste, and regarded by her illustrious peers as one destined for fame and fortune, we follow her pilgrimage as she encounters her rendezvous with the fateful question: What would Jesus do?

Those of us blessed with even an average allotment of twenty-first-century savvy would have little difficulty answering the question for her, especially if we were permitted to modify it slightly into its more plausible counterpart, "What would I do?"

We would, of course, save up our money while counting the days in anticipation of our pilgrimage to Mecca (aka Nashville). Armed with a demo tape in one hand and our pastor's recommendation in the other (optional in Nashville, of course), we would proceed to knock on every door (doors open to those who knock) of every recording studio until we got the big break we knew "the Lord had for us."

From there it is fairly predictable...fame, fortune, bookings, ministry, and, of course, all for the glory of God. Not to mock our beloved Christian brothers and sisters in the music industry. Many are called, after all. Of course, far fewer are chosen...

But Brother Sheldon would have us asking ourselves this question: Are *all* called? Are all who think they are called actually called? To Nashville? To fame? Fortune? "Big time" ministry? One has to wonder, if such is really the case, then why are so few chosen? And what of those who are not? Are they God's rejects? Or Nashville's?

These words must be painful to read for the many who, understandably, do not take kindly to having their cherished dreams mocked or made light of. But such is not Sheldon's purpose, and neither is it mine. The tragedy is that so much is wasted by such a narrow definition of success. We are all the products of our culture, whose values and aspirations permeate every facet of our society, even, seemingly, the very air we breathe.

The desire to see one's gift used for the glory of God is both good and noble. Unfortunately, we are often victims of a kind of tunnel vision when it comes to seeking the path best suited for fulfilling God's dream in our hearts.

In the case of Rachel, we find that the Lord has something very different in mind than passing through Graceland en route to Music City. She began to feel stirred within herself to reach out to the very lowest of society's refuse, the discarded remnants and dregs of humanity, cast off and forgotten by the important people of the world. She conceived a plan to bring her considerable talents to bear on the cause of lifting up the spirits of those broken and shattered on the rocks of modern civilization's sterile indifference.

So she started singing in the rain, in the low places, in the forgotten and forsaken places. In dark alleys where was heard only the sound of despair and desperation, a new sound began to fill the air. The sound of an angel sent from heaven, with a voice empowered by love to bring hope and, dare it be whispered, courage to begin again, to even…dream again. Who can say what power God infuses into the voice of one who has placed herself on the altar of his divine calling?

To sing where the Lord sends you, to bring music to gladden the hearts of those who, but for the grace of God, would wear our shoes and we theirs. The question calls to us, each in its own way, God's way, for us…what would Jesus do? Where would Jesus sing? Who would he sing to? What would he sing for? For those so gifted among us to be singers, musicians, why aren't you singin' in the rain?

Chapter Five

The Carpenter's Workshop (for Butchers, Bakers, and Candlestick Makers)

Someone once said that the greatest source of talent, creativity, and innovation in the world resides in the body of Christ. Considering that we have been redeemed from our fallen state and made into new creatures in Christ, restored into the image of God's glory we were made to reflect, it seems hard to argue with that statement.

We who have been born again want to use our God-given talents for his glory. The world is not short on talent, but nonreligious people use whatever they have in the way of talents, skills, and abilities to further their own interests, with no regard for the glory of God.

Yet it seems that much more could be done to honor God with our talents, if only we had a mind to. Many Christians scarcely realize the potential their gifts and abilities hold for benefiting mankind in ways that could honor the Lord. This holds true even aside from any consideration for "ministerial" gifts or callings. Our true talent, possessed by every single member of the body of Christ, is our capacity, desire, and willingness to give of what we have and what we are to the benefit of others.

One vast field of possibility for doing this, overlooked (or at least neglected) by many, is the art of giving in the area of our vocational talents. That is, our knowledge, our expertise, and our vocational experience put to use for the benefit of others with no thought of self-aggrandizement in return. How might this translate in practical terms, in our everyday lives? The possibilities are unlimited. Just a few examples will be enough to make the point. Substitute in place of these your own vocational skills (or artistic, recreational, or educational areas of expertise), and you'll begin to get the picture. Here are just a few of the endless possibilities:

If you are a mechanic, place an advertisement in your local paper announcing free seminars (or workshops) teaching laymen how to do their own brake repairs, or tune-ups, shock absorber replacements, or small engine work, etc.

If you are a professional interior decorator, place a similar AD announcing your own seminar to dispense free advice and suggestions for those desiring to redecorate their homes "on a budget."

Following this pattern, so too the carpenter, gardener, cosmetologist, plumber, stock broker, the butcher, the baker, and the candlestick maker! Photography experts, professional or otherwise, this includes you, too. Likewise the bird watchers, mathematicians (and teachers galore), antique collectors, salesmen and saleswomen, ecology experts, sportsmen and sportswomen, roofers, farmers, pet groomers, accountants, dress makers, and so on and so on.

You can just imagine the impact such a movement might have on a world driven by selfishness and the desire to get ahead regardless of who gets in the way. The greatest antidote for selfishness is unselfishness. The greatest power of the gospel lies in its ability to transform lives. What greater way to demonstrate this to an unbelieving world than by giving with no thought of receiving anything in return?

If you find the thought of doing so intriguing and feel that this may indeed be something God would like you to consider, here are some tips to help pave the way:

Robert Davis

How to Hold "Free" Workshops for the Glory of God

1. Prepare your seminar. Since you will be teaching on something that is second nature to you, whether career or job related, or something you do as a hobby or on the side, putting together a teaching plan should not be too difficult for you. Make an outline listing the main parts and the highlights you wish to cover.

2. Decide how you will advertise. The newspaper, posters, flyers? Many radio stations will allow you free airtime for short "spots" of fifteen to thirty seconds. Try to choose a day and time (for your seminar) of convenience to the greatest number of people.

3. Prepare a schedule for your participants. You will want to list the title of each section, the starting and ending times, and the break time(s). Even if your workshop is only an hour and a half (three hours is usually a good limit for any one meeting, depending, of course, on the complexity of your subject and depth of your presentation), you will want to schedule a break in the middle to give yourself and everyone else opportunity to mingle. Be sure to serve coffee, soft drinks, and some refreshments.

4. Begin your presentation by introducing yourself and telling the people two things: 1) *What you will be doing*—that is, the topic you will be covering; and, 2) *Why you are doing it*. This is your all-important "moment of truth" in which you will inform your participants that you are doing this "as a service to your community for the glory of the God whom you serve." You need say little more than this. Certainly, you will not want to preach.

5. Having identified yourself as one of God's people and having declared your reason for doing your workshop (his glory), your seminar/workshop will be your "sermon" and your testimony! All will understand that you are performing this service out of a heart of Christian benevolence. Most people will appreciate and respect this. They will also be impressed by God's Spirit, as he will be working alongside you and long after you have finished. In the unlikely event that someone resents your stated reason for offering your workshop, he will probably keep it to himself. If someone were to be so crass as to express open hostility, stay calm and respond with meekness and grace. Others will not hesitate to put the malcontent in his place. After all, they are not there to listen to his prejudices, but to be the beneficiaries of your good graces!

6. After you have finished, thank your participants for coming and inform them that you would like to make some spiritual literature available for those who might be interested. Better yet, a personalized tract from you, sharing your testimony (see "The Tract Nobody Is Using" from Part One of this manual) would be a very effective means of sharing your faith. Rest assured, these people will be quite interested in knowing more about you. After all, you just gave them your services for free! You might mention that this literature is "on the table" for those who would like to help themselves. This is more discreet than simply handing it out, but if you do want to hand them out, that is perfectly okay. (It would be advisable to also offer a handout reviewing the highlights of your seminar.)

7. You are done! You have brought glory to God and left a lasting impression on your participants, some of whom may even become your friends! Who knows what God may do?

Chapter Six

Start the Revolution without Us! (for Teenagers…and the Young at Heart!)

If you are a young person, the years you spend as a teenager, though they can be difficult, may well be among the most exciting and adventurous days of your life. The future, with all of its promise and mystery, lies opens before you like an endless highway filled with magical possibilities. While you are living them, these years will seem to stretch on into eternity. But you will look back, not long after they are gone, and wonder how, oh someone please tell me, how did they fly by so quickly? But that is for later…

I am going to tell you five reasons why the years you are living through right now are the most crucial seven years you will ever have to determine your destiny.

1. You will never be stronger than you are right now! Having freshly emerged from childhood, you now live in a (hopefully) healthy, fully developed, brand new adult body. Your energy reserves are higher now than they will ever be again. Even if you workout strenuously and run religiously well into your twenties, you may increase your physical stamina and endurance and feel as though your energy level has risen. But in fact, you will still have aged by several years, your heart will have used up a few million more of its allotted beats, your immune system will have fought off a few hundred or perhaps a few thousand more diseases,

and you will have lost a few mil—well, let's just say, some more brain cells, and you will have breathed a few million more of whatever number of breathes providence has allotted for you on your earthly sojourn. The fact remains that, though you may be in better physical condition in the future by making healthy lifestyle changes today, you will still be older then than you are now.

2. You will never be more adaptable than you are right now! Already, even as a young teenager, you are *past* your "adaptability prime" in several key areas. For example, if you start learning a foreign language at the age of thirteen and stick to it, you will doubtless become very proficient in several years. But you will never approach the absolute mastery of the language as, say, a child who begins at the age of three or four. You will likely always have an accent. You will always feel more at home with your native tongue. Not so the child. She will feel equally at home with either language, reading, writing, speaking, and even thinking… and without the slightest trace of an accent.

   The situation is much the same for learning a musical instrument. You may become extremely proficient if you work hard for many years beginning as a young teenager. But most of the world's great musicians started much earlier than the grand old age of thirteen. To this list, we might add nearly every form of athletic endeavor, many academic skills such as reading and mathematical ability, and a wide variety of unrelated skills such as artistic ability, manual dexterity, and so on.

   However, during your teens, you still retain a near unlimited capacity to develop healthy habits, character traits, and social graces—all attributes of far more importance than any academic, athletic, or artistic talents.

Robert Davis

3. It will never be easier for you to believe God's promises than it is right now! It is the common experience of mankind that with the advance of years, so advances our awareness of our own sinfulness before God. Certainly this is the case for those who are outside of Christ, a fact easily demonstrated by the story of the woman caught in adultery. It was the oldest would be condemners who first dropped their stones. A lifetime is more than long enough to establish in the mind of the old sinner the recognition of his own guilty conscience. But even the humble Christian, set free from the tyranny of sin's rulership, is all too aware of the fact of his own guilt outside of the redeeming blood of Christ.

   The fact that the oldest recognized their guilt first, and then afterward the younger, illustrates the truth that, as a young person, though still guilty before God as a sinner (if you have not yet come to Christ), you are less weighed down by the guilt and burden of long years in sin. Having lived fewer years as a sinner, the teenager has a heart more inclined and enabled to trust in the promises of God. His heart is less battered and less hardened by sin and the fruit of sin, which is unbelief. As a young person you are, therefore, more capable of believing God and of confidently trusting him with your life and your future.

4. You will never have more freedom to launch out in new directions than you have right now! You are likely not yet tied down with cares and obligations and responsibilities. As you survey the wide-open vistas before you, life presents itself as a world full of endless possibilities. And it is! You may have made mistakes, perhaps some serious ones. But you are still young. You can begin again. You can start anew!

5. You will never be as daring as you are right now! Besides being more able to believe God, as a young person, you are more able to launch out into exciting and daring new paths because your spirit has not been dampened by years of mediocrity and disillusionment. Even if you have grown up in a broken home, under less than ideal circumstances, you still have a heart that *wants* to believe, to hope, to dream, and to venture out into the wild blue yonder!

These five magnificent advantages are, more than for any other age group, the special treasure and rightful inheritance of the young person, the teenager—you! But there is an enemy waiting in the shadows ready to strike, but not with the sound of trumpets or of the pounding hooves of apocalyptic horses. No, his approach is silent and stealthy, unseen and unheard, unannounced and unwelcome, but a sure intruder who has already marked out a day and an hour when he will come calling...on you. His name is entropy.

> Entropy: 1. Thermodynamics, the measure of the amount of energy unavailable for work during a natural process; 3. Hypothesized tendency toward uniform inertness, especially of the universe. (The Random House College Dictionary, Revised Edition, 1980)

In biblical terminology, this is referred to as the law of sin and death. As mortal beings (in the flesh), our bodies are breaking down, weakening, aging...dying. All of us are subject to this slow, dying death. We have a promise from God, however: "But though our outward man perish, yet our inward man is renewed day by day" (2 Corinthians 4:16).

As a born-again, Spirit-filled child of God, you are assured that the power of God living inside of you is renewing you in your inner spiritual being day by day. As Christians, therefore, we need have no fear of growing old, for our inner spirit man is ever and forever being made new again by the law of the spirit of life, which is in Christ Jesus. However, we still "have this treasure in earthen vessels." And in spite of all we do to keep ourselves young and young at heart, we are destined to die. Meanwhile, even as we live, we are slowing dying in our physical bodies, as the clock of our mortality swings inexorably toward the midnight of our of earthly existence.

What that means to you, my young friend, is this. In this one earthly life that has been given to you, you will never be more alive than you are today, right here and right now. If in these next few years you determine to grow "strong in the Lord and in the power of his might," you will lay the foundation for a life that may truly bring great glory to his name. David slew his greatest enemy when he was a mere shepherd boy. But before he ever faced the mighty Goliath, he had spent time alone with God in green pastures and beside still waters.

There are Goliaths loose in the land today, and who knows but that it may be only our young people who might summon the strength and the faith of God to slay them. We who have gone before have not been strong enough or able enough to bring prayer back into our public schools. Nor have we been able to bring creation science, a true science with provable tenants, into the classroom to do hand-to-hand combat with the lying dragon of Darwinianism, a doctrine that has driven millions into apostasy, agnosticism, and despair. And now it appears to be only a matter of time before "one nation under God" may be ordered out of our Pledge of Allegiance. Who will rise up and run to face this enemy with the boldness and power of God and say, "No! I will not be forced to be silent about my God"?

Who will recapture our universities from the clutches of a godless, amoral humanism bent on defaming and slandering our priceless historical heritage? How long will those who deliver our nightly news be cloaked with the colors of contempt for our religious and moral values? Will the pro-abortion, criminal sympathizing, pro-pornography, homosexual-agenda endorsing, voluntary prayer in public school and Ten Commandments in public buildings opposing, anti-Christian ACLU always be the official voice writ large of our nation's legal professionals? Will these moral relativists forever be the breeding ground from which we spawn that select company appointed to don black robes and decide for the rest of us concerning matters of right and wrong?

We may have to answer the preceding questions in order: no one; indefinitely; yes; and very likely…unless you and others of your generation decide *while you are still young* to take these matters firmly into your own hands. "The kingdom of heaven suffers violence, and the violent take it by force" (Matthew 11:12).

Not the violence of guns or hatred, but the violence of a faith that defies all opposition because it is persuaded that "with God all things are possible" (Matthew 19:26). Only a faith working by a fearless, tireless love could believe this big.

I will not be able to fight this battle. I have too many other battles to fight as it is. Nor as I scan the horizon of my generation, or even the one coming up behind me, do I see anyone who might be capable of leading the charge. Too be sure, there are those who are sounding the trumpet and crying in the wilderness. But leading the charge…? I simply do not believe we are young enough, strong enough, daring enough, or perhaps even hopeful enough (I ask my peers to forgive me, for I certainly do not wish to appear to be speaking for you or anyone but myself).

But I do see one crowd in the camp who are capable. If they wait too long, it will become for them what I believe it may have become for us…too late. Not that we have not won our victories in Christ and will yet win. But some battles are not meant for old warriors to win. Other troops must surge to the front lines if the enemy is to be put to flight. He is entrenched, hunkered down, yet not defensive, for his weapons are not silent.

In the military, there is a term reserved for combat fighters uniquely trained and equipped for special assault operations.

They are called shock troops. I am convinced that teenage believers are God's shock troops in this holy war we are engaged in with his enemy. All you need is the training. The Heavenly Father is calling his young ones to green pastures and still waters where, like David long ago, you might sit in his presence and learn at his feet and taste and see that the Lord is good. And in so doing, grow strong.

If I were a teenager I would want to be among the shock troops of God's army. Young, strong, energetic, daring, I would want to fight the battles that seem lost and turn the tide where the enemy has come in like a flood. I would want to—if I were younger…if I were stronger, and more daring to believe God, and more courageous—to believe the impossible.

Part Four

To Go or Not to Go?
That Is the Question

Why Are We Stalling ?

There is a line in a contemporary gospel song from a few years ago (DC Talk's "Say I Love You!") which, reflecting on God's greatness and all he has done to equip us for the task of world evangelism, poses the question, "Tell me why, then, are we stalling?" It is a question as relevant today as it was back then. Christians are stalling. The *Random House College Dictionary* defines the word *stall* as follows: "to bring to a standstill; check the progress or motion of, esp. unintentionally; be brought to a stop."

That seems like a pretty fair description of what's happened to many. As Christians, it is impossible for us not to want to share our faith. The willingness is there somewhere, hidden beneath the surface fears and uncertainties. But the doing of it presents us with problems. The will to do what God wants is always present as an inward expression of our new natures. However, God has so designed us for permanent dependency that in order to actually do what we want to do we must, in the here and now of each situation, actively place our faith in Christ to help us perform the doing of his will.

This is very much the case when it comes to sharing our faith. Yet we must still get past the excuses and rationalizations that have become crutches to lean on (or to stall) so that, setting these aside, we may lean on him. Faith to do the will of God is leaning on Jesus—"trusting in, relying upon, and adhering to him" as the Amplified Bible puts it.

While it is widely recognized that the church needs to get out of its rut of procrastination (stalling) and make a serious *rededication* to fulfilling our individual callings in the Great Commission, there remains an almost tangible sense of acceptance that this will not happen. That simply has to change. There is only one way this can be accomplished: *We must change the culture in our churches and make sharing our faith the number one priority in our relationship to the world!*

Of course, when it comes to changing the culture of the church, the buck stops with the leadership. If God's leaders do not agree to this and allow the change to start with themselves, it will never happen. Pastors are not exempt from winning the lost! And we are not just referring to the lost souls inside the church. Some pastors are fond of saying, "Shepherds don't give birth to sheep. Sheep do!" This is misleading. God's shepherds are sheep too! In the words of T.L. Osborne, one of the greatest missionary evangelists of the twentieth century, "A soul-winner first, then a pastor" (teacher, music minister, usher, greeter, children's worker, pew sitter, et al)!

There is a way to begin again. This is not to say that a great deal has not been done. But who can deny that a great many have done little or even nothing insofar as contributing to the cause of world evangelism is concerned? And we're not talking money here! I believe that God is willing to ignite a passion in the church to reach the lost on a worldwide basis. Before this can ever happen, however, we must want it to happen! The question is, do we really want it?

Chapter One

Why Bother? Jesus Is Coming Back Soon!

I remember the first time that I really thought that Jesus was coming back. It was 1982, and the cool autumn air was turning cold, heralding the first approach of winter. I was knocking on a lot of doors around that time and reading a lot of W.V. Grant books, getting convicted for various sins I'd been struggling with and just knowing in my heart that Jesus was coming back any time, probably that winter and certainly no later than the next. The signs were everywhere: war with the Soviet Union was bound to happen any day, the Middle East was as turbulent as ever, a pope- inspired Poland was defiant in solidarity, and God's people were in agreement at last, at least about the one thing that mattered most: Jesus is coming back soon! Except that he didn't.

It is now more than thirty years later and we are all still waiting. Certainly we are that much nearer. In spite of the "end" of the cold war, the crumbling of the Berlin wall, and even the demise of the dreaded Soviet Union, the world, if anything, seems more dangerous and unpredictable than ever. Of course, 9/11 didn't exactly contribute to our sense of security and stability. The war on terror, with its shadowy, borderless enemy lurking we know not, nor ever will know, where; Islamic militance spreading throughout the world; Israel hated and surrounded by enemies who want to destroy her; anti-Americanism; North Korea; the reemergence of Russia; and the rise of China haven't exactly allowed us to "make the world safe for democracy."

We see and hear of "wars and rumors of wars," "distress and perplexity of nations," but "the end is not yet." The truth is, we just can't be sure. Unfortunately, however, many seem to be doing what many before them did whenever events in the world seemed to conspire to "prove" that Jesus's return was imminent: they pack up their spiritual bags and sit by the door waiting for him to come calling.

But this is not the plan Jesus gave us for preparing for his return. True, he did tell us to "Watch therefore, for you know neither the day nor the hour in which the Son of man is coming" (Matthew 25:13, NKJV). So we are to be watchful. But notice that this state of perpetual readiness is adjured upon us because we do not know either the day or the hour. This lifestyle of preparedness is not the only instruction Jesus left us concerning our manner of conduct as we look for him to come back. He also told us to, "Occupy till I come" (Luke 19:13).

When it comes to the cause of world evangelism, many seem to have become preoccupied with the first part and left the other out in the cold. It does seem that many in the church have quietly concluded that the job is more or less done and that there's little left to do but stand around waiting to "clock out." But did Jesus say we're done yet?

No matter how late in the day it may seem, no matter how many clouds in the sky, it is never so late as to justify ceasing to pray for lost people, to stand in faith for their salvation, and to do all within our power to "compel them to come in" (Luke 14:23).

If you had told me in 1982 that thirty years later we would still be waiting for Jesus to come back, I would not have believed you. There was simply no way that could have been possible! Yet here we are.

What if there are still ten years left before Jesus does come back for us? It seems just completely unbelievable that there could still be that much time...but can we be sure? Do any of us really know? We do not even know whether we will still be breathing ten years from now, or even tomorrow, much less whether Jesus will have come by then. What would you want to accomplish to do your part in the Great Commission if you really did have ten more years to serve him? Have you thought it out? Written it down? Prayed for godly wisdom?

Whatever you hope to do, it seems unlikely that coasting, floating wherever the current takes you, or drifting aimlessly would rank high on your "to-do" list. Yet many do just that. They rarely plan ahead, set goals, or establish deadlines for meeting them. If you have not sat down to put your God-inspired hopes and dreams in writing, what are you waiting for? If you do not do so soon, today or tomorrow, while it is still fresh in your mind, when will you? What would it take to get you motivated?

If you are like me, you could use all the help you can get. Here are some permanent goals I have set for myself, goals I will be striving to reach and exceed for as long as a live.

1. I want to become stronger in prayer the longer I live. I want to become more reverent and worshipful, more grateful and thankful, more dependent and trusting, and more watchful over the souls of others, especially (but not only) my loved ones. I will never be satisfied that I have arrived in my prayer life. I can always go higher.

2. I want to become more confident in my identity in Christ. That is, I want to trust in, rely upon, and adhere to Jesus more and more the longer I live and to grow ever more confident in who I am in him, in what I have in him, and in what I can do through him.

3. I want to become more faithful in reaching out to tell others about Jesus. I want to do more, not less, as I get older, to help people come to know Christ as their Savior.

These are some of my lifetime goals. I have others, but I have chosen to share these because we know that every Christian should aspire to greater devotion in prayer, in reliance upon Christ, and in reaching out to others. Each of us must decide for ourselves how to achieve these aspirations. We should settle for no less if we hope to bring honor and glory to our Creator; for in pursuing these desires, we are seeking first the kingdom of God and his righteousness. And this will keep us safely occupied with the Master's business until we see him face-to-face.

Robert Davis

Chapter Two

Ambassadors,
(Re)Take Your Mark (16:15),
Get Set, Go Ye!

If you were to take a poll of Christians who have been saved for say, five years or more, asking them to name their biggest regret since coming to Christ, it is likely that many would respond by saying that they wish they had "done more" to reach the lost. As in most spiritual endeavors, so also in sharing our faith…our actualizations never seem to rise to the level of our aspirations.

There is the temptation to become discouraged. We see people all around us going down. It can, quite honestly, be overwhelming. We wonder if we can really make a difference. Since most of us feel far less than the mighty man or woman of God that we would like to be, we find ourselves prone to minimizing the capabilities we do have.

It's sort of like the emotions we've all felt as we watched the images on our television screens of the starving people in third-world countries. So many of them! And we're just one person!

What can we do to make any difference in the face of such numberless tragedy?

Yet many of us have learned that by making a commitment to sponsor that one hungry little boy or girl, hope had been birthed in our heart. Our sadness for the millions did not go away, of course. But it was no longer alone. For right there in the midst of the sorrow was gladness and relief, a joy for the one that we could help. And herein we find a perfect metaphor for our plight in coping with the myriad lost souls in the sea of humanity surrounding us. There is one somewhere, perhaps not far, likely within arm's reach, whom we may help. A lost soul floating aimlessly in the ocean of life, searching for a way out, something to grab hold of, to keep from going under.

We have the lifeline they are looking for: Jesus. True, we can't save everyone. But nobody can! Should that stop us from trying to save anyone? What a horrible thought...to despair of saving anyone because we can't save everyone! A sorrow that would debilitate us from trying in the face of so much need is truly a sorrow that "worketh death."

We must summon both the courage and the humility to accept our limitations without allowing them to become debilitations. Someone out there will listen to us. Someone will listen to what you have to say about Jesus. Someone will listen to what I have to say about Jesus. I think we are all tired of making excuses and of pacifying ourselves with good intentions. We're almost out of time. Everything is ending, but it hasn't ended yet. Now is the time, the only time we have left.

Maybe what the church needs to do is make a collective decision to break away from the slough of despond with regard to the Great Commission. Maybe we need a fresh start. Years ago I heard the following imaginary scenario that I'd like to share with you here:

You're sitting at home relaxing in front of the television. Somewhere in the background the phone is ringing. Reluctantly, you get up to answer it. You are surprised to hear someone on the other end of the line asking if you'll hold for the president. Thinking it's a prank caller, you start to hang up the phone, but an impulse, curiosity or humorous indulgence perhaps, causes you to respond, "Oh, well, if it's the president, sure, I'll hold." (This scenario assumes, of course, that the candidate of your choice won the election, a necessary assumption in the days we are living in.)

After a few seconds, you hear the voice of, low and behold, the president of the United States. As it begins to sink in that he really is talking to you (he even called you by name), you realize that he is asking you a question…something about your ethnic roots and family lineage (your great-grandparents were from Tahiti). This has been brought to his attention (somehow), and he has been informed that you speak fluent Tahitian (of course), and so he was wondering, would you consider being his special ambassador to Tahiti?

Now if you are at all like me (I've have always wondered what it would be like to go to Tahiti, and suddenly, here is the president of the United States of America on the phone asking you not only to go there, but to go for your country and for your president, as his special ambassador no less) it seems reasonable to assume that you would be fairly thrilled at the prospect.

Imagine, an ambassador representing the most powerful country in the world, a special envoy for the president himself. Why you would probably answer with awe and humility, "Yes, Mr. President! Of course! I'd be honored, sir! Just tell me what you want me to do!" Then, after receiving your marching orders, you'd hang up the phone in a state of euphoric ecstasy as you ran to tell your family members, your friends and neighbors, maybe even your enemies (for the more vindictive among us), of the incredible turn of good fortune that had befallen you.

After you had a chance to calm down, you would start to carefully plan out each and every step in preparation for embarking upon your great calling—new clothes, new hairstyle (ladies), Tahitian lessons (to "brush up," of course), travel arrangements, and so on. Each step would be painstakingly planned from start to finish.

Above all, you would spare no effort to study the message received from your nation's leader and to ponder any and all ways and means at your disposal that might be of assistance to you in communicating that message to the people to whom he has sent you. As you traveled to your destination, all of your thoughts would be focused on how best to conduct yourself, taking care that every word, every gesture, every expression, and every action were such as would most accurately represent your leader and bring honor to your country.

By now, you know where all of this is leading. We are ambassadors for Christ, a much higher calling. Ours is no mere earthly kingdom. We have been called as representatives of heaven, highest over all. And our king, the King of the entire universe, has chosen us, you and me, to be his ambassadors, his representatives, his messengers! What was I thinking? What were you thinking? What were *we* thinking?

When will we see the true greatness of the honor God has bestowed upon us? If we could search to the farthest reaches of the universe, we would find no greater calling than that of "Ambassador of Christ to the Lost"! And the only place under God's heaven where the gospel may be preached is right here on planet earth. Angels cannot preach the gospel. If there are other intelligent beings in the universe, however lofty and noble they might be, it has not been given to them to preach the gospel to lost souls. Only to you and me has this unparalleled "one time only" mission been given.

How curious we must seem to the angels as they behold us, citizens of the most powerful kingdom in this or any other universe, representing our King…hesitantly, haltingly, fearfully, and even, wonder of wonders, reluctantly. Here we have God's ambassadors, armed with all of the invincible weaponry of heaven itself, behaving with timidity and (self-imposed) inferiority—and this in the presence of helpless, hapless, lost souls who, for the most part, are clueless as to the meaning of their own existence.

Sinners are filled with fear, whether they acknowledge it or not. They are afraid of the unknown, afraid of their seeming insignificance in a world that will scarcely notice when they're gone, afraid of what might happen today, afraid of what might

Robert Davis

happen tomorrow, afraid for themselves, afraid for their loved ones, and in the midst of all this fear, the ever present and inescapable shadow of death, waiting, out there, somewhere, ready on a moment's notice or with no notice at all, to lay his cold hand of finality upon their shoulders…to end it all, forever.

And we're afraid? We whose lives are no longer lived in the darkness of uncertainty, insignificance, or fear of things present or things to come, or even of death, come though he may, and will, for us also someday. None of these things terrify us anymore. We know that God is with us, that he is for us, and most of all, that he loves us. This ought to give us the courage and compassion to want to reach out to others, even in the face of fear. After all, we have all overcome other fears in our lives, especially when our desire to do so was strong enough. With so many around us facing death and eternity without Christ, who would suggest that we are lacking in motivations?

The resources for overcoming our fear and inertia are available, if only we will avail ourselves of them. Prayer is only a breath away. Who could ask God for "divine appointments" and doubt that he would answer such a request? Our testimony is clear to each one of us who has placed our faith in Christ. And the message of God's redeeming love is neither confusing nor ambivalent.

Furthermore, though we may have failed to recognize it, there *are* good teachings, books, tapes, and resource materials to instruct anyone desiring to receive training in the "how-to" dynamics of sharing our faith. And what about all of the wonderful, anointed gospel tracts available for anyone who is willing to distribute them? Could we perhaps hand someone a simple piece of lifesaving literature with a smile and an expression of friendly interest?

Most of us know at least someone in our church or our community of faith who has stood out as a believer, unafraid to share his faith with others. Would it be so hard to ask such a person for some pointers? If you cannot find such a person, then why not get together with one of your Christian friends who is struggling with the same problem? Lord knows you'll not have to look far. Why not help each other, knowing that "where two of you are gathered in his name" Jesus will be there in the midst of you?

You can overcome your fears. We do know what Jesus means to us. We do understand the message that God has communicated concerning his saving grace in Christ. So take courage and resolve to conquer your fears, for God's honor and glory and for the sake of those perishing around you.

Remember what's at stake. We may not safely assume that "someone else" will reach the heart of the lost person beside us. It is not so important what that person thinks of you or me, but it is all important what she thinks of the one we represent. Be willing, if need be, to look foolish, silly, uncertain, even fearful for the sake of someone's eternal soul. And know that as you do, a spirit will come upon you, a spirit will move within you, and yes, a spirit will move upon those you reach out to, calling, drawing with gentle love, even the Spirit of God within you, who "is not willing that any should perish but that all should come to repentance."

Chapter Three

What If We Were All to Get Baptized Again?

As I begin to write the words to this chapter, I feel lost, as though I were searching for something in the dark. The light switch on the wall, the lamp on the night table, the door leading to the hallway. I've had this thought for a while now, more like a question really. I've been thinking about how soon the history of the church on earth will be finished. And I'm struck by the fact that it seems there is no record anywhere, at least that I know of, in the two-thousand-year history of the body of Christ, chronicling even one instance where all of Jesus's followers decided to get together with one mind, in one accord, to proclaim with one united voice to the world, "We have found the Messiah."

I guess the closest we ever came to having one voice was when Peter stood up on the day of Pentecost and boldly preached Christ to the thousands. What strikes me most painfully about this realization is the fact that that day, the Day of Pentecost, was the very first day of the church! And here we are, two thousand years later, and we have not even once since then been able to unite as one body, of one mind in one accord, to proclaim as one that Jesus Christ of Nazareth is the Messiah the world has been waiting for! And now the story is almost over.

Please don't get me wrong. I'm not saying we haven't been proclaiming Christ. Of course we have. Down through every century, the church has been the light of the world, pointing the way to mankind's Savior. But even as we did so, that very same light exposed our differences, our divisions, our disagreements, and finally, enshrined in towering temples and sanctuaries of stone, our denominations. We had to solidify them...our differences, our divisions, our disagreements...with brick, mortar, and stone. Permanent altars to our own inability to see eye to eye!

Which brings me back to my question. Is it possible that just once, or should I say just once more, before it is too late, before Jesus comes back and the record books on the history of his church are closed forever, that there might be one more chapter written—about the time when all of Christ's followers set aside their differences, their divisions, their disagreements, and for just a moment, their cherished denominational doctrines to join upraised hand in upraised hand—brother and sister, mother and father, parent and child, neighbor and stranger, black and white, rich and poor, countrymen and foreigner, and dare we even say, friend and foe—to shout with one voice to the entire world, "*We have found him! The Messiah! The one foretold in the Scriptures,* Jesus of Nazareth!"

Could this happen? Might we make it happen? Dare we believe to do such a thing?

And if we really did this, really and truly set aside our differences in some profound, universal demonstration of love, what might our impact be on a world grown cynical about the church, the Christians...and their Messiah? Would they see God in it all? Would it occur to them that just maybe, perhaps, he was trying to tell them something? Which leaves me wondering, what would Jesus think ?

I find it hard to imagine that he would disapprove. In fact, I am more inclined to wonder, could it be something stirring around in the back of his mind? An idea that comes to him now and then but that he pushes away because he thinks, *Oh, my people... No. They would never do that...not even for me.*

I doubt that we've ever really thought of it that way. But still, you kind of have to wonder. It's not like we haven't disappointed Jesus before, if you know what I mean. Of course he loves us way too much to be disappointed in us. So please don't get me wrong. After all, he has declared us to be new creatures in him, his Father's workmanship and all. Obviously he has a very high opinion of us.

Still, just imagine if we did it. You know, if all of our very famous and influential leaders were to get together (just this once, of course) and decide to do something, make a...uhh... statement of sorts. Hmmm...what could we do? What would we say? *Maybe we could all get baptized again...* I mean if we all, *all,* got together on a worldwide basis to do this, or do *something...*so that the world would hear us and know...

"By this shall all men know that ye are my disciples, if ye have love one to another" (John 13:35).

P.S. Where Are the Jesus People?

(Or, Keith Green, We Miss You)

[Note to the reader: I decided to include this tribute to Keith Green because, like many of my generation, he was a true inspiration to me in my walk with the Lord. I wrote it with the voice of the young man that I was back in 1979, when on a dark, lonely stretch of Interstate 80, I first encountered the man through his music.]

It was the middle of the night, around two or three in the morning, in the early fall of 1979. I was hitchhiking the interstate in the middle of nowhere, to New Jersey from Wyoming, thumbing it fifteen hundred miles across the country to see my family for the first time in two years. I was young and single, carrying all of my earthly belongings in a beat up forty-year-old suitcase, my sleeping bag rolled up and tied to the outside of it.

I have no recollection of where I first saw him. Just that I turned around and he was there, like a ghost, approaching me from the shadows. Like me, he was hitching rides down the highway, and as luck would have it, heading east…like me. I wasn't scared really, just a little bit apprehensive about this stranger in the dark. But he was tall, a full six inches taller than me, and lean, with broad shoulders and a dark countenance and, to make matters worse, an air of suspicion about him that left me feeling uneasy. There were no cars on the road, and we were alone.

It didn't help matters any when, after exchanging rather perfunctory greetings, this shadow man asked me what I had in my suitcase. *Why does he want to know that?*, I wondered. The creep. I was frankly suspicious of him now and told him in no uncertain terms that he didn't need to know. That seemed to satisfy him for the moment. We talked then, for a while, about where we had come from—me, Wyoming; him…I don't remember—and where we were going—me, New Jersey; him, about "a hundred miles down the road," wherever that was. There were still no cars, and I'm beginning to wonder, *How in the world am I going to get a ride with no cars, this sinister-looking, serial-killer type hitch-hiking here beside me, in the middle of the night, in the middle of nowhere?*

I was tired, frustrated, and ticked off at this guy for just being here and for looking like a serial killer and for asking me what I had in my suitcase. My already bleak prospects for getting a ride had suddenly taken a very bad turn for the worse. But I had had an idea about what to do from the moment I first saw him. I knew. And now seemed like as good a time as any to start. So I began to tell him about Jesus.

And he listened. After a while, he said that, "Well, yes," he knew that God was going to "get a hold of him someday" but it was clear from his demeanor that "that day" had not yet arrived. By now I knew I had to shake this guy, so I came up with the idea of offering to buy him a cup of coffee. There was a Holiday Inn or some place like that with an all-night restaurant back off the interstate a quarter of a mile or so. I figured that since there were no cars, what did I have to lose?

I guess it sounded pretty good to him because he accepted my offer. So I headed down to the restaurant with this guy for coffee, to sit down and rest for a while and to try to figure out what I would do next. We went inside for coffee, sat awhile, and talked. I told him about my life and how much it had changed since I met Jesus. He listened, but seemed distracted. He asked me again about my suitcase. I asked him, "Why do you want to know? It's my clothes and a few other things, and in case you were wondering, there's no money in it. I have a few dollars left to get me home, and I'm spending some of it now so we can have coffee. And I'm ready to go."

I got up, hoping he would stay for a couple of more refills since they were free. But no. He got up to go with me. So back out the door we went, me feeling more frustrated than ever and praying under my breath, "God, please, I've told him about you. He's more interested in my suitcase than he is in you. I'm tired, and I really need a ride. And could you please do something?"

We had been on the exit ramp for about five minutes, maybe less, when some guy pulled over, rolled down his window, and asked us if we needed a ride. I was closer to the window than shadow guy, so I answered, "Yeah, thanks!" and started to reach for the front door. Suddenly, I changed my mind. It was the music. I had never heard it before, but I "knew" it. I couldn't make out the words to the song, but someone was definitely singing, and my heart was telling me that God was here. I could feel him in the air.

I knew that I should get in the backseat so that the driver could witness to my twilight companion, which I somehow knew that he would do…and so that I could listen to this music. I told the guy with me to get in the front. As I hopped in the back, with shadow man climbing into the front, I asked the driver, "Is that Christian music?" He answered that, "Yes, it was," and that "if I liked it, there was more where that came from." So I proceeded to get settled in the back of the car and to turn my ear toward the rear speaker behind me as the driver began to, you guessed it, witness to Mr. "What's in Your Suitcase?" in the front. And that music, from, not earth, I was sure, began to filter into my ears: "Do you see? Do you see? All the people sinking down? Don't you care? Don't you care? Are you gonna let them drown?"

I had heard a fair amount of Christian music, having been saved for about three years at the time. But I had never heard anything like this before: "How can you be so numb, not to care if they come? You close your eyes and pretend the job's done!"

I had to know…who was singing this? I wanted to ask the driver, but I couldn't very well interrupt him. After all, he was witnessing to this person whom I had just been witnessing to! So I waited, and I began to listen to the driver as he shared his testimony of how Christ had changed *his* life. And as I listened, I began to realize something. There was nothing really remarkable about what he said, not unless you considered a person declaring that his life had changed as a result of starting a relationship with someone who had died on a cross two thousand years ago remarkable. What I mean is that he told of no supernatural miracles or of any divine manifestations of any kind. Unless, of course, you considered deliverance from despair and hopelessness and a meaningless life of selfishness and sin to be a miracle or a manifestation of the divine.

What struck me more than anything the man said (after all, I knew all about Jesus changing people's lives!) was the almost palpable sense of…drama. I couldn't help feeling that this simple encounter, in which one person was telling another about how Christ had changed his life was, in the grand scheme of the universe, a drama of cosmic proportions. Though I couldn't put my finger on it at the time, I know now that angels were in attendance, divine witnesses watching with an interest so keen as to conjure images of a dazzler, a Svengali waving his magic wand of hypnotic power over a spellbound audience hanging breathlessly on every word. Angels fascinated, hypnotized, mesmerized by the power of Christ to transform yet another one of those spectacles of the ages—a sinner, a rebel, a God-rejecter—into a child of the Most High God!

I know what you are thinking, but no! I'm not talking about the passenger in the front (you thought I was referring to him as having been led to the Lord, didn't you?) No. The impression I recall with absolute clarity more than three decades afterward is that the angels were fascinated with *the testimony of the driver who had been saved by the redeeming power of Christ.* This was what fascinated them, captivated them, and held them in spellbound silence and reverent awe before God…a lost sinner, now saved, testifying of how the power of the risen Christ had saved him, changed him, transformed him, and healed him. For those words of testimony, of the power of Christ to transform a lost sinner into a devoted child of God, were to the angels, I believe, the most amazing and unfathomably wonderful demonstration of the power and glory of God in all of creation!

After he was done sharing his testimony, the guy who wanted to know what was in my suitcase responded by remarking that he was sure that "God was going to get a hold of him one day." (déjà vu all over again!) He did add, however, his suspicion that "whenever God hits me, I know he's going to hit me hard!" as he put it. (Hmm.) The driver declined, as I had before him, to try to coerce any kind of artificial response from the man. He would come to Christ when and if he ever he decided that he wanted Jesus in his life badly enough to stop running. I suspected that day would come. We drove on. My thoughts returned to the music: "I want hearts of fire, not your prayers of ice. And I'm coming quickly to give unto you, according to what you have done, according to what you have done, according to what you have done!"

In all the years I have been a Christian, I have not found a place in the world where I can go to sense the presence of God and the fire of a heart so passionate for Christ, merely by popping in a CD, as I do when I listen to the music of *Keith Green*. I love the music and songs of many brothers and sisters of the Lord, and please don't get me wrong, I'm not comparing.

But anyone familiar with Keith's life and his music knows that he was very different. He was a twentieth-century psalmist whose music lives on well into the new millennium in the hearts of those of us who came to know and love him, as did so many from my generation. To hear him singing was to be forgiven, restored, renewed, uplifted, ready again to take up the Master's cross, and follow once more in his footsteps. He was a prophet, a genuine bona fide messenger from God, sent to lift us up out of the sloth of our despond, to rebuke us for our sins, and to call us to a life of holy consecration to God and to the cause of saving the lost.

He laid down his music early in his Christian life and vowed to God never to pick it up again, unless Jesus bid him to. Thankfully for the rest of us, *he* did, and he did. I think Keith would be most *proud*, in the completely unsinful sense of the word, if he were remembered more than anything else as someone who was, to use his own words, "bananas for Jesus." I sometimes wonder if he might not have been more bananas for Jesus than anyone else from my generation. He made us all feel so humble…thankful… obligated…responsible…indebted…on fire, and, just plain electrifyingly glad to be called, chosen, commissioned to fulfill our part in the mighty master plan of God for humanity.

I want to be on fire like that again, no longer content to just rest in the blessings. When I was young, I dreamed that with God inside of me anything might be possible. Now, many years later, I find myself wanting to return to that dream. Why not dare to dream big again? Why not believe in a God who never tires of doing "a new thing in the earth"? That's what I want to do… something new, something bold, something, anything, if God might use it to arouse sleeping sinners or slumbering saints. I think what I am really trying to say is, "I want to be bananas for Jesus!" Like when I was young. Like Keith was.

The Appendix...
Not Just an Afterthought

The topics covered in this Appendix are intended to help you "(have) your feet shod with the preparation of the gospel of peace" (Ephesians 6:18).

Though they are presented last, they are not least. Some were put here to facilitate a smoother transition from one subject to the next ("More Stuff for Children"; "More Fear Busters for the 'Feint' of Heart"). Others were placed in the appendix as reference materials ("Lists That Levitate," "What Would Jesus Say?" and, "Survey Says...").

A book dealing with practical teaching and "how tos" faces the challenge of balancing readability with nuts-and-bolts instruction. I have sought to preserve such a balance.

As we strive to be faithful in our efforts to share Jesus with people, we can rest assured that "the Lord (will be) working with (us), confirming His Word with signs following" (Mark 16:20).

(Appendix A)

Lists That Levitate

Therefore every scribe who is instructed unto the kingdom of heaven is like unto a householder, who brings forth out of his treasure things new and old.

Matthew 13:52

For out of the abundance of the heart the mouth speaks.

Matthew 12:34

In Colossians 3:16, we are exhorted to "let the Word of Christ dwell in (us) richly in all wisdom." This admonition, when followed, brings great blessing and confidence to our hearts.

We are not the only beneficiaries, however. As we follow this injunction God will use our efforts to "establish us in every good word and work" (1 Thessalonians 2:17).

If we want faith to come into people's hearts, we must give them the Word (Romans 10:17). God uses his Word to pull down strongholds, not in our lives only but also in the lives of those we minister to. To this end, we need to be prepared with more than just four or five "salvation" scriptures. The needs of people vary greatly. Everyone is different. Each case is different.

In order to help facilitate a means by which we might be better prepared to minister to the wide variety of situations and circumstances we find in people's lives, we offer the following "lists." Each is intended to provide spiritual ammunition to help pull down strongholds, provide motivation to strengthen our wills, and wisdom to help light the way.

List Number One:
Why I Witness to People

These scriptures will keep you motivated to share Christ with people. They may also be useful as means for explaining to them *why* sharing your faith is important to you. The Word is its own best explanation and brings God's authority to your witness. (Perhaps you might write these scriptures in the back of your Bible or in the form of a "chain" reference, along with the other lists provided.) Here are just a few scriptures telling us why we need to share Jesus with people.

1. Jesus commands us to preach the gospel to every creature (Mark 16:15).

2. People need to hear the gospel in order to be saved (Acts 4:12).

3. Those who receive Christ will inherit eternal life (John 3:16).

4. God created us for his pleasure (Revelation 4:11).

5. God's Word contains the solution for all of man's problems, and he has ordained us to proclaim his Word to others (2 Timothy 3:16; 4:2).

6. Jesus is coming back soon, and people must be ready (Matthew 24:44).

7. We want to offer friendship to others so that we might help them discover a relationship with God (1 John 1:3).

Note: Observe that each of these "reasons to witness" may be used as:

Robert Davis

A statement of purpose…to explain to others why you have approached them.

The basis of a question…to help you establish rapport.

The focus of your conversation…both the reason and the accompanying scripture may serve this purpose.

A final thought…to leave with the person as you depart.

The same usage may be made of the list that follows.

List Number Two:
Blessings We Receive in Christ

People need to know what God desires to give them through his Son. As we share these blessings under the guidance of his Spirit, they will be enabled to see how God can help them.

1. We are brought back into a restored relationship and fellowship with the One who made us (1 John 1:3).

2. We receive eternal life and a home in heaven (1 John 5:13).

3. We find meaning and purpose for our lives (Psalm 16:11).

4. We have all of our needs met—spiritually, emotionally, socially, etc. (Philippians 4:19).

5. We receive power over sin; Christ sets us free (Romans 6:14).

6. We receive the fruit of the Spirit: love, joy, peace…replacing hatred, sorrow, fear (Galations 5:22-23).

7. We receive a new self-image in Christ (2 Corinthians 5:17).

8. We now have the privilege of serving God (Romans 6:22).

9. We now have a genuine ability to help others (1 Corinthians 3:5).

List Number Three: Important Scriptures for New Christians to Know

It is exposure to the Word of God that will keep the new believer on the right path. These scriptures are essential for every Christian to know. While one person's list might differ from another's, the important thing is that we introduce new believers to those truths that will help them build a firm foundation for their walk with God.

1. Repentance: Matthew 3:2, 8; Matthew 4:17; Mark 1:5; Acts 3:19; Ezekiel 14:6

2. Faith: Romans 10:17; Ephesians 2:8-10; Hebrews 11:6; Colossians 1:21-23; 1 Timothy 6:12

3. God's Word: 2 Timothy 2:15; Isaiah 28:10; Acts 17:11; Colossians 3:16; Proverbs 2:1-5

4. Our identity in Christ: 2 Corinthians 3:18, 5:17, 5:21; 1 Corinthians 1:30; Philippians 2:5

5. Prayer: Ephesians 6:18; 1 Corinthians 14:15; Matthew 26:41; Luke 21:36; 1 Thessalonians 5:17

6. Church fellowship: Hebrews 10:25; 1 Corinthians 12:12-27 and 14:26; 1 John 1:3 and 2:18-19

7. Water baptism: Matthew 3:1-17 and 28:19; Acts 8:12 and 10:47; Hebrews 6:2

8. Holiness: Ephesians 1:4; Colossians 1:22; Hebrews 12:14; 1 Peter 1:16; 2 Peter 3:11

9. Witnessing: Mark 16:15; Matthew 12:30; Proverbs 11:30; 1 Peter 3:15; 2 Corinthians 5:19-20

10. Giving: Genesis 4:1-8; Malachi 3:8-12; 2 Corinthians 8:9-15 and 9:6-7; Luke 6:38

11. Love: 1 Corinthians 1-13; 1 John 3:16 and 18; 4:20, 5:4

12. Satan: Genesis 3:1-24; John 10:10; 1 Peter 5:8-9; James 4:7; Job 1:1-3

13. Christ's return: 1 Thessalonians 5:1-6; 2 Peter3:3-14; Matthew 24:3-51; and 25:1-46; Mark 13:32-37

14. Spiritual gifts: 1 Corinthians 12:1, 4-31; 7:7; Romans 12:3-8; Ephesians 4:7-16

15. Being led by the Spirit: Romans 8:1-14; Galations 5:16-18; 1 John 2:27-28; James 3:17; Hebrews 12:14

List Number Four:
Questions to Help You Relate to People

Questions are means to an end—to help you "connect" with people while gathering necessary information to assist you in knowing how to steer the conversation. The important thing is to establish rapport, making the other person feel comfortable enough to open up to you. Be careful to avoid asking too many questions or questions of too personal a character. You don't want to make the person feel like he is being given "the third degree."

"Nonspiritual" Questions

Have you lived around here long? Or, Are you from around here?

Are you happy with your life?

If you could change one thing in (your life, the world) what would it be?

Do you believe in the existence of evil?

Are you afraid of death?

What is most important in your life?

What kind of people do you most admire?

What do you want your children to believe?

How do you hope to be remembered after you are gone?

Do you like to read? (Could lead into, "Have you ever read the Bible?")

"Spiritual" Questions"

Do you believe Jesus is alive today?

Do you ever talk to him?

How can you know God's will for your life?

Does the Bible have any relevance to modern problems?

Have you ever had any people from one of the churches in your community visit you?

If you were to consider visiting a church, what would you look for?

Have you ever had a close friend who was a devoted Christian?

Do you believe what the Bible teaches about an after life?

Do you believe there will be a judgment day? What do you think will happen to you on that day?

What would you change in your life if you knew Jesus was coming back in six months?

(For additional questions, consult Appendix G: "Survey Says…" and other examples given throughout this book.)

List Number Five:
Twelve Questions the Holy Spirit Causes People to Ask Themselves When We Witness to Them

1. God – Does he really exist?

2. The Bible – Is it really the Word of God?

3. Jesus – Is he really who he says he is?

4. The cross – What is its meaning in my life?

5. Eternal life – Can I really live forever?

6. Heaven – Is it real?

7. Hell – Is it real?

8. Salvation – What must I do to be saved?

9. Bible prophecy – Are we really living in the last days?

10. Their lifestyle – Am I living right?

11. The last judgment – Am I ready to meet my maker?

12. Their loved ones – What about their souls?

And when he (the Spirit) is come, he will reprove the world of sin, of righteousness, and of judgment (John 16:8).

List Number Six:
Twelve Means the Holy Spirit Might Use to Remind People of Your Witness to Them

1. Seeing a Bible

2. Seeing or hearing a preacher on TV or radio

3. Seeing a picture of Jesus

4. Seeing a Christian bumper sticker or T-shirt

5. Hearing a Christian song

6. Reading or noticing Christian literature

7. A personal or family crisis

8. Hearing about a friend or acquaintance getting saved (or dying)

9. Thoughts about their mortality

10. Thoughts about their loved ones' mortality

11. The memory of your face

12. The Holy Spirit himself

And when he (the Spirit) is come, he will reprove the world of sin, of righteousness, and of judgment (John 16:8).

"Bonus" List: The Five Ws of Jesus

Remember in grade school when they taught us the "five Ws"? This is a simple, effective way of telling the important points about a thing, or in this case, a person.

Who? *Who is Jesus Christ?*

He is the son of God (Matthew 3:16&17)

the light of the world (John 8:12)

the way, the truth, and the life (John 14:6)

the only one who can save us (Acts 4:12)

What? *What has Christ done for us?*

He died for us (Romans 5:6)

took our punishment (2 Corinthians 5:21)

gave us power over sin (1 John 5:3-4)

reconciled us to God (2 Corinthians 5:19)

Where? *Where does Christ want to dwell?*

In our hearts (Revelation 3:20)

On the throne of our lives (Romans 10:9-10)

In our thoughts (2 Corinthians 10:15)

In our actions (2 Corinthians 3:2)

When? *When will Christ return?*

In such an hour as you think not (Matthew 24:44)

Quickly (Revelation 22:20, Matthew 24:27)

Soon (1 Timothy 3:1-5)

When will you receive him?

Now is the acceptable time (2 Corinthians 6:2)

How shall we escape? (Hebrews 2:3)

Why? *Why should we live for Christ?*

He gave his life for us (1 John 3:16).

He that loses his life for Christ's sake gains it (John 12:25).

So that we can stand (Matthew 7:24-27).

(Appendix B)

What Would Jesus Say?

Have you ever talked to someone about the Lord and found yourself suddenly stumped by a question or a remark or faced with a situation in which you wanted to give the right response, but the words eluded you? Most of us have experienced this more than once.

God does not expect us to become Bible experts before we can talk to someone about Jesus. If you can say, "Jesus loves you," God can use you to witness to people. With all of the teachings and suggestions you will find in this book, the following statement remains true:

If You Can Open Your Mouth, You Can Share Your Faith

We really don't need to be "taught" how to do this any more than we need to be taught how to have conversations with people. We only think we do. Once we get even a little experience talking to people about Christ, witnessing becomes as natural as breathing. Like riding a bike, once you know how to pedal, and to keep your balance, you are going to go forward.

On the other hand, this does not mean that we cannot grow in wisdom through practice and experience. While looking to God to do his part, we should also be seeking to grow in knowledge—to hone our skills and to sharpen our swords. We should be constantly striving to "preach the word, [and] be instant in season, out of season; [and to] reprove, rebuke, exhort, with all longsuffering and doctrine" (2 Timothy 4:2). This book is about moving forward in that direction.

People Need Our Prayers

The two most important weapons for waging spiritual warfare in the area of winning souls are prayer and the Word of God. Concerning prayer, we have maintained throughout that, "Except the Lord build the house, they labor in vain that build it" (Psalm 127:1). Only as we seek the Lord's help and guidance and petition him through our prayers and intercessions on behalf of lost sinners can we see any fruit come of our labors. And we must abide in him, drawing our life from him as the branch draws its life from the vine. Then we will have his life to give to others.

> Abide in Me, and I in you. As the branch cannot bear fruit of itself, unless it abides in the vine; neither can you, unless you abide in me. I am the vine, you are the branches: He who abides in me, and I in him, bears much fruit; for without Me you can do nothing.
>
> John 15:4-5 (NKJV)

And They Need God's Word

Our other spiritual weapon, the Word of God, is the means through which God has ordained to reveal himself. As this is a book on witnessing rather than prayer, our focus here will be on the Word of God and how we can sharpen our skills in using it so as to be ready to point people in the right direction on the road of life.

It is God's Word that will open the eyes of those whose minds are blinded. Our own words may bring comfort, hope, and encouragement. But only the words that come from God can give life. Only his Word can bring someone to conviction and repentance.

> For the Word of God is living and powerful, and sharper than any two-edged sword, piercing even to the division of soul and spirit, and of joints and marrow, and is a discerner of the thoughts and intents of the heart.
>
> Hebrews 4:12 (NKJV)

> All scripture is given by inspiration of God, and is profitable for doctrine (right believing), for reproof (exposure of wrong believing), for correction (pointing the way back to right believing), and instruction in righteousness (teaching uprightness of character and conduct).
>
> 2 Timothy 3:16

When we are confronted with error, we must be prepared to expose it with the light of truth. God's Word is the truth he has revealed to man. We have an obligation to equip ourselves with the armor of his Word so as to be able to combat the errors and deceptions being noised abroad in the world today.

The Spirit of God Uses the Word of God

God backs up his Word with the witness of his Spirit. When sinners are exposed to the truth, God will stamp his seal of authenticity upon their conscience. Unless the listener chooses to override the Spirit's testimony with delusions of his own preference, he will recognize the truth as coming from the mouth of his Creator.

Knowing this, as God's ambassadors, we should purpose to recognize at least the more popular errors running loose in the minds of those who are out of the way. By arming ourselves with appropriate scriptural remedies, we increase our effectiveness in overcoming the deceptions that blind people from the truth of the gospel.

More to the point, we need to know the excuses people are hiding behind to avoid God's call. Sinners will go to great lengths to find errors and false philosophies to justify their rebellion. The Lord's method for dealing with darkness is to shine his light on it. When sinners are confronted with what God has to say about their delusions, some will "lay down their weapons" and surrender to his call.

This is not to suggest that we hurl scriptures at sinners like lightning bolts. To the contrary, we are called to humility and gentleness: "In humility correcting those who are in opposition, if God perhaps will grant them repentance, so that they may know the truth" (2 Timothy 2:25, NKJV).

As a strategy for dealing with "those who oppose themselves," we may ask ourselves the following question as a compass to help navigate our way through the maze of excuses and objections we are likely to encounter when dealing with sinners. Put simply: What would Jesus say?

This appendix will present some of the more common excuses that lead people astray and then offer some scriptural responses for dealing with them. We will first look at some of the spiritual "conditions" frequently encountered in people whom we minister to. That is, most people fall into one of several broad categories with reference to their standing with God. While these "categories" may vary in name and description, depending on who is doing the naming and describing, most believers will agree with the idea that, as reference points for understanding people and their different spiritual needs, categories are useful, provided we do not use them to stereotype anyone or desensitize ourselves to the uniqueness of each individual. People will reveal themselves to us and, based upon their responses, we may with a high degree of accuracy "diagnose," if you will, the spiritual condition of each.

Recognize a Person's Spiritual Condition

For our purposes, we will use six categories for describing people with reference to their relationship to God, as follows: 1) Committed Christians; 2) Lukewarm Christians; 3) Religious

Professors; 4) Backsliders; 5) The Unsaved Ignorant; 6) The Unsaved Rejector.

Allowing that the reader might prefer a different choice of descriptions, we will at least agree on two broad categories universally accepted by those who believe in the inerrancy of Scripture: namely, those who are saved and those who are not. We go further in the belief that unsaved people have drastically different backgrounds and attitudes toward God.

Allowing for our differences, some observations are offered here for each of the categories listed, with the intention of encouraging you to study these things out for yourself and draw your own conclusions. Doing so will help you be better prepared to deal with individuals based on these insights and the leading of God's Spirit. It should be emphasized that the guidelines offered here are not foolproof formulas. At best, they are merely reference points to stimulate your own reflection. Our goal is to rely upon God, keeping ourselves sensitive to his direction while recognizing that *the end of all preparation is to be more ready and able to follow his lead.*

Committed Christians

We can usually recognize a brother or sister in the Lord without much difficulty, especially when we are talking to him about Jesus. The subject of the Savior will evoke a positive response from those who are trusting him. Such people will frankly confess their hope in Christ.

Bear in mind, however, that even among the brethren, not all will be eager to show a receptive manner, especially to a stranger. Some might wonder if we are trying to pull them from their church. Others, seeing our example of dedication to reaching the lost, may experience pangs of conviction over their own lack of willingness to share their faith, causing them to be reserved in their responses toward us. Or perhaps we might have just caught the person at a bad time.

Still, we may gain an overall impression about a person's spirituality from his manner, his responses, and the inner intuition or "instincts" of our spirits. While we can never see completely into another person's heart and should never be quick to judge, Jesus did declare that "by their fruits you shall know them" (Matthew 7:20).

When we meet fellow Christians, we should consider such encounters as opportunities to offer encouragement and edification. The Lord may want us to minister to a brother or sister in some way. He may also have purposed for that believer to minister to us. We are called to "love one another and to provoke one another unto good works." Often the Lord will use such encounters to stir fellow believers through our example of reaching out, as we said before. Yet a humble attitude on our part requires that we be as willing to receive as we are to give—never assuming that we are the ones with "more" to offer.

We must be sensitive. Perhaps the person needs fellowship. Elderly and handicapped saints, as well as other believers, will usually welcome the opportunity to spend time with a visiting Christian out doing the Lord's work. You might read or study the Bible together or just enjoy each other's fellowship. Don't just chalk such a person up as "saved" and, therefore, not worth spending any more time with. We are called to minister as well as to witness (Acts 26:16). Let God be the one to decide what you do.

Though you will usually have little trouble identifying those who are trusting in Christ, here are a few questions to help: (These should only be asked if you have "doubts." It would be wise to use only one or two of these questions in any given encounter.)

1. "Can you tell me how you know you are a Christian?"

(Compare the person's answer to what the Word says.)

2. "Do you know for sure that if you died tonight you would go to heaven?" (One of the more well-known "diagnostic" questions.) If the person answers "Yes," you may ask, "Can you tell me why?" (Compare her answer to what the Word says.)

3. "What is a Christian?" (From C.S. Lovett) If the person answers by telling you what a Christian *does*—"I go to church; I believe in God; I believe in the Bible; I was baptized," etc.—explain that these are things a Christian does but you want him to tell you what a Christian *is*, i.e., someone who has received Christ into his heart as Lord and Saviour, or someone who has been born again by trusting Christ. These or similar words will describe what a Christian is. (Compare the person's answer to the Word.)

4. "Are you trusting in Christ alone for your salvation and living for him the way the Bible tells us to?" (Compare answer to the Word.)

5. "Are you still close to the Lord, or would you say that you have drifted away from him?"

   Do not ask this question unless the person is showing signs of conviction or discomfort talking about the Lord. If the person indicates that she is still close to the Lord, be ready to give her the benefit of doubt. If you still feel uneasy about the matter you might follow up by asking something like, "Could you tell me how your relationship with the Lord has changed you?" (Compare her answer with the Word.)

Lukewarm Christians

Sometimes these believers will come right out and tell you that they are "not as dedicated as they should be," or some such comment, while denying that they are backslidden. Usually, however, it will be necessary for you to look for some of the telltale signs of this condition. These people will usually declare their faith in God but upon questioning, one or more of the following will come to light:

> They are no longer going to church
>
> They demonstrate a worldly attitude about things
>
> They seem to lack evidence of committed discipleship
>
> They seem to show a lack of zeal for the Lord; and/or,
>
> While claiming to believe in the nearness of the return, there are hints of a lack of true concern or conviction about it.

Of course our churches are filled with people who might demonstrate any number of these characteristics, and we know that church attendance alone is not an indication of true commitment to the Lord. Yet it is also important to remember that all of us go through dry spells and desert experiences during which our zeal, our dedication, and our commitment may wax feeble and even appear to be extinguished.

The observations suggested here are not offered as instruments for judging or condemning anyone who claims loyalty to Jesus! On the contrary, our motive is to discern people's needs so as to be better able to minister to them. It takes experience, wisdom, discernment, and prayer to be able to recognize many peoples' true spiritual condition. And even then we may still get it wrong. If our heart is motivated by the compassion and love of God, however, we may be confident that the words we speak will bring life and encouragement to those who are struggling in areas most of us are familiar with—through our own experience.

Having said this, here are some questions that may help you to "identify" those who may have fallen into this condition. Use only as many as you need to do so.

1. "Can you tell me what it means to serve God?"

2. "Is going to church important?"

3. "How would you describe your relationship with the Lord?"

4. "What is God wanting to do with your life?"

5. "How can we know whether we are living to please God or following our own desires?"

6. "How should we be different from other people?"

Questions such as these must be asked in a spirit of humility and compassion. Realize that those who are in this condition often desire to hide it from other believers. Even so, such questions, if ventured in a loving, nonjudgmental manner, will compel people in this condition to face their situation, whether they admit it or not. "Brethren, if a man is overtaken in any trespass, you who are spiritual restore such a one in a spirit of gentleness; considering yourself, lest you also be tempted" (Galations 6:1, NKJV).

The lukewarm Christian needs the Spirit's conviction in the area of commitment. He has left his first love. Those who persist in this condition are in danger of being rejected, unless they repent (Rev. 3:16). We must not deceive ourselves about this. If we would help those who are "following Jesus from afar," we must recognize the danger and do what we can to help them get back on track. We are called to speak the truth in love so that those who have become lukewarm may recover themselves from the snare of the devil.

Some useful scriptures to keep in mind when dealing with the lukewarm: Revelation 3:15-16: "I would that you were hot or cold..."; Matthew 6:24: "No man can serve two masters..."; Luke 9:24: "whosoever will save his life shall lose it..."; Matthew 7:21: "not everyone that saith unto me Lord, Lord, shall enter into the kingdom of heaven..."; Revelation 2:2-5: "thou hast left thy first love..."

Avoid the appearance of "pointing" these or any other scriptures at the person. If the shoe fits, the Holy Spirit will make sure that the person "wears it"—though you ought not let on that you are aware of the matter. The same holds true for those described below.

Religious Professors

These are people who think that they are saved because they involve themselves in some outward show of works—going to church, paying tithes, devotion to some social cause, etc., without ever really having given their hearts and lives over to the Lord in trusting, obedient faith. They either live to please themselves (not withstanding their good works) or they harbor some secret sin or sins that they are unwilling to let go of. There is something or someone they love more than God. Ultimately, such affections are an indication of choosing self over God. To pacify their consciences, such people have substituted faith in Christ (if they ever had it) with faith in rituals, traditions, works, i.e., "having a form of godliness but lacking the power thereof."

These people need to be shown the futility of justification by works, or self-righteousness, and that they cannot come to God on their own terms. Many have confused mental assent to the *identity* of Christ with actually surrendering *in faith* to his lordship.

Questions To Help You Identify Religious Professors

1. "Do you believe that people are saved by going to church?"

2. "Do you think that a person can do good works for the Lord and still be lost?"

3. "Can a person believe in Jesus Christ without ever really giving him his heart?"

4. "What must we do to be saved?"

Useful scriptures for dealing with religious (self-righteous) people: Galations 2:16: "for by the works of the law shall no flesh be justified"; Isaiah 64:6: "all our righteousness are as filthy rags"; Romans 3:10-20: "As it is written, there is none righteous, no, not one"; Ephesians 2:8-10: "For by grace are you saved by faith"; Luke 9:23: "If any man will come after me, let him deny himself"; Luke 6:46: "And why call ye me Lord, Lord"; Matthew 7:22-23: "Many people will say unto me in that day…"

Backsliders

It is impossible for the backslider to be happy. When we encounter one who has fallen away from the Lord, we should view such a meeting as divinely appointed. The Father loves his backslidden children and, like the father of the prodigal son, looks "out the gate" longingly, eager to welcome them home.

Backlidden believers have returned to Egypt and found that the promises of pleasure and ease were lies…"the way of transgressors is hard" (Proverbs 13:15). While most backsliders do not need conviction for their sins, they do need conviction for their duty to repent. They also need assurance that God's mercy, forgiveness, and restoring grace are available to them, if they will but return to him. The following are the most frequent causes of backsliding:

1. Doublemindedness – lack of spiritual commitment

2. Procrastination – neglect of the Word and prayer ("Means" of grace)

3. Worldliness – love of money, things, and worldly pleasures

4. Rejection – forsaking Christian fellowship and corruption from evil companions

5. Discouragement – looking at self (and the self's weaknesses) and circumstances instead of to Christ and his sufficiency

Here are some questions to help you recognize those who may be "backslidden." As before, use such questions with discretion (that is, only if you need to), and ask only as many as necessary to help you in your spiritual "diagnosis."

1. "Are you still as close to the Lord as when you first came to him?"

2. "Are you still in fellowship with God's people?"

3. "Is there any area where you have been unable to gain victory?"

   It may be wise to omit direct reference to sin here. People are usually reluctant to admit to sin. However, such responses as, "Well, everybody sins," or, "Nobody's perfect," may be an indication of compromise. While such responses are true in that none of us are perfectly sin-free, we are promised victory from sin's mastery.

Robert Davis

Before we were saved, we desired only sin and chose self-ishness exclusively over God, though we may have done "good things." After salvation, we desire righteousness and want to please the Lord. Of course we struggle with sin and are defeated many times. Yet though we fall, we rise again to renew the struggle. As we learn to regain the victory through faith, our reliance transfers more and more to God and his power. Our heart wants to follow after God, and 1 John 1:9 is a faithful friend and comforter rather than a cloak for hiding affection for sin.

While the sincere Christian will have frequent and long battles with his flesh, he continues hoping in faith for grace to overcome. The backslider, however, has given up the struggle. He has thrown in the towel and is no longer trying to please his Lord. He has gone back to his former devotion to self and selfishness.

4. "Are you are living the way the Bible tells you to live, trusting Jesus to help you?"

Regardless of whether these or similar questions are answered truthfully, conviction will come if the person has lost his first love. Usually, his manner or tone in answering will tell you more than just his words alone.

The following scriptures address the issue of backsliding: Isaiah 1:18: "Though your sins be as scarlet…"; Proverbs 14:14: "The backslider shall be filled with his own ways"; 2 Peter 2:21-22: "For it were better never to have known the way of righteousness…"; Jeremiah 29:13: "You shall seek me, and…find me when you shall search for me with all your heart"; Hosea 14:4: "I will heal their backslidings…"; Isaiah 55:6: "Seek the Lord, while he may be found…"; Isaiah 1:18: "Come now, and let us reason together, says the Lord…"

The Unsaved Ignorant

This refers to those unsaved people who have never heard the gospel, as distinguished from those who have heard but rejected the truth. Most people in America have heard the gospel, probably many times. However, many have not had a personal encounter with Christ through a one-on-one witness from a Christian. Many teenagers, and children especially, have never received a personal witness of what Christ has done for them. There are also many immigrants and foreign visitors who need to hear the good news.

Hearing a salvation message from a television evangelist or a radio preacher, or even through a well-written gospel tract, is not the same as a one-on-one witness from a living, breathing, testimonial of God's grace. A personal invitation to receive Jesus can have a far greater impact than a "general" call.

Those who are ignorant of what the Bible has to say about Christ need to hear a faithful presentation of the truth. Too often Christians get sidetracked when witnessing by issues not directly related to the central message of "Jesus Christ, and him crucified." Sometimes these distractions are caused by the sinner, who is prone to throw up a smokescreen of objections and questions in order to avoid facing his personal need of salvation. But other times, the Christian himself, having no clearly defined objectives when sharing his faith, is vulnerable to pursuing every "rabbit trail" that strikes his fancy!

While we need to be able, as best as we can, to deal with the questions and objections of those who are out of the way, we also need to stay focused on the most important thing—namely, presenting the person of Jesus and urging the lost sinner to receive him. Suggestions for handling the more common excuses and objections are offered below (after the last category, "Unsaved Rejecters").

Unsaved Rejecters

These are people who respond negatively to your invitation to receive Christ. Perhaps they have just listened to a presentation of the gospel from you and have indicated in one way or another that they are not interested. Or maybe you attempted to present the plan of salvation but were not able to because the person would not allow you the opportunity to share the truth with him.

In either case, rejecters need to be warned of the consequences of their rejection. We should show such people what God's Word has to say about the future consequences for those who refuse his offer of mercy. Those consequences are: 1) death; 2) judgment; and 3) hell.

Not every believer will have the fortitude to do this. If you witness to someone and that person refuses your invitation to receive Christ, you are not obligated to take the matter further. If you can do so, well and good. If not, you have still been faithful to present Christ, and God reckons you as a faithful witness. Not everyone has the personality strengths required to warn people. If this is you, you may benefit from rereading the suggestions for leaving one last thought in the chapter on street witnessing.

A word of caution for those who do give "warnings." Use the utmost tact and grace when doing so. Never speak in a strident or imperious manner, and never sound angry. We are never to provoke needless resentment. It is not always possible, however, to avoid such reactions from those who are resisting God's Spirit. In such cases, do not push. Just share what you can, and do your best to leave on a note of grace and good will.

Questions to Help You Identify Rejecters

1. Would you like to invite Christ into your heart today?

2. Do you understand that by saying you are "not ready" you have made a decision to reject Christ, even if it is only for the next five minutes?

3. Do you understand the consequences should you decide not to receive Jesus?

Useful scriptures for dealing with rejecters: Matthew 7:24-27: "Therefore whosoever hears...and does not..."; Matthew 10:28: "...but rather, fear Him who is able to destroy both body and soul in hell"; Mark 9:43-48: "...to go into hell, into the fire that shall never be quenched"; Proverbs 1:24-33: "Because I have called, and you refused..."; Revelation 20:11-15: "And I saw a great white throne..."

A final note of caution: The scriptures above are very terrifying. It is better to read them in such a manner as will help the sinner understand that these are words that God declares to people in general when they choose to reject or turn away from his offer of mercy. Take care not to use these, or any other warning scriptures, as a dagger or sword. This will never happen if such scriptures are shared with gentleness and compassionate concern.

Common Obstacles That Hinder People from Following Christ

There are many things that keep people from committing their lives to Christ. God addresses all of these obstacles either directly or in general terms in his Word. He wants us to arm ourselves with his words so as to be able to pull down the strongholds and barriers sinners erect to hide from him as they seek comfort and fulfillment in their chosen vanities. Only the Word of God can penetrate these barriers of the heart and separate lost sinners from their delusions. Never underestimate the power of God's Word to pierce and divide.

> For the Word of God is quick and powerful, and sharper than any two-edged sword; piercing, even to the dividing asunder of soul and spirit, and of the joints and marrow; and is a discerner of the thoughts and intents of the heart.
>
> Hebrews 2:13

The obstacles listed below form a basic catalogue of problems you will encounter when dealing with people about their need of salvation. One person's list will, of course, differ from another's. Still, most Christians will agree that the obstacles mentioned below would fall in somewhere on their own list of things that commonly hinder sinners from coming to Christ.

This list is followed by a second one listing common excuses and objections that are frequently heard when dealing with the unsaved. A third list, of the parables of Christ, is included with a brief comment on each.

A. Common Problems

1. Procrastination: Putting off the decision to receive Christ (if unsaved); neglecting discipleship (if lukewarm).

   Internal thoughts: "I'm not ready yet..."

   "Maybe when (this or that) happens..."

   Scriptures: Luke 14:16-24: A certain king made a great supper...

   Hebrews 2:3: How shall we escape if we neglect...

   Proverbs 27:1: Boast not thyself of tomorrow...

Luke 12:45: But, and if that wicked servant saith, My Lord delayeth...

2. Worldliness: Lust of other things

   Internal thoughts: "I need to get established financially..."

   "I want (this, that, the other, etc.)"

   Scriptures: Luke 4:7: And some fell among thorns...

   1 John 2:15-16: Love not the world, neither the things ... in the world.

   Luke 18:18-26: And a certain ruler...

3. Cares of this world: Poverty, worldly responsibilities, concerns, etc.

   Internal thoughts: "I have more important things to think about right now."

   "I have to attend to (this and that)."

   Scriptures: Matthew 6:25-34: Seek ye first the kingdom of God...

   Matthew 6:19-21: Lay not up for yourselves treasures on earth...

   Mark 8:36: For what shall it profit a man if he shall gain the whole world...

4. Rebellion: Self-will and self-seeking

   Internal thoughts: "I won't..." (toward God)

   "I will..." (toward self)

Scriptures: Matthew 16:25: Whosoever will save his life shall lose it…

1 Samuel 15:23: For rebellion is as the sin of witchcraft…

2 Thessalonians 1:8-9: In flaming fire taking vengeance on them…

5. Idolatry: Loving anyone or anything more than God

Internal thoughts: "(This or that) is what I (really) want…"

"If only I could have (such and such [or] so and so)"

Scriptures: Romans 1:25: Who worship and serve the creature more than the Creator…

Exodus 20:3: Thou shalt have no other Gods before me.

2 Timothy 3:4: lovers of pleasures more than lovers of God

6. Wrong companions: Consorting with ungodly people

Internal thoughts: "(These) are my kind of people."

"(They) do what I want to do."

Scriptures: Proverbs 13:20: He that is a companion of wise men…

Matthew 7:24-27: He that hears my word and does it… [Note: If we are companions of doers of the Word (wise men), we shall be wise (doers of the Word).]

1 Corinthians 15:33: Evil communications corrupt good manners.

Proverbs 1:10: My son, if sinners entice thee…

2 Corinthians 6:14; What fellowship hath righteousness with unrighteousness

1 John 2:19: If they had been of us, they would...have continued with us.

Hebrews 10:25: Not forsaking the gathering of ourselves together...

7. Fear of man: Being more concerned with man's opinion than God's.

    Internal thoughts: "What will my (friends, family, neighbors, coworkers, boss, etc.) think?"

    Scriptures: Proverbs 29:25: The fear of man bringeth a snare...

    Acts 5:29: We ought to obey God rather than man.

    Mark 8:38: Whoever is ashamed of me, and of my words...

8. Unforgiveness/Bitterness: Against others, self, God

    Internal thoughts: "It's (their/his/her) fault."

    "I (won't/can't) forgive (them/myself/God, etc.)."

    Scriptures: Ephesians 4:32: Forgiving one another, even as God...hath forgiven you.

    Philippians 3:13: forgetting those things which are behind...

    Hebrews 12:15: Lest some evil root of bitterness...

    1 Samuel 45:29: All that are incensed against him shall be ashamed.

9. Rejection: Ruined or lowered self-esteem

Internal thoughts: "I'm not good enough/I hate myself…"

"I don't deserve it…"

"Nobody cares…"

Scriptures: 2 Corinthians 5:17: Therefore, if any man be in Christ…

Ephesians 1:6: …wherein he has made us accepted in the beloved

Philippians 4:13: I can do all things through Christ…

Philippians 1:6: having begun a good work in you, will perform it …

1 John 4:4: greater is he that is in you…

Romans 8:37: in all these things we are more than conquerors…

2 Timothy 4:18: And the Lord shall deliver me from every evil work…

10. Discouragement: Fear of Failure

    Internal thoughts: "I can't make it…"

    " I can't go on…"

    " What if (this or that) happens…"

    Scriptures: Galations 6:19: Let us not grow weary in well doing…

    Romans 14:4: God is able to make him stand…

    Jude 24: Him that is able to keep you from falling…

    Isaiah 54:17: No weapon formed against me…

2 Timothy 1:7: For God hath not given me a spirit of fear...

11. Sexual sins: Lust, fornication, adultery, perversion, etc.

Internal thoughts: Sinful sexual fantasies of every variety

Scriptures: Galations 6:7-8: Be not deceived; God is not mocked...

1 Corinthians 6:9-10: no fornicator, nor unclean person...

Galations 6:19-21: they which do these things...shall not inherit the kingdom

Ephesians 5:5-7: because of these things cometh the wrath of God...

Galations 5:16-17: walk in the spirit and ye shall not fulfill...

12. Vain philosophies: False doctrines and false religions

Internal thoughts: "I have my own (beliefs, religion, etc,)

"There's more than one way to God."

Scriptures: Proverbs 16:25: There is a way that seemeth right...

John 14:6: I am the way, the truth, and the life...

Galations 1:8: But though we or an angel...preach any other gospel...

1 Peter 1:16: we have not followed cunningly devised fables...

Matthew 7:13-14: broad is the path that leadeth to destruction...

B. Common Excuses and Objections

This list of excuses and objections, as well as the obstacles mentioned above, are not intended to be complete. They are sufficient to serve as a basic reference guide. To utilize them to maximum effect, you may wish to list each "problem," "excuse," and "objection" neatly in the back of your Bible, along with the appropriate scriptures for dealing with them.

If you have limited space, then you may do one of two things: Either list the first scripture for each situation in the back, using the "chain" method for the remainder (list the second reference alongside the text of the first, the third reference alongside the text of the second, and so on), or you may make your lists on paper, reducing the size as necessary on a copier, until the sheets are compatible with the size of your Bible. (You may also use Microsoft Word or some other program on your computer and print it out.) When you are done, simply tape them together on one side (as a little "carry along" insert) or tape them into the back of your Bible for easy reference. This will greatly enhance your ability to be "instant, in season and out" with the Word!

1. "I have my own opinions…"

    John 14:6: I am the way, the truth, and the life…

    Mark 16:15-16: He that believes not shall be damned…

    Acts 4:12: …there is no other name under heaven…

2. "I'm busy right now…"

    Hebrews 2:3: How shall we escape if we neglect…

    Luke 14:16-24: they all with one consent began to make excuse…

3. "I go to church…"

John 3:3-6: except a man be born again…

Matthew 7:24-27: He that hears my word and does it…

Romans 2:13: …not the hearers of the word shall be justified…

4. "I believe in God…"

James 2:19: …devils also believe, and tremble…

James 2:14-17: faith, if it hath not works, is dead…

5. "I don't think we should push religion…"

Mark 16:15: Go into all the world, and preach the gospel to every creature…

Luke 11:23: He that gathers not with me, scatters…

6. "There's too many hypocrites…"

Romans 14:12: So then, everyone of us shall give account of himself

Romans 2:1: wherein you judge another, you condemn yourself…

7. "I have to think about it…"

Hebrews 3:15: Today, if you will hear his voice, harden not your heart…

2 Corinthians 6:2: Now is the acceptable time, today is the day of salvation.

Isaiah 55:6: Seek the Lord while he may be found…

8. "My time will come…"

James 4:13-14: Go to you that say…

Tomorrow we will…

Proverbs 27:1: Boast not of tomorrow…

2 Corinthians 6:2: Now is the acceptable time…

9. "The Bible was written by man…"

2 Timothy 3:16: All scripture is given by inspiration from God…

2 Peter 1:21: for the prophecy came, not by the will of man…

Mark 13:31: Heaven and earth shall pass away, but my Word…

Psalm 138:2: For you hast magnified your Word above all your name…

Hebrews 4:12: For the Word of God is quick and powerful…

Psalm 12:2: The words of the Lord are pure…

Psalm 119:89: Your Word is settled forever in Heaven.

Isaiah 40:8: The grass withers, and the flower fades…

10. "What if I try and fail?"

Proverbs 24:16: A righteous man falls seven times and rises again.

2 Timothy 4:18: the Lord shall deliver me from every evil work…

Philippians 4:13: I can do all things through Christ…

Romans 14:4: is able to make him stand.

Matthew 19:26: With men this is impossible; but with God all things are possible.

11. "It's too hard to be a Christian."

    Matthew 11:29-30: my yoke is easy and my burden is light.

    Proverbs 13:15: The way of the transgressor is hard.

12. "I can't give up my evil ways."

    Luke 13:3: Except you repent, you shall all likewise perish.

    Ezekiel 36:25-27: a new heart also will I give you…

    Proverbs 29:1: he that being often reproved…

    Hebrews 3:8: harden not your heart…

    Matthew 3:9: God is able of these stones…

13. "I don't understand."

    Proverbs 3:5: Trust in the Lord with all your heart…

    Philippians 2:5: Let this mind be in you which was…in Christ Jesus.

14. "What will my friends think?"

    Proverbs 29:25: the fear of man bring a snare…

    Mark 8:38: whosoever is ashamed of me…

15. "My (pastor, teacher, parents, friend, etc.) says…"

    2 Timothy 2:15: Study to show yourself approved to God…

    Isaiah 2:22: Cease from man…

Acts 17:11: These were more noble than those of Thessalonica…

16. "There are other things in life besides religion."

Matthew 7:13-14: broad is the path…that leads to destruction…

Mark 8:35: For whosoever will save his life shall lose it.

Mark 8:36: For what shall it profit a man if he shall gain the whole world…

17. "I'm too young to think about it…"

Ecclesiastes 12:1-7: Remember now thy Creator, in your youth…

Isaiah 55:6: Seek the Lord, while He may be found…

Proverbs 27:1: Boast not yourself of tomorrow…

18. "What about the heathen in Africa…"

Romans 8:29-30: those whom He foreknew, He also called…

Romans 9:20: who are you that replies against God?

Romans 14:12: So then, every one of us shall give an account of himself to God.

19. "I don't feel that (this or that) is wrong.

Proverbs 21:2: Every way of man is right in his own eyes…

Jeremiah 17:9: The heart is desperately wicked and deceitful…

Proverbs 14:12: There is a way that seems right to a man…

2 Timothy 3:16-17: All scripture is given by inspiration of God...

20. "Why did God allow (such and such) to happen?

    Job 4:17: Shall mortal man be more righteous than God?

    2 Samuel 22:31: As for God, His way is perfect.

    Job 33:13: He gives not account of any of His matters...

21. "Why do all the preachers talk about money?

    Romans 14:12: everyone shall give account of himself...

    Romans 14:13: judge no man; but judge this, rather...

    John 21:22: What is that to you? Follow me.

22. "Everybody sins..."

    1 John 3:8: He that commit sin is of the devil.

    Romans 6:7: He that is dead is freed from sin.

    Proverbs 28:13: He that covers his sins shall not prosper.

    Romans 6:10-11: For in that he died he died unto sin once...

    Romans 6:2: how shall we who are dead to sin...

    Romans 6:14: For sin shall not have dominion over you...

    Colossians 3:3: For you are dead and your life is hid in Christ.

23. "Why does everybody interpret the Bible differently?"

    2 Timothy 2:15: study to show yourself approved unto God...

2 Timothy 3:15: the scriptures, which are able to make you wise…

24. "The Bible is full of contradictions."

2 Timothy 3:16: All scripture is given by inspiration of God…

Psalm 12:6: The words of the Lord are pure words…

Psalm 19:7: The law of the Lord is perfect…

25. "I'm not a bad person."

Isaiah 64:6: all our righteousness is as filthy rags…

Romans 3:10-20: there is none righteous, no, not on.

Isaiah 53:6: All we like sheep have gone astray…

26. "I don't believe in hell."

Mark 9:43-46: where the worm dies not, and the fire is not quenched…

Matthew 13:40-42: shall be cast into a furnace of fire…

Revelation 20:15: and whosoever was not found written in the book of life…

27. "God's too good to send people to hell."

Luke 12:5: Fear Him who has power to destroy both body and soul in hell.

Revelation 20:15: and whosoever was not found written in the book of life…

Galations 6:7: Be not deceived; God is not mocked…

Numbers 14:18: The Lord is longsuffering...yet that shall by no means clear the guilty.

2 Thessalonians 1:8: in flaming fire taking vengeance...

Romans 9:22: What if God, willing to show His wrath...

28. "Obedience isn't necessary to be accepted."

Hebrews 5:9: gives eternal salvation to all who obey Him.

Matthew 7:21: Not everyone...shall enter...but he who does the will of the Father...

29. "I'm an (atheist/agnostic)."

Psalm 14:1: The fool has said in his heart, There is no God.

John 7:16-17: If any man will do the doctrine he will know...

30. "I don't care to discuss it with you."

1 John 4:6: he who is not of God does not hear us.

Matthew 10:40: He that receives you receives me...

C. The Parables of Jesus

The following is a list of Christ's parables, in which he clarifies the conditions and requirements for being his disciple. The parables of Jesus are among the most neglected and yet most powerful weapons we have been given to pull down the strongholds Satan has erected in the hearts of people to keep them from coming to, and walking with, Christ. The themes dealt with are universal in their application, exposing hidden motives as well as right and wrong priorities and values in the light of God's coming kingdom.

1. Matthew 22:1-14: The Parable of the Marriage Feast

   (Illustrates the need to respond when God calls)

2. Matthew 13:3-9, 18-23: The Parable of the Sower

   (Illustrates the need to let the Word take root in our heart)

3. Matthew 13:44: The Parable of the Hid Treasure

   (Illustrates the properness of forsaking all to follow Christ)

4. Matthew 13:45-46: The Parable of the Pearl of Great Price

   (Illustrates the properness of forsaking all to follow Christ)

5. Matthew 13:31-32: The Parable of the Mustard Seed

   (Illustrates effect of sowing to the Spirit)

6. Matthew 13:33: The Parable of the Leaven

   (Illustrates effect of sowing to the Spirit)

7. Matthew 7:24-27: The Parable of the Two Houses

   (Illustrates the need to be doers and not hearers only)

8. Matthew 21:28-32: The Parable of the Two Sons

   (Illustrates the importance of doing the will of the Father)

9. John 15:1-6: The Parable of the Vine and the Branches

   (Illustrates the need to abide in Christ)

10. Luke 15:11-32: The Parable of the Prodigal Son

    (Illustrates God's mercy to repentant backsliders)

11. Luke 18:9-14: The Parable of the Pharisee and the Publican

    (Illustrates rejection of the self-righteous)

12. Matthew 13:47-50: The Parable of the Good and Bad Fruit

    (Illustrates the need to bring forth good fruit)

13. Luke 16:1-12: The Parable of the Unjust Steward

    (Illustrates the need for faithful stewardship)

14. Luke 18:1-7: The Parable of the Importunate Widow

    (Illustrates the need for steadfast prayer)

15. Luke 10:30-37: The Parable of the Good Samaritan

    (Illustrates responsibility for our neighbor's welfare)

16. Matthew 18:21-3: The Parable of the Unforgiving Servant

    (Illustrates the necessity of forgiving others)

17. Matthew 25:14-30: The Parable of the Talents

    (Illustrates the need to be faithful and diligent)

18. Matthew 20:1-16: The Parable of the Laborers in the Vineyard

    (Illustrates equality of the saved and mercy toward sincere latecomers)

19. Matthew 25:31-46: The Parable of the Sheep and the Goats

    (Illustrates the importance of loving in deed and truth)

Robert Davis

20. Matthew 25:1-13: The Parable of the Ten Virgins

(Illustrates the need to abide in Christ and be ready at his appearing)

(Appendix C)

Survey Says…

The following suggestions are offered as guidelines to help you make your own surveys. Surveys, except when used as tracts or as inserts in letters (both great ideas!), should be used as a means to an end…namely, to help you converse with and witness to people. Therefore, it is important to be flexible when using surveys, or petitions, so as to be sensitive to people's needs. Do not be in bondage to your surveys, but allow them to be tools to help you relate to people and to communicate the gospel.

Step One: *Determine the theme of your survey*. You may, for example, just want to have a general survey to inquire about peoples' church affiliation and spiritual background. Or you may wish to develop a more specific survey to inquire about a person's particular beliefs on a given topic. Surveys may be used to focus a person's attention on any part of the gospel or on any subject of the Bible. Some examples:

1. Your questions may deal with a person's *attitudes about the Bible.*

2. Your questions may deal with a person's *beliefs about the return and Bible prophecy.*

3. Your questions may deal with a person's *beliefs about what it means to live for Christ.*

Step Two: *Develop questions related to the subject* and form them in such a way as to direct people's thoughts to the importance of the subject to their own lives. Questions may be constructed in such a way as to leave little room for a wrong answer. This will tend to cause the person, when answering, to become convicted by his own responses. For example:

1. If the Bible is God's Word, what should that mean to us?

2. Can we form an opinion about Jesus without reading what he says in the Bible?

3. If Christ really rose from the dead, what should that mean to us?

4. What should a Christian be like?

Step Three: *Start with questions which are "less threatening,"* and increase the "spirituality" with each one. In other words, move from questions of a general nature to ones that are more personal.

Step Four: *Close with a question about the person's spiritual condition.* (Usually, but not always.)

The following surveys may serve as examples, or you may use them as they are. As you ask the questions compare the person's answers to the Word and adapt your responses accordingly.

Example Survey One

1. Do you attend church anywhere? Are you a regular attender?

2. What do you like most about your church? (Or, if not attending church) Why not?

3. What role do you feel God has called you to play in your church fellowship? (Or, if not a church goer) What would cause you to want to go to a church?

4. Do the other people in your family attend church with you? (Or, if not attending) Does anyone in your family go to church?

5. Do you believe in your heart that you would go to heaven if you died today? Can you say why you feel this way?

Example Survey Two

1. Do you believe that the Bible is the Word of God

2. Do you believe what the Bible teaches about the fall of man? About Christ? About heaven and hell?

3. Can we know God's will for our life without a knowledge of his Word?

4. What does God want you to do?

5. Are you ready to give an account of yourself to God?

Example Survey Three

1. What does it mean to be a true Christian?

2. What is your understanding of Jesus's declaration: "If anyone will come after me, let him deny himself, and take up his cross daily, and follow me"?

3. How should the lifestyle of a Christian be different from that of an unbeliever?

4. Do you feel that you are living the lifestyle of a true Christian?

5. What would Jesus say to you if he were standing right here?

Example Survey Four

1. Have you ever thought about the Bible prophecies in the book of Revelation?

2. What do you think will happen in the last days if the book of Revelation is true?

3. Do you think we are living in the last days right now?

4. Do you believe in the literal return of Christ?

5. What will happen to you when Jesus come back?

Keep in mind that each of these questions has the potential to develop a fruitful conversation. Allow the person sufficient time to respond, and be sure to listen so as to relate to what he says before moving on to the next question. If the person is not responsive and does not show interest, you may simply ask the last question. Leave on a positive note. (If you have copies of your survey, you might offer one to the person to take with him.)

How to Make and Use Petitions

Petitions are effective instruments for promoting "Christian consciousness" in areas of concern to us as believers. Of course, the Holy Spirit will also use our petitions to address the spiritual condition of each person with whom we converse.

Petitions may be circulated to promote awareness of various issues of moral and social concern, or simply to stimulate people to give thought to the underlying spiritual significance of the particular issue raised. In other words, petitions of a "Christian" nature (related to issues of social and personal morality) will tend to cause people to reflect upon their relationship to Christ.

While abortion, school prayer, and pornography are perhaps the "big three" that first come to mind when referring to "Christian" petitions, there are any number of other candidate causes that may be promoted. Revitalizing decaying communities, clearing out drug dealers from local parks, protesting the secularization of public school textbooks, and many other issues have been legitimate causes for petitioning civic, governmental, and even spiritual action within the church community. Here are some guidelines to assist you when making your own petitions:

1. Look up scriptures related to the issue to be addressed by your petition so you will know what the Word says.

2. Study Christian literature on the subject, and be prepared to distribute this or some other related information with your petition.

3. Formulate your own petition based on your study, or use one already in circulation.

4. Practice on a friend if you need to, and then *go out and do it!*

Soliciting petition signatures may be a preliminary means of reaching your community with the gospel, or a means of revisiting those already contacted. By using different approaches (surveys, petitions, offers of Christian literature, etc., see Part Two, "Dwelling in Ceiled Houses: Does God Really Go Door to Door?"), you increase the possibility for establishing relationships that may lead people to Christ and hopefully into active fellowship with your church as well.

(Appendix D)

Letters in Lights

The following three example letters are short messages to be distributed by different means. Your letters may be short or long, one page (even one sentence) or many pages, covering multiple topics. Do what you like, and use your own style. That's what God wants!

Example Letter #1

Dear Friend,

Today I chose your name out of the phone book. There were thousands of names to choose from, but I find myself writing to you. I do not know you. But God does. He has been watching over you all of your life, and he is watching over you now.

Jesus wants you to let him love you. I would like to write down some scriptures for you to look up in your Bible. If you will do this and believe what you read, God will make himself known to you *in a new way*. Jesus wants to give you a life of love and joy and peace. Will you let him?

[List scriptures you feel impressed to write down. Avoid limiting yourself to "salvation" scriptures only.]

Example Letter #2
(Given Directly to a Teenager)

Hi,

You're wondering what this letter is about and why I gave it to you. I wrote it last night and asked God to show me who to give it to. You're the one! He was thinking of you when he told me to tell you in this letter that...*he loves you!* You were asleep while I was writing, but God was awake, watching over you. There is someone he wants to send into your life to help you find your way safely home to him. This person is *the only one who can bring us back to God.* I think you know his name. He was thinking of you when he died. If you have never met him, he is knocking on the door of your heart right now. Just ask him. He will hear you, and when he comes in, *he will be with you forever.* He will never leave you or forsake you. So go to the door and open it. He's standing there, waiting...

Example Letter #3 (Left in a Public Place)

Hi ! I'm sure you're surprised to find this message in your hands. I asked God to give it to you. *That's why you found it before anyone else did!* God wants you to know how much he loves you and how very special you are to him.

Have you talked to him today? God wants to be your heavenly Father. He sent Jesus (you remember him, don't you) to bring you back to himself. Do you remember why Jesus died on the cross? I think you do...our sins made it necessary for him to suffer our punishment because God did not want us to have to pay the price ourselves.

Eternity is a long time. Our time on the earth is very short. Christ's return is very near. Are you ready to meet him? If he lives in your heart, you will look forward to his return. But don't wait until it is too late! God loves you, and he wants you to choose life. Choose Jesus and live!

Example Letter Questionnaire

The following questionnaire may serve as an example to guide you in making your own, using the technique demonstrated here. Formulate a series of provocative spiritual questions and then give the reader some appropriate scripture references to look up the "answers." The powerful impulse of curiosity (energized by the Spirit of God) will compel her to look up the scriptures on her own. Questionnaires such as these may be used as supplementary material included with your letter, or as letters in their own right.

What Do You Think?

1. Does the Bible indicate that there are many ways to God? (John 14:6)

2. Will God be pleased with our good works if were are sincere and do our best? (Isaiah 64:6)

3. What if I have different religious beliefs than what the Bible says? (Proverbs 16:25)

4. What does Christ say about my life if I am building it on something besides his Word? (Matthew 7:24-27)

5. What if I think the idea of Christ actually returning to the earth is unlikely? (2 Peter 3:3)

6. What did Jesus say would become of those who choose not to follow him? (1 Thess. 1:8-9)

7. Where can I find hope? (Matthew 11:28)

(Appendix E)

More Stuff for Kids

Guidelines For Making Your Own Teaching Lessons

The following suggestions may be helpful when you are preparing your own teaching material. Remember, you do not need to have a "special gift" with children, just a willingness to be used and a simple trust in God to guide you.

1. *Pray and ask God to impress upon your heart a theme or a topic.* Ask yourself such questions as, "What is important for these children to know about God right now?"; "What stories in the Bible illustrate lessons of special significance to children?"; "What scriptures seem to be especially useful for helping children to trust in Jesus?"

2. *Choose a scripture verse that best illustrates the meaning of the Bible lesson or story.* Use this scripture as your "memory verse." (Note: Be sure to choose a translation or rendering of the verse that is easily understandable.)

3a. *If you are doing a Bible lesson*, examine the verse closely and think of one or two practical examples of how this verse may be positively applied to one's life; then, think of one or two examples of how the verse might be negatively "applied" to one's life, either through neglect of the principle taught or direct disobedience of it.

3b. *If you are doing a Bible story*, use the central actions or responses of the main characters as the source for your positive and negative examples and illustrations.

4. Follow your illustration with *a challenge for the children to give examples from their own lives* of how they might positively or negatively apply the lesson.

5. *Share one or two examples of blessings* that come to us through obedience to the principle or lesson taught, *and one or two examples of possible negative consequences* of neglect of, or disobedience to, the principle or lesson.

6. Have the children thoroughly memorize the memory verse.

7. *Pray with the children.* You may have each child pray individually or as a group, asking God for help to apply the lesson she has learned.

8. *Pass out any review materials at the end of the meeting.*

Guidelines For Sharing Your Testimony

Occasionally you may wish to share part of your testimony with the children or have one of your helpers do so when it seems to be appropriate for the lesson theme. The suggestions that follow are offered to help you to relate your testimony to the Bible lesson.

1. *Consult the person who will be teaching to find out what the lesson theme will be.*

2. *Pray and ask the Holy Spirit to show you how your personal life experience relates to the lesson being taught.* (For example: If the lesson is on obeying your parents, reflect upon incidences of both obedience and disobedience in your

relationship with your parents; if the lesson is on faith, recall examples of when you experienced victory because of your faith and also times when you experienced setbacks because of your doubts or unbelief.)

3. *When sharing with the children, cite these past experiences* in which you either applied or failed to apply the lesson or principle taught by the teacher. Be sure to share the consequences of your actions, both good and bad. Reinforce the lesson by relating it in practical terms to your testimony.

4. *Tell the kids how you learned to obey in the area the lesson dealt with and how Jesus helped you.*

5. If time permits, *ask some children to share experiences of their own.* Be sure to keep them focused on the theme of the lesson.

6. *Pray with the children.* Encourage them to confess any disobedience to God, trusting him for forgiveness and help to grow.

Guidelines For Leading Children to Christ

This outline emphasizes God's love for his children, our broken relationship with him, his desire for the restoration of that relationship, and the provision he has made for us in Christ. Every Christian should understand the importance of being able to clearly present the truths of the gospel. It is, after all, the good news we are called to give to the world.

Children, many of whom will be hearing the truth for the first time, deserve to be given a worthy and well thought-out presentation of the gospel so that from life's beginning they can know the comfort of God's love and his provision for their everlasting happiness.

I) Who is God? He is our creator and the Creator of all of the earth, the universe, and all living things. Describe the beauty of creation and God's loving hand in making us. Be sure to emphasize that when God made the world, he pronounced it "good," and after making man, he declared that creation to be "very good." This is important because the evil we see in the world today was not there in the beginning of God's creation.

II) Why did God make us? God is love, and because of his loving nature, he wanted to share the gift of life with beings who would be capable of having a love relationship with him. This is why God made us, so that we could be loved by him and love him in return. This is the reason we exist. Tell the child that God longs to be our heavenly Father. He wants to love us, watch over and protect us, and lead us and guide us into all good things. In return, he desires our love and reverence.

This is a good time to tell the children about heaven, the special place that God has prepared for us to live forever with him at the end of our earthly lives. Describe what heaven will be like, a place where everyone will be happy all the time, where everyone will be kind and loving to each other, and where there will be no more death, sorrow, or suffering of any kind. (Note: It is important to describe heaven before the story of man's fall because heaven should be introduced before telling children about the "other" place.)

III) Something has happened to prevent this relationship. When God made man, he placed him in a garden paradise called Eden. At the dawn of man's history, he chose to turn his back on the very one who had made him by rebelling against his Maker. Tell the children the story of man's fall from grace. Describe how Adam and Eve, our first parents, chose to listen to and follow the evil suggestions of the serpent (embodied by Satan) over the will of God. They chose to forsake God's way and to follow their own way of selfishness. This is what the Bible calls sin—choosing our way over God's. Point out that the motive of all sin is selfishness, preferring our own selfish way above God's, which is always unselfish and good. Help the children to understand that all human beings, including themselves, have sinned and are, therefore, guilty before God. Give some examples that each child can relate to, incidents in which *he* has sinned.

It is important that children know this story because it is the reason why the world is full of evil, tragedy, and death; these things came as a result of sin. Young children are gradually awakening to the darker side of life—some all too soon. The fall explains the reason things are this way while also setting the stage for God's loving provision to restore man to his former state of honor and right standing with his Maker.

IV) Explain the consequences of sin: separation from God forever. Because God is holy, just (fair), and good, he cannot have fellowship with those who choose to sin and rebel against his goodness. Therefore, He has made a place to separate those who choose to reject Him from His presence and from the presence of those who choose to follow him. This place of separation is called hell. Tell the children that this is a place where no one is happy because they are separated from God forever. Help them to understand that this is fair of God because those who go to hell did not want anything to do with him or his people in their earthly lives. These people must be separated from those who chose to love and follow God because he does not want them to hurt his people by their sinful behavior. (Do not linger on the topic of hell. Briefly describe it and move on.)

V) Because of God's great love for us, he has made a way for us to be restored into a right relationship with him. Though our sins have separated us from God and deserve his just punishment, he has made a provision for us to be forgiven through the death of his Son Jesus Christ on the cross. Explain to the child that Jesus took the punishment that our sins deserved. During his earthly life, Jesus lived in perfect obedience to the will of his heavenly Father. He never sinned, not even once. And so he did not deserve to be crucified. Yet he allowed sinful men to put him to death, knowing that in the eyes of God, his death would be an acceptable sacrifice and a substitute for the punishment that we deserved.

Emphasize that no one can deserve to go to heaven by being good enough because we are already guilty sinners. Each of us has committed many sins in his lifetime. Give some examples the children can relate to, i.e., lying, disobeying our parents, being mean to others, etc. Salvation is available to us, however, as a free gift from God, by receiving Christ into our hearts and trusting in his sacrificial death on our behalf.

VI) Explain that each person has a choice to make: to receive Christ or to reject him. God desires for all to be saved. He wants us to receive his Son into our hearts and to trust in the sacrifice that he made for our sins. But he will not make us do so.

Explain what it means to receive Christ. Tell the child that Jesus wants to come into his life and to live inside of him (in his heart). He wants to be our best friend always.

And he wants us to trust him with our lives. To receive him, we must repent of our sins (by no longer wanting to do them) and turn to Jesus in faith that he receives us and forgives us. We must want Jesus and his will for our lives more than sin and our old, selfish way of living. When we do this, God accepts us, forgives our sins, and makes us his very own children.

God also gives us a new heart and a new spirit that desires to follow him. Our old, sinful nature will still try to lead us into sin and wrongdoing, but God forgives us when we confess our sins, and he will help us as we trust in Jesus. And as we learn to rely on the Lord to help us, instead of trusting in our own strength, God will cause us grow stronger and stronger.

VIII) Invite the child to receive Christ. Tell her how to invite Christ into her heart…by simply asking him to come in. Help her to understand that though she cannot see Jesus (he is invisible), he is still a real person and he will come into our hearts when we ask him to.

Do not force or coerce the child to pray. If she wants to receive Jesus, prayer is just a way for her to ask him to come into her heart. Be sure to point out that it is not the prayer that saves, but the person of Jesus Christ. The prayer is an invitation we give to Jesus to come into our hearts if we really want to trust and follow him. If we don't want to trust and follow him, then saying the prayer would be meaningless. (Saying this will keep the child focused on the person prayed to rather than on the prayer itself.) If we are sincere, however, Jesus will hear our prayers and come into our hearts. As we trust and follow him, he will lead us safely on the path that God has for our life.

VIIIa) If the child refuses to invite Christ into his heart, gently remind him of the consequences of his decision, emphasizing the resulting separation from God more than the reality of hell (you already mentioned hell). Do not linger over the point. Tell the child that he can still change his decision but that no one is promised tomorrow—not even children. You may ask the child one more time after explaining this, but again, avoid coercion. The decision must come from his heart because of his appreciation for the truth and the Spirit's conviction, not because of your persuasiveness or pressure.

VIIIb) If the child does receive Christ, explain that he now has a wonderful home waiting for him in heaven and that Jesus also has a whole new life in store for him here on earth, a life planned out for him by his loving heavenly Father who wants only the best for him. Tell the child that God will begin to teach him what his will for his life is—through his Word, through Bible teachers, and by impressing his heart. The Lord will teach him to follow after what is good and to turn away from evil. Explain that God blesses us as we obey him and, because he loves us, he disciplines us if we sin. He does this so that we will learn to choose the good and refuse the evil. Close by telling him that the angels in heaven are rejoicing over him because of his decision to receive Christ!

Ten Important Truths For Children to Understand After Salvation

All of these truths are familiar to us. They are offered to help inexperienced teachers focus on foundational lessons which children, like all of us, need to understand as early as possible in their new life in Christ.

I) God is now our heavenly Father, watching over us, loving us, and protecting us. When we received Christ, we were "born again." Our first birth was to our earthly parents. Our second birth is to our heavenly Father. Our earthly parents are our parents only as long as we are on this earth. Our heavenly Father, on the other hand, will be our Father throughout all eternity. As important as our relationship to our earthly parents is, our relationship to our heavenly Father is even more important. He is our Creator, our Savior through Christ, and our heavenly Father. While we love, respect, and obey our earthly parents, our first love should be to our heavenly Father who gave us our parents!

II) Christ is now in us, leading us and guiding us. When we received Christ, he came to live on the inside of us. Now, wherever we go, he is not only with us, but in us. He will lead us and guide us as a shepherd guides his sheep. He is the Good Shepherd, who gave his life for the sheep (us). We can trust him who died for us to lead us in ways that are best for us. We should thank the Lord every day for his guidance and protection. He has promised he will never leave us or forsake us.

III) We are now in Christ, receiving his nature, his ability, and his provision. Not only is Christ in us, leading and guiding and protecting us, but we are also in him. This means that, 1) we are who God says we are in Christ... he says that we are new creatures, with God's nature and love on the inside of us; 2) we have what God says we have in Christ. He says that we have everything we need in and through him. This means that we will not lack for anything because God supplies all of our needs in (and through) Christ; and, 3) we can do what God says we can do through Christ. His Word says that we can do all things (that God wants us to do) through Christ who strengthens us!

IV) God talks to us through his Word, the Bible. God tells us that the sincere milk of his Word will cause us to grow. We need the spiritual nourishment of God's Word just as much as a baby needs her mother's milk. The Bible reveals to us, 1) Who God is. Without the Bible's revelation of who God is and what he is like, we might simply end up worshiping a god of our own imagination. Millions of people do just that; they make up their own ideas about God and what he is like and how to please him. God, however, only accepts those who worship him according to his Word, the Holy Bible; 2) What God has done for us through Christ—how Jesus became our substitute, dying on the cross for our sins; and how he (God) gives us a new life in Christ, a life of holiness and obedience to his will for our lives; and 3) What God expects from us, that we give ourselves in faith and submission to Christ who died for us, committing ourselves to follow him and his plan for our lives no matter what the cost. God's Word not only shows us how to live a life that is pleasing to him; it also enables and empowers us to do so because his words are spirit and life to us!

V) We talk to God in prayer. Fellowship is a two-way sharing. God created us to have fellowship with him. Therefore, our highest calling in life is to fellowship with God. He is the reason for our existence, and he alone can satisfy our souls. We should talk to God first every day, thanking him for his many blessings and loving him for who he is. Our heavenly Father wants to be loved for himself, and not just for what we can "get" from him. He does want us, however, to tell him our needs and to ask him for our daily provisions. We need to know that we may go to God at anytime and in any place, being confident that he will hear us. When we worship God, telling him that we love him and singing songs of praise to him, we are filled with the sense of his presence and blessing and peace. We may then face all of the uncertainties of life with confidence, knowing that God will be there to bring us through to victory.

VI) We have an enemy: the devil. The devil is God's archenemy—and ours! God is good, and he loves us. The devil is evil, and he hates us. God did not create the devil evil. He was originally a chief angel in heaven, Lucifer, who sought to overthrow the throne of God. He chose his own way, instead of God's. When he did so, God cast him out of heaven, and he became an evil being called the devil and Satan, and the god of this world. Now Satan, together with the fallen angels who rebelled against God with him, seeks revenge against God by trying to steal from us, to kill us, and to destroy us. Satan does this by trying to get God's people to choose his ways instead of God's. However, through Christ we have the power to resist the devil and his temptations. We are to stand against Satan by relying upon the power of God and by using the name of Jesus against him. When we do this, the devil must flee, for Christ has brought us victory over him (and sin) through his death and resurrection.

VII) God wants us to honor him by loving and obeying him. God wants us to show our love for him by doing what he tells us to do: "For this is the love of God, that we keep his commandments" (1 John 5:3). If we sin, we are to confess our sins to God, trusting him to forgive us and to cleanse us from all unrighteousness (1 John 1: 9). We show God that we love him by obeying him, confessing our sins when we do wrong, and choosing to resist sin by trusting in Jesus to help us. We have no ability of our own, but we receive all that we need through relying on Jesus. God "works in us both to will and to do of his good pleasure" (Philippians 2:13). Our loving obedience to our heavenly Father honors him and glorifies him, because the goodness of his will and plan for all men and women is only revealed in the lives of those who choose to love and obey him. The lives of those who reject God grow darker with each passing day. But we who choose to love and serve our Maker see our paths become "like the shining sun, that shines ever brighter unto the perfect day" (Proverbs 4:18, NKJV).

VIII) God wants us to love our brothers and sisters in Christ, and to become a part of a local church. In 1 John 4:20, God tells us that we prove our love to him, whom we cannot see, by loving our brothers (and sisters), who we can see. The only way we can love our brothers and sisters in the family of God is by being around them and by doing good to them. If we deliberately (by our own choice—obviously children whose parents do not take them to church or allow them to go are not responsible) separate ourselves from our brothers and sisters in Christ, we are separating ourselves from any opportunity to show love to them, and therefore, we are missing any opportunity to show God that we love him! "And this commandment we have from Him: that he who loves God must love his brother also" (1 John 4:21, NKJV).

IX) God wants us to be his special representatives to those who do not know him, to those who have not received Jesus and who therefore are not saved. We love them by showing kindness to them and by telling them about Jesus, trusting God to help us do this. We also show our love for unsaved people by praying for them to come to know Christ.

X) God wants us to obey our parents. This is one of the most important ways that we can please God. We are commanded to obey our parents. This is the first commandment God ever gave with a promise attached to it—that if you obey your parents, "it may be well with you and you may live long on the earth" (Ephesians 6:3, NKJV).

God's promise is that we may have a long and happy life when we honor and obey our parents. The only exception to this rule of obedience is if our parents deliberately try to make us commit sin or do wrong. In such instances, we are to obey God instead. Yet even here we are to maintain a humble and submissive attitude toward our parents, as we respectfully explain why we do not want to sin against God. When this happens, we will also want to pray for our parents so that the Lord may work things out for us.

Guidelines for Creating Puppet Skits

The following suggestions are offered to help when you need or want to create your own puppet skit material. Consult the person who will be teaching to find out the lesson theme.

Format One

A. Create two puppet characters—one representing a person who is obedient to the lesson; the other representing a character who is disobedient.

B. Have the obedient character teach the lesson to the disobedient one by briefly summarizing what was taught.

C. Have the disobedient character either reject the lesson and show forth bad fruit as a result of doing so, or have him receive the lesson and show forth good fruit as a result.

Format Two

A. Create a puppet character who plays the role of someone who has just learned the lesson with the kids.

B. Have the puppet review the lesson by affirming its value in his life and how the application of what he has learned will help him in the future.

C. Have the puppet ask the children questions that will cause them to think about how they may apply the lesson to their own lives.

Format Three

A. Create a puppet character who plays the role of someone who wants to know what the teacher just taught.

B. Have the puppet ask the children questions about the lesson that will allow them to "teach" what they have just learned to the puppet.

C. Have the puppet ask the kids simple questions that will allow them to teach the puppet how to apply the lesson to his own life.

Format Four

A. Create a character representing the devil, who comes on the scene to oppose the Word that just went forth.

B. Have him ask questions, attempting to get the children to misunderstand the lesson; make the errors obvious. Let the children catch him in his lies and resist him with the truth.

C. Have the devil try to talk the children out of obeying the lesson.

D. Have the class leader encourage the children to reject the devil's suggestions and tell him to leave in Jesus's name.

Format Five

A. Have the children teach one or more of the puppets the memory verse from the lesson, after they have learned it themselves.

B. Have the puppet(s) ask the kids to explain the meaning of the verse. (If none of the children volunteer to explain it, have the puppets offer "right" and "wrong" interpretations of the verse, and have the kids agree or disagree.)

Format Six

A. Have a puppet share her testimony to an "unsaved" puppet friend in such a way that the benefits of the lesson are reviewed.

B. Then have the "Christian" puppet lead her unsaved friend to receive Jesus.

Format Seven

A. Have three puppets in a "To Tell the Truth" format, each claiming to be the "true" believer.

B. Have another puppet play the role of game show host who asks each of the three contestants, in turn, questions about the lesson and its importance.

C. Have one of the contestants give only "wrong" answers.

D. Have another contestant give some right and some wrong answers.

E. Have the remaining contestant give all right answers.

F. Have the children write down who they think the real "true believer" is (#1, #2, or #3) on a piece of paper. Give a balloon, sticker, or some other small prize to those children who correctly identified the true believer.

(Appendix F)

More Fear Busters for the "Feint" of Heart!

1. Take your watch off during your lunch break. While out, ask a strange whenever you want to know what time it is.

2. Tie a colorful string around your finger. Whenever anyone asks you what it is for, answer that it is to remind you to pray for whoever asks you that question (from "The Small Group Idea Book"; author's name unknown).

3. When food shopping, ask customers their opinion about different food items or brands in the section you are in.

4. Re-record your answering machine or cell phone message. Include a short scripture or brief word of spiritual encouragement in your new one.

5. Put your thoughts on paper about an important social or moral issue relevant to your community. Send it to the editorial section of your newspaper. Sign your name!

6. Share a testimonial in your church about something God is doing in your life. Tell the people that you have resolved to reach out to at least one person you have been hesitating to witness to because you are tired of holding back from fear.

7. Do what you told the church you would do in # 6.

8. Bake some cakes or cookies and take them to your neighbors for "no reason at all."

9. Write a short little essay to yourself entitled, "Why I Want to Share Jesus." Print it up in flyer form, and pass out copies to people at church—and to people outside of church as well!

10. Set up a booth in a flea market with a boldly lettered sign announcing, "Free Literature." Offer pamphlets, flyers, tracts, etc. to anyone who shows curiosity. Be prepared to answer questions about the literature.

Robert Davis

(Appendix G)

A Doubt-Proof Prayer to Help You Witness…If You Dare

Many times Christians struggle to "have faith" to believe God for one thing or another. We know that Jesus told us "all things are possible to those who believe." Some things, however, do not present such a challenge to our faith if only we give ourselves over to see them from God's perspective.

Often we fail to realize that, not only do we not have God's point of view, we even prefer our own for the comfort we imagine this gives us. In the case of witnessing, many fall into a rut of inactivity because of insecurity and lack of confidence. This holding back can even be a sort of safe haven in which we hide from the challenge of facing our fears.

From God's perspective, though, the things he calls us to do are not dependent upon mere human capabilities. Therefore it is not his will for us to view the performance of these things as dependent on our own strength or weakness. To do so is to trust in the arm of the flesh, which, when it comes to spiritual pursuits, is an exercise in futility.

The truth we all know, but are often reluctant to embrace, is that *everything we are commanded to do by God is accompanied by his enabling power*. If, in spite of this knowledge, we choose to view our spiritual responsibilities from the vantage point of our weaknesses, we are choosing doubt over trust. When we fail to see God's faithfulness to empower us, we block ourselves from receiving his ability. We should remember what Jesus told us: "…without me you can do nothing" (John 15:5).

This would seem to invalidate the excuse of weakness. Indulging in self-pity because of self-focused insecurity is, from heaven's point of view, disobedience. After all, if we can do nothing without Christ, then clearly the Lord has invalidated self-reliance. This being the case, to plead inability is to deny the provision that has been made in Christ to enable us.

So we must relinquish our inability in favor of God's ability. In so doing, we declare ourselves to be the children of a faithful Creator. Moreover, our reliance upon our Heavenly Father is the very essence of the faith that brings him glory.

Which brings us to this prayer, offered to help maintain this perspective, that what God commands us to do, he enables us to do. And that it is only through our dependence upon him that we can bring glory to his name. As you pray with this in mind, you will receive the boldness, wisdom, and compassion to face down your fears. Instead of your weaknesses, you will see the needs of other people. As you become Christ-conscious, aware that he is with you in every situation, your self-consciousness will subside, and you will find the freedom and fearlessness you long for. So then, pray...if you dare!

Heavenly Father,

I am tired of allowing fear and insecurity to hold me back from reaching out to the lost souls in my life. I know I cannot continue to do this and be obedient to what you have commanded me to do. Therefore, I'm giving my fears, my insecurities, and my worries about what to say or do, and my fear of rejection, to you. I'm casting my cares upon you, and I'm asking you to lift them off of my shoulders. Please help me, Lord, to look past my fears and see the needs of those who are perishing.

Lord, give me words to say, show me what to do, give me favor, and help me to reach out to these people. I know that your perfect love in my heart will cast out any fear. I trust you, and even though I feel weak and helpless in myself, I won't worry. Because I know that you are with me. I'll take courage by looking to you. And I'll rely upon you to help me reach out to people with the wonderful news of your saving grace! In Jesus's name I pray. Amen!

CPSIA information can be obtained at www.ICGtesting.com
Printed in the USA
LVOW10s0246051015

456906LV00021B/313/P